# The Quest for the Historical Satan

# THE QUEST FOR THE HISTORICAL SATAN

Miguel A. De La Torre
and Albert Hernández

Fortress Press

Minneapolis

THE QUEST FOR THE HISTORICAL SATAN

Cover art: © SuperStock
Cover design: Laurie Ingram
Book Design: PerfecType, Nashville, TN

*Library of Congress Cataloging-in-Publication Data*
De La Torre, Miguel A.
  The quest for the historical Satan / Miguel A. De La Torre and Albert Hernández.
      p. cm.
  Includes bibliographical references and index.
  ISBN 978-0-8006-6324-7 (alk. paper)
  1. Devil—Christianity—History of doctrines. 2. Devil—History. I. Hernández, Albert.
II. Title.
  BT982.D4 2011
  235'.4709—dc22
                              2011009185

The paper used in this publication meets the minimum requirements of American National Standard for Information Sciences—Permanence of Paper for Printed Library Materials, ANSI Z329.48-1984.

Manufactured in the U.S.A.

15   14   13   12   11        1   2   3   4   5   6   7   8   9   10

*To our children Anthony, Christina, Sara,*
*Steven, Victoria, and Vincent*

May your generation discover a more balanced vision of Good & Evil;
always looking upon the Other with understanding, compassion, and love.

# CONTENTS

# Preface

T his book is the product of a conversation that took place over several years between a historian, Albert Hernández, and an ethicist, Miguel A. De La Torre, concerning the ethereal, specifically the spiritual force of evil. The historian was interested in how evil has been manifested throughout the centuries; the ethicist was interested in how moral agency is constructed in response to how evil is defined and which people-group signifies said definition. We entered the conversation with different backgrounds and different goals, sharing with each other—and now with you—our own testimonies concerning our encounter with the Evil One, or better yet, the evil ones.

## Albert Hernandez

I am a deeply religious man who grew up Roman Catholic in the Cuban exile community of Miami, Florida. My love for historical studies began early; the memories of so many relatives who passed away longing to return to a vanished world and time haunted my ethical sensibilities, making me highly suspicious of romanticizing the past. I learned the contested story of ideological division between Cubans who supported their former capitalist dictator, President Fulgencio Batista, with deep loyalty and Cubans who sided with the alleged Communist liberator, Fidel Castro, with a sincere hope for a better future. Each was certain that absolute good was on their side and that absolute evil resided in the twisted hearts and minds of their opponents. These tendencies came to a head in Miami during the late 1980s and early 1990s as Soviet Communism collapsed and scores of disillusioned former revolutionaries "tired of Communism" and, believing it to be "a lie," began arriving in Miami after the fall of the Berlin Wall. Such are the outcomes of ideological obsessions for many men and women; whether one is possessed by the ideas of the "left" or by the ideas of the "right," sooner or later one's excessive passion for the noble cause simply runs out of fuel and one enters a state of disillusionment. The twentieth century witnessed an enormous level and intensity of such ideological struggles, and I recall how my maternal grandmother, a Cuban peasant with a fourth-grade education, compared this type of excess, whether from the "left" or the "right," to demonic possession.

A small but significant aspect of the early Cuban exile experience was the generous support and empathy received from the Jewish community and its leaders in the 1960s. Some of my parents' Jewish friends and neighbors were Holocaust survivors. In my early thirties, I attended a public presentation that affected me deeply. During the presentation, a conversation focusing on the problem of evil drifted to the question of madness as a means of explaining the violence and evil of the Nazi concentration camps. Some in the audience were convinced that such atrocities could be explained by reference to psychoanalytic theory or mental illness. Others believed that the key to understanding such inhuman cruelty lay in the role of demons and Satan corrupting the human soul and turning it against all that God represents. Finally, an elderly Jewish man from Nuremberg, Germany, told his story. According to him, if we had seen with our own eyes how some of the camp guards could play with little children in the morning, bounce them on their laps and give them candy at noon, and then stand coldly at the selection line to decide who lived for another day and who went to the gas chambers for an alleged shower, the answer was easy. "Then, my dear friends," he said, "you would never doubt that *the demonic is real* and what an extremely dangerous force it is when unleashed upon the world!" The man's words have stuck with me through the years, moving me to explore the question for myself. How could an all-loving and all-powerful deity allow evil things to happen to otherwise innocent men, women, and children? Does postulating absolute, sentient Evil—as represented traditionally in the form of Satan and his demons—offer a partial answer?

## Miguel A. De La Torre

I went to Blessed Sacrament Catholic School in Jackson Heights, New York, and I attended Mass every Sunday. I was baptized and confirmed in the church, but at night I would offer sacrifices to Obatalá (my mother's *santo*), Changó (my father's), and of course Elegguá (my *santo*). I was a child of Ellegguá, best known within the Santería faith tradition as the trickster. I wore his *elekes*—beaded necklaces—kept his image in a dish behind my front door, and was in line to become a *santero*—a priest of the faith.

Like many Hispanics, I grew up in a hybrid spirituality where I could be a good Catholic boy who prayed the rosary by day and a faithful Santería devotee by night. Although theologians will be quick to point out the contradictions of my religious practices, those of us who participate in the faith of the people recognize and hold a more fluid understanding of spirituality. In my early twenties, motivated by a youthful desire to assimilate to the dominant culture, I walked down a Baptist church aisle and gave my heart to Jesus. Eventually, I would go to seminary and pastor a rural church in Kentucky.

During my spiritual journey as a Southern Baptist, I did more than simply put aside my previous religiosity. I learned from spiritual mentors that Catholicism, due to all the statues of saints in churches, was idol worship and that the Pope was akin to the Anti-Christ. As to my Santería, this was clearly of the Devil. All of the *santos* venerated were in fact demons, with Ellegguá as the head demon, Satan. I accepted these interpretations without question, and turned my back on my spiritual roots with the zeal of a new convert. I was now walking with God, no longer a servant of the Devil.

Yet as I read scripture, I was struck by how little mention Satan receives in the Hebrew Bible and how sparse were the New Testament bases for the fuller understanding of Satan that would later develop in Christian faith. Also, as I saw the evil that good Christian folk were committing in the world, or with which they were complicit through their silence, I began to wonder about the role Satan might be playing in their lives. Added to this was the witness of non-Christian faith traditions that seemed in their praxis to be more faithful to the ideals of Christianity than some of those within my own faith tradition.

I began to question Satan, wondering how he developed and how he is used to define those who did not believe as I did. I began to wonder if it was a good idea to have such a strict dichotomy between absolute Good and absolute Evil, a concept that did not seem to be the norm in the Hebrew Bible. Furthermore, reaching back to my Ellegguá, I began to wonder how an ethics based on the concept of trickster—a concept that appears all too often in the biblical text—would differ from an ethics in which we are with God and those who disagree with us are with the Devil.

As I reclaimed the hybrid spirituality of my people, seeing and defining myself as a "Baptecostal Catholic Santero," I moved away from a rigid understanding of faith and instead boldly began to wrestle with faith concepts that bring oppression to the most vulnerable. One such concept, which was the primary motivation for me to engage a historian in the present project, is how the demonization of others facilitates and justifies their disenfranchisement and dispossession. As a liberative ethicist, I am compelled to seek out the face of evil if I truly want to work toward the dismantling of oppressive social structures.

From these social and intellectual contexts began the conversations that led to the beginnings of our quest for the historical Satan. As the years went by we discussed the manifestation of evil across the pages of history and in the works of different philosophers and ethicists. What exactly is evil? Is it the byproduct of demonic beings? An antithesis to the goodness of God? A consequence of a cosmic battle between the forces of Christ and those of Satan? Or is it part of human nature? Is it an innate predisposition or the result of learned immoral behaviors? Why is the history of Christianity punctuated with so many episodes of unnecessary violence and intolerance of other traditions in the name of goodness and light? We each wrote on the topic and shared our work with each other, allowing our coauthor to add, delete, or challenge our work. Pages went back and forth between us as together we shaped the conversation into the book you are presently holding.

## Acknowledgments

We recognize the many hands that made this book possible. Specifically, we wish to thank our research assistants, Adriana Tulissi and John Bechtold, who helped gather data and proofread earlier drafts. We are also grateful for the editing help provided by our administrative assistant, Debbie McLaren. We also thank our employer, the Iliff School of Theology, for allowing us time off from regular administrative and teaching duties during the completion of this project. The staff members of Iliff's Ira J. Taylor Library and the University of Denver's Penrose Library were exceedingly helpful in the procurement of key primary texts and relevant secondary resources. A special thanks goes to our editor, Michael West, who was patient with us as we tried to meet deadlines and supportive when we fell short, as well as Susan Johnson and Marissa Wold at Fortress Press. We are appreciative to Neil Elliott, Henry Ansgar Kelly, and Irfan Omar for reading portions of the manuscript and providing constructive criticism. And finally, we recognize that if it was not for the encouragement and support of our families, none of this would have been possible. ✳

# DESPERATELY SEEKING SATAN

O n the west coast of Florida sits a small fishing village called Inglis. Originally called Crackertown (from a term used for white Southerners that can be taken as either derogatory or complimentary, depending on context), Inglis is but a few minutes north of the Crystal River, nestled among densely populated forests, waterways, and wildlife. With a population of only approximately 1,500 and located about an hour north of Tampa, Inglis achieved national attention in 2001 when it became the spiritual epicenter of a conflict between the forces of Satan and the servants of God. Inglis's Mayor, Carolyn Risher, made international news when she signed a city proclamation banishing Satan from her community. Specifically, the proclamation issued by the town of Inglis, carrying the town's seal and logo, states:

> Be it known from this day forward that Satan, ruler of darkness, giver of evil, destroyer of what is good and just, is not now, nor ever again will be, a part of this town of Inglis. Satan is hereby declared powerless, no longer ruling over, nor influencing, our citizens.
>
> In the past, Satan has caused division, animosity, hate, confusion, ungodly acts on our youths, and discord among our friends and loved ones. NO LONGER!
>
> The body of Jesus Christ, those citizens cleansed by the Blood of the Lamb, hereby join together to bind the forces of evil in the Holy Name of Jesus. We have taken our town back for the Kingdom of God.

We are taking everything back that the devil ever stole from us. We will never again be deceived by satanic and demonic forces.

As blood-bought children of God, we exercise our authority over the devil in Jesus' name. By the authority, and through His Blessed Name, we command all satanic and demonic forces to cease their activities and depart the town of Inglis.

As the Mayor of Inglis, duly elected by the citizens of this town, and appointed by God to this position of leadership, I proclaim victory over Satan, freedom for our citizens, and liberty to worship our Creator and Heavenly Father, the God of Israel. I take this action in accordance with the words of our Lord and Savior, Jesus Christ, as recorded in Matthew 28:18-20 and Mark 16:15-18.

Signed and sealed this 5th Day of November, 2001

Carolyn Risher, Mayor

Sally McCranie, Town Clerk. (Leary 2001)

Mayor Risher and her pastor placed copies of the proclamation in hollowed-out four-foot fence posts situated at the four entrances to the village. Each post was inscribed with the words "Repent, Request, and Resist." Subsequent to the posts being stolen a few months after installation, the Mayor's pastor replaced each with an eight-foot fence post—buried four feet into the ground and anchored with concrete.

Mayor Risher, a devout fundamentalist Christian, refused to rescind the proclamation against Satan, even when nationally ridiculed. When sued by the American Civil Liberties Union (ACLU) on behalf of Inglis resident Polly Browser, who claimed her U.S. Constitutional Rights to the separation of church and state were violated, the Mayor and the City Council stood steadfast. Neither remorseful nor repentant, Risher justified her position by declaring that "You're either with God or you're against Him" (*St. Petersburg Times* 2002). For the Mayor, there exists no middle ground, no subtle differences, and no nuances. You're either with God or with Satan—and few are those who take the narrow path, but many are those who traverse on the wide road to perdition. It would appear that unless individuals share the same form of faith as the Mayor, they are against God. The danger of such thinking is that it all too easily defines everything that is suspect, unfamiliar, or ambiguous—such as the stranger, the alien, the racial or ethnic other, or dissenters from the norm—as belonging to Satan's domain. One is left wondering if indeed the enormity, intricacy, and complexity of evil are simplistically reduced to the image of Satan.

For many living in the twenty-first century, news of city officials partnering with the church to cast out demons from their town appears somewhat out-of-place, a practice long exorcised from public and religious consciousness since the end of the Middle Ages. Yet the actions of Mayor Risher and her fellow citizens may appear more at home in our alleged modern times than most Americans care to admit. According to a nationwide *Newsweek* poll conducted by Princeton Survey Research Associates[1] on April 13–14, 2000, 75 percent of those surveyed declared their belief in the reality of Satan, while 19 percent denied Satan's existence, and 6 percent were unsure. An opinion poll conducted by Fox News[2] on September 23–24, 2003, discovered that 71 percent of Americans believed in the Devil, while 24 percent denied the existence of Satan, and 5 percent were not sure. A Baylor Religion survey conducted in 2007 showed that 73 percent where either absolutely sure (53.6 percent) or probably sure (19.4 percent) that Satan was real, while 27 percent doubted Satan's existence.

These poll numbers might help explain the success and popularity of such supernatural thrillers as Frank E. Peretti's novels—specifically, *This Present Darkness* (1986) and its sequel, *Piercing the Darkness* (1989), the latter being the winner of the Evangelical Christian Publisher Association (ECPA) Gold Medallion Book Award in 1990 for best fiction. Both books together have sold over 3.5 million copies worldwide. Written by an Assembly of God minister, Peretti's novels tell the tales of spiritual battles conducted between the angelic warriors of Heaven and demonic spirits from Hell for control of the citizens of the small fictitious towns of Ashton and Bacon's Corner. The novels create a dualist cosmology where the characters are either fundamentalist Christians called by God to provide "prayer-cover" for the angels to win the spiritual struggle manifested in the physical world, or else non-Christians who are demon-influenced, if not possessed. These demons seem to flourish in multicultural settings (1989, 140), public schools (1986, 197; 1989, 31); school boards (1989, 216), colleges and universities (1986, 48; 1989, 248), the government (1986, 190; 1989, 22), multinational corporations (1986, 205), non-Christian religions such as Taoism, Hinduism, Buddhism, and Native American spirituality (1986, 315; 1989, 366); liberal Christian ministers (1986, 238); and finally, organizations such as the United Nations (1986, 165), the World Bank (1986, 205), and the ACFA (the American Citizens'

Freedom Association, which seems eerily similar to the ACLU (1989, 71).[3] The true Christians are the real persecuted minority (1989, 82) who face the full power of secular society and the government, both of which are influenced by the forces of Satan.

Peretti paints for us a picture of absolute Evil engaged in a cosmic death-struggle against the forces of absolute Good, concepts rooted in how many Americans define Satan and God. Mayor Risher's proclamation to the residents of Inglis compares well with the novel's prayer warrior who also geared her proclamation to Satan, exclaiming "whatever your plans for this town, I rebuke you in Jesus' name, and I bind you, and I cast you out!" (1986, 113). What Inglis's Mayor does through decree, the fictionalized character in the novel does through prayer. Both of them rebuke, bind, and cast out Satan, in Jesus' name, from their towns.

The quest for the historical Satan is an endeavor not only to deal with the problem of evil but also to understand evil and shed new light on Christianity's age-old emphasis on absolute Good versus absolute Evil. The idea of a *quest* comes to us from the Medieval Latin term *quaestio*, meaning "to question." To begin a quest is to set off on a spiritual journey or a philosophical search for answers to questions dealing with ultimate meaning in human life. As the embodiment of light, goodness, and truth, Jesus Christ has been juxtaposed for centuries against the figure of the Anti-Christ as a representative of Satan, signifying the opposite qualities of darkness, evil, and falsehood. This cosmic and earthly dichotomy of Christ versus Anti-Christ has been central to the Christian imagination since the early Middle Ages whenever it confronted anxiety and fear about the approaching "not-yet" of the future and dealt with looming social changes that were forcing the church to alter its exclusivist doctrines or reform its hierarchical organizational structures.

In our quest for this historical and moral understanding, we must avoid the pitfall of limiting how many perceive Satan's role in the world today to small out-of-the-way towns, whether they be the fictional towns of Ashton and Bacon's Corner or the real town of Inglis, Florida. Satanic and demonic powers have been blamed for many of the atrocities of the past century, such as the two World Wars, the horror of Nazi concentration camps, numerous acts of genocide, detonation of atomic bombs, and the spread of terrorist attacks around the world. Indeed, whether we search the archives for modern examples or gaze back into the past for further evidence of our predisposition for evil, acts of violence in the name of religious ideals aimed at defeating cosmic or absolute Evil are more numerous than most readers imagine.

Our quest for the historical Satan cannot rest content with an overview of the satanic origins of Judeo-Christian demonology, or by merely compiling another summary of how Satan has been presented in the Hebrew and New Testament scriptures, or with another academic analysis of the medieval witch-craze and the injustices of the Spanish Inquisition. If we are to be honest, then our search for the origins of Satan must also take on the larger and perhaps more ancient question about the origins of evil and the degree to which many of our images of evil were derived from popular culture and Christianity's struggle against rival religious beliefs and philosophical ideals. Just as important is the unsettling historical reality that greater atrocities have been committed in defense against various conceptions of the forces of evil personified in Satan and his demonic servants. Declaring the "Other" as Satanic or demonic has been effective for both religious and political leaders. Identifying the Other as a tool of Satan differentiates them from their political adversaries (those representing the evil in the world).

We see these persistent tendencies at play nationally in the way President Obama has come to be demonized—horns and all (see Figure 1)—as well as globally in the rhetoric of security and containment that led up to Operation Desert Storm in 1991 when Saddam Hussein's capacity for evil was compared with that of Adolf Hitler's Nazi regime as the embodiment of absolute Evil in modern times. We see the pattern repeated when Iran's President Mahmoud Ahmadinejad states that former U.S. President George W. Bush is inspired by Satan (Harrison 2003), or when Venezuela's President Hugo Chavez, speaking from the same lectern as President Bush during a United Nation's address, said: "The devil came here yesterday, right here. . . . It smells of sulfur still today." And what was the reaction of the United Nations? First gasps, then horrified giggles, then finally loud applause that lasted so long that U.N. officials had to instruct the cheering group of delegates to stop (Cooper 2006).

Simple name-calling, while providing provocative sound-bites for the evening news, still misses the persistent role some perceive Satan plays in horrific world events. Take for example the tragedies that occurred on 9/11, when four planes were hijacked—two flown into the World Trade Center in New York City, one into the Pentagon outside of Washington D.C., and the last crashing in a field in rural Pennsylvania, falling short of its intended target. The nineteen al-Qaida hijackers who commandeered the jets, armed only with boxcutters, saw themselves as holy warriors combating what they perceived to be the "Great Satan"—a term first applied to the United States in the late 1970s by the Ayatollah Khomeini of Iran during that nation's Islamic Revolution.

The poverty and misery experienced by many within the Muslim world is understood as a consequence of Zionism and its major sponsors, the United States and Great Britain. When we consider how the United States benefits from economic globalization at the expense of the majority of the world's population, it is not surprising that many Muslims in our world, among others, view the U.S. as the major exporter of evil. It matters little if Americans fail to see themselves as global aggressors—many throughout the world do. By dismissing the Muslim world as the real evil, the Christian West can ignore the causes of their resentment and any validity their grievances may have.

But can such dismissals work both ways? Not surprising, the hijackers of 9/11 saw themselves mainly as fervent believers choosing to enter martyrdom. As demonstrated by Palestinian suicide bombers, the extreme act of self-sacrifice is conducted as a religious and patriotic expression against the forces of evil. By dying for God and country, they achieve redemption while defying unjust powers. Fueled by the consequences of the U.S. position in the world, these young men—and many other young men and women throughout the world—understand salvation from the forces of Satan as linked to attacking what they perceive to be the root cause of evil in the world: America, "the Great Satan."

The 9/11 hijackers were not the only ones who saw the U.S. as an evil nation deserving judgment from the Almighty. On Friday, September 14, 2001, the imam of the Red Mosque in Islamabad, Pakistan, delivered his weekly message, focused on the 9/11 attacks that occurred three days earlier. "This is the wrath of Allah," said the imam, his voice ringing over a loudspeaker. "You Americans commit oppression everywhere, in Kashmir, in Palestine, and you do not see the blood spilled." No Arab country had the means to launch such attacks, the imam declared, "But when Allah catches hold of you, there is no escape" (Constable 2001).

But just as some within Islam perceive the United States as the "Great Satan," so too does the United States perceive some Muslim factions and nations and their people as evil and satanic. Since the collapse of the Berlin Wall and the start of "the War on Terror," George W. Bush provided us, during his 2002 State of the Union speech, with a new term: the "Axis of Evil" (Iraq, Iran, and North Korea). A similar scenario played out when President Ronald Reagan's eagerness to revitalize the U.S. defense industry and halt the spread of communism around the world compelled him to describe the Soviet Union as "the evil empire" while denying the validity of international research suggesting this alleged empire was already on the verge of bankruptcy, internal collapse, and open revolt among its Islamic eastern provinces by the time of his election in 1980 (d'Encausee 1979). Euro-American fears of Soviet aggression, which Moscow's expansionist and reactionary behaviors often encouraged, drove American public opinion about the future safety of the free world to agree with President Reagan's characterization of the U.S.S.R. as an "evil empire." Reagan's use of this phrase, and its echo across the world of newspaper and television media, as well as in living rooms and dinner tables across America, made it one of the most successful rhetorical ploys ever used in focusing U.S. foreign policy on a global enemy.

Labeling opponents of the United States as evil is not limited to those who participate or advocate acts of violence. All who reject the U.S. position in the world, specifically Muslims or Arabs, are seen as demonically led. Franklin Graham, son and successor of evangelist Billy Graham, created a furor by describing Islam as a "very evil and wicked religion" (Kristof 2002). Meanwhile, Jerry Vines, former head of the Southern Baptist Convention, declared the Prophet Muhammad to be a demon-obsessed pedophile, which echoed earlier medieval projections of Islamic evil and serious disrespect about the religious message and ministry of Islam's merciful and revered founder. The true followers of Satan are thus identified and stereotyped as those who practice "Radical Islam" (Kristof 2002).

To counter such evil, the self-proclaimed believers in the "real" God enter into a crusade against God's enemies, similar to the fictionist yarn spun by Peretti. The invisible spiritual battle taking place around us, which is won or lost by how many believers drop to their knees in prayer, directly impacts the physical battles between true Christians and the rest of the world. According to Mayor Risher, the evil committed on September 11 inspired her to pursue the proclamation against allowing Satan into her town: "It gave me the inspiration that [her constituency] needs to be ready if something like this was to happen to the town of Inglis. We need to be ready to meet our maker." Even though a terrorist attack on a small Florida village is highly unlikely, manipulating fear allows the Mayor to call her fellow citizens to repentance.

She goes on to say that "if our churches band together and pray, our nation and our town can be a godly nation and a godly town" (Tuchman 2002).

For some religious leaders, whether dealing with Christianity or Islam (or any other faith tradition for that matter), the Other is either the personification of evil or demon possessed. It cannot be denied that evil was, and continues to be, committed throughout the world by men and women of all religious orientations. But to reduce the Other to an ultimate representative or personification of evil justifies cruelties and atrocities committed by those engaged in the battle to save humans from Satan's corruption. No evil ever dreamed-up by Satan can outdo the atrocities committed by good, decent people attempting to purge such evil forces from this world. Any "crusade to rid the world of evil," once and for all, is a misguided endeavor fraught with deep peril for both the self-appointed warriors of goodness, as well as for the alleged evildoers who will be on the receiving end of these projections. Some of the most diabolical actions, enough to make the very demons of Hell cringe in shame, are committed by those who consider themselves to be God's righteous chosen ones in the spiritual battle against the forces of evil. David Frankfurter states it best, "historically verifiable atrocities take place not in the ceremonies of some evil realm or as expressions of some ontological evil force, but rather in the course of *purging* evil and its alleged devotees from the world" (2006, 224).

To paraphrase the immortal words of the cartoon character Pogo the Possum: "We have met Satan, and he is us!" Whether it be flying planes into skyscrapers or U.S.-based mercenary companies that kill unarmed Iraqi civilians, such acts are justified as a form of self-defense against an invincible satanic Other. Unfortunately, the spiritual battle against the alleged forces of darkness, which often becomes a physical battle in the political or military arena, masks any actual evidence of evil supposedly existing in the accused Other. Naming the Other as "satanic" or "demonic" effectively short-circuits moral arguments, political critiques, or social analysis. By definition, the individual, group, or nation accused of manifesting or personifying Satan's vices and desires can never be in a dialogue of mutual edification or a meaningful compromise. Pure and virtuous warriors in a cosmic spiritual battle against the forces of Satan need not consider, understand, or explain the root causes of the opponent's actions. To do so demonstrates a lack of resolve or an acute moral weakness. Even those who attempted to articulate a more nuanced elucidation as to the causes of the 9/11 events, an understanding that considers the grievances of the hijackers, are dismissed as "coddling terrorists" or attempting to "psychoanalyze" evil. In either case, a critical exploration of the causes of evil fails to occur. Instead, in the name of God, or Allah, and in defense of the highest good (*Summum Bonum*), evil—with few or no constraints—is perpetrated in order to resist evil. Fire always seems to be fought with fire.

Still, even though many Christians may rail against Satan—casting him out from influencing their lives—they still need Satan. Inglis's Mayor Risher may "bind the forces of evil in the Holy Name of Jesus" and cast Satan from her fair village, but nevertheless Risher, along with many Christians, desperately need Satan. For, you see, how else can she, or we for that matter, explain the presence of evil before a God whom we claim to be all-loving and all-powerful? Reading any major local or international newspaper section, on any given day, is to read about evil on a global scale (for example, Darfur, the most recent in a long line of genocidal hotspots) and on a local scale (for example, the abused body of an innocent child recently discarded in a garbage dumpster). In a world overflowing with injustices, one must ask: "Where is God?" Surely an all-loving, all-compassionate, and all-merciful "Father" would act protectively and proactively upon hearing the agonizing cries of a child. The existence of evil raises what theologians call "the theodicy question," best articulated by the eighteenth-century philosopher David Hume, who asked concerning God: "Is he willing to prevent evil, but not able? Then he is impotent. Is he able, but not willing? Then he is malevolent. Is he both able and willing? Whence then is evil?" (1948, 196).

The word "theodicy" is derived from two Greek words: *theos*, which means God, and *dikē*, which symbolizes justice. The word argues that God is just despite the presence of evil. For evil to exist, and God to be acquitted of complicity and retain an all-loving and powerful nature, injustice must somehow be reconciled with God. For many, evil exists because (1) human depravity makes no one innocent (hence the concept of Original Sin rooted in Adam and Eve's fall from grace); (2) it is as part of some master cosmic plan whose end purpose is to produce mature followers of Christ (as Paul would say: "all things work for good to them that love God"—Rom 8:28); and/or (3) because there is a devil, a father of misery and darkness who can be blamed for all the evil and injustices that exist in the world. Satan literally becomes a necessary evil—an evil that excuses God. Satan allows the Rishers of the world to hold on to a faith in an all-loving and all-powerful God while evil runs rampant. Indeed, the history of several major religious traditions is punctuated with examples of acts of violence and policies of intolerance carried out in the name of the one, true God of power and might. Nevertheless, regardless of how we wish to imagine or construct Satan, regardless of what powers we may wish to bestow upon him, in the final analysis there must remain on God's office desk a sign that reads "the buck stops here."

As necessary as Satan may appear to be for Christians, attempting to understand Satan via the theodicy question may conclude with the justification of evil. Terrence Tilley would argue that to seek answers to the theodicy question is to attempt to make God's providence complicit with injustices. Evil becomes an abstract concept that ignores pain and suffering (1991, 210–14). The mother whose daughter was raped before her eyes by an invading army; the father who holds his son in his arms as he dies of hunger due to the poverty faced by a population located in the midst of rich, fertile land; or the child who loses his or her parents to a drunken driver going home from a Christmas party—all these find little solace in doctrinal positions on the theodicy question. For those who suffer unjust situations, explaining away evil so that God's limitless love and power can remain unquestioned falls short of any meaningful and honest discussion about Satan.

It matters little if Satan exists—evil definitely does. And maybe our response to Satan is a recognition that the evil he causes, or represents, is beyond human comprehension. No simple theological answer for the reason of Satan's existence will satisfy the one suffering unjustly. Our quest for the historical Satan is meaningless unless we also develop a response to the disturbing examples of evil committed in the name of goodness and justice—an ethics—that seeks to counteract the forces of Satan.

Our concern is not whether Satan is believed to be physically or symbolically present. The fact of the matter is that Satan, in the minds of many, is both physically real and symbolically at hand; and that presence has and continues to influence human moral agency. Any understanding of human nature, religious beliefs (specifically Christianity), or morality must touch upon Satan and the evil he represents. This is why this book was developed. It is not our goal to prove or disprove Satan's existence. Such exercises fall short of our real goal concerning Satan: understanding the reality that we have traditionally called Satan, its actual origins and influence on humanity, and our call to overcome the injustices caused in Satan's name. Our interest is to understand Satan as symbol and what this symbol signifies. Our hope is to move beyond the numerous existing dichotomies that oppose those who seek to rid the world of Satan's presence to those who seek to define who/what is Satanic and who/what is not.

Redefining what Christianity, and Euro-American society, is trying to signify when claims about Satan's existence surface will help us to discuss and confront the concept of evil. The questions we pose at different historical stages of our investigation include: Who exactly is Satan? What are his origins? Does Satan have power over humans? How has he evolved throughout history? Is he the evil counterpart to God? Does Satan contain similar attributes as God—all-knowing, all-powerful, ever-present? These historical questions raise other theological and philosophical questions: If Satan is imagined as almost as powerful as God, can Christianity really claim to be monotheistic? Where does evil come from and what can be done about it? Are the origins of evil supernatural, or is evil the result of human free-will and desire? Or is evil simply a human projection? Is Satan more a figment of our imagination than an actual being—as the caricatures of Satan wearing red tights, with horns and a pitchfork, signify? Or was the nineteenth-century French poet and literary critic Charles Baudelaire correct when he stated: "the Devil's cleverest trick is to persuade [us] that he does not exist"? (1975, 135).

The purpose of this book is to explore the problem of evil as historically and morally constructed by Christianity through the changing image and symbols of Satan. The traditional dichotomy between an absolute Good (personified by God and Christ) and absolute Evil (personified by Satan and his demons) is a development within Christian thought and civilization that has negatively influenced how moral reasoning is normatively conducted. Yet a more biblically rooted understanding of the developing conception of Satan, what we might call his trajectory from the ancient Hebrew tradition to early Christian thought, and throughout the Medieval Era, is quite different than our prevailing contemporary understandings of Satan. Rediscovering how Satan was originally envisioned and developed can provide modern-day Christians with insights for comprehending the ambiguities of right and wrong and perhaps for living a more balanced moral life. ✳

## Chapter 1

# SATAN IN THE MODERN WORLD

I n 1977 rumors started circulating among Christian churches that Ray Kroc, owner of the McDonald's fast-food chain, had appeared on the Phil Donahue show in May of that year to claim that the corporation's success was due to his pact with the devil. According to the rumors, he was donating 35 percent of the restaurant chain's profits to the Church of Satan. A few years later, in 1982, rumors spread that the Proctor and Gamble logo depicting a moon and star was a satanic symbol. It was alleged that the company president, "a major twentieth-century Satanist," also appeared on the Phil Donahue show confessing that all the company profits went to the Church of Satan. Even though the events never occurred—Kroc had appeared on the Phil Donahue show, but only to promote his book—rumors of Satanic activities continue. An Internet search of the names of these companies with the added word "Satan" reveals how persistent these rumors are.

Who is this Satan who supposedly profits from major corporate contributions? Close your eyes and try to picture what Satan might look like. What do you see? Do you see a man in red tights with a forked tail, cloven hooves, horns on his head, and holding a pitchfork?—something akin to the logo found on cans of Underwood Deviled Ham Spread? If so, such a modern appearance is rooted in an early attempt of Christianity to demonize the gods of those they considered pagans. In this particular manifestation, Satan is eerily similar to the Greek god Pan (whose Roman counterpart was Fauna), who possesses the hindquarters, cloven hooves, goatee, wrinkled skin, and horns of a goat, representing indulgence in music, worldly pleasures, and sexuality (see Figure 3).

Or maybe you envision Satan wearing a $600 business suit, with manicured fingernails, looking like he just stepped out of *Gentlemen's Quarterly* magazine. Such an understanding of Satan as a CEO is best captured in the popular C. S. Lewis Christian apologetic novel *The Screwtape Letters*, which consists of instructional correspondence written by a managing demon to a bureaucratic subordinate charged with leading a newly converted Christian astray. The image of Satan as a corporate figure was also portrayed in the 1997 film *The Devil's Advocate*. Keanu Reeves played the role of an ambitious and highly talented young lawyer recruited to join an elite New York law firm run by John Milton, played by Al Pacino, who turns out to be Satan. Pacino's character wreaks havoc on the souls and moral integrity of the firm's partners, as well as on the lives and legal affairs of all who come in contact with his law firm.

In most European literature or works of art, Satan appeared hideous—a creature that had different animal body parts. For example, he would be portrayed as a person with goat legs, or pig teeth in his mouth, or duck feet, thus symbolizing an unnatural creature, an abomination of creation. In the United States, racist attitudes have historically seeped into how Satan is viewed by Americans. In many movies and plays, Satan is usually played by a black man. So, for example, while early nineteenth-century artist William Blake could depict Satan in luminous hues as an angel of light, the first cinematic portrayal of Satan, in *Dante's Inferno* (1911)—a film to which we return below—depicted him as a black creature. After all, we find "black" defined by *Webster's New World Dictionary* as "dirty, evil, wicked" and "white" as "pure, innocent," leaving us to wonder how color can possess moral qualities.

Satan has been pictured by Christians throughout the ages in multiple fashions, from a grotesque and hideous creature to a beautiful being masquerading as light. For many Christians—specifically those whose exclusive views of Christian doctrine and identity do not accept the identity and views of others—Satan can be perceived behind the faiths of unbelievers and outsiders. During the Reformation of the sixteenth century, both sides—Catholics and Protestants—each viewed the other as being in league with the Great Deceiver, who was bent on destroying and corrupting the church of Christ. Luther eventually believed that he was participating in a cosmic struggle against the Anti-Christ, who was acting through the office of the

Roman Papacy. In turn, King Charles I of Spain, whose vast empire included the Americas and the German territories of the Holy Roman Empire, accused Martin Luther of being the real Anti-Christ. The king and his allies were deeply concerned that the German princes, many of whom supported the Protestant Reformation, would break away from the growing territories and provinces of the Spanish Empire. For them, and still for many Christians today, not believing the correct teachings of the church means worshipping the enemy's doctrines—Satan's lies. Even to question the church's doctrine or authority is to oppose God!

A more recent example of equating another's faith with the satanic can be found in a speech given to Christian churches by Army Lieutenant General William Boykin, then deputy under-secretary of defense for intelligence and war-fighting support. The Lieutenant General, in full uniform, addressed church groups while conducting the "War on Terror." According to Boykin, the U.S. battle against Muslim radicals is a fight against Satan. Recounting a story of a Somali Muslim fighter who said that U.S. forces would never capture him because Allah was protecting him, Boykin responded by saying, "Well, you know what I knew—my God was bigger than his. . . . I knew that my God was a real God, and his was an idol." These militant Islamists, according to Boykin, sought to destroy the U.S. "because we're a Christian nation." For him, "The enemy is a spiritual enemy. He's called the principality of darkness. The enemy is a guy called Satan" (*The New York Times* 2003).

For others, however, Satan has been reduced to a profitable, humorous caricature, a symbol or image used as jewelry, displayed on clothing, used for decoration and costumes on Halloween, engraved on bodies as tattoos, and praised in certain music styles marketed to "wanna-be" rebellious youth. Even though most of these concepts of Satan come from popular culture, they remain rooted in the age-old theological and moral attempt to explain why individual human beings and human societies participate in evil. Take, for example, the way Saturday morning cartoons depict a character struggling with temptation. A miniature devil, usually looking like the character but with horns and a pitchfork, sits on the left shoulder of the one being swayed, whispering temptation in her or his left ear. Of course, there exists a counter to these evil persuasions, usually in the form of an angel, again a miniature copy of the character, but this time in a white gown with a halo and holding a small harp, sitting on the person's right shoulder. It is interesting to note that this popular portrayal, which we have witnessed since childhood on such well-liked television shows as *Popeye* or *Tom and Jerry*, has its grounding in the writings of the third-century Alexandrian Church Father Origen. Basing his views on the early second-century manuscript the *Epistle of Barnabas* (18:1) and the late second-century work the *Shepherd of Hermas* (*Mandate* 6.2.1-10), Origen argued that each individual is attended by two angels. When good thoughts arise in our hearts, they were suggested by the good angel. But if instead bad thoughts arise, then they were suggested by the evil angel (*De principiis* 3.2.4).

So how *should* Satan be imagined? We begin our quest for the historical Satan by realizing that there exists no single, universal representation of Satan. Different groups across the centuries and within modern society, with competing agendas and goals, have created Satan to meet their own needs, justify certain actions against demonized opponents, or provide answers to the unanswerable fact of what can appear as the total moral depravity of humans and creation. In this chapter we explore some of the many ways Satan is imagined and manifested by our popular culture and how these manifestations shape not only our view about evil but also how we have come to know the Divine.

## Satan Goes to Hollywood

With the demise of the medieval worldview in the eighteenth century came the increasing secularism and materialism of modern civilization. As the scientific rationalism of modern society increased, the once popular belief in demons, fairies, and angels had waned in favor of the promise of new inventions and industries that became mingled with turn-of-the-century ideas about unlimited progress and the perfectibility of human nature. What happened to humanity's primordial fears of Satan and the forces of evil?

On December 10, 1911, Satan and the themes of evil and human suffering made a dramatic comeback at Gane's Manhattan Theater in New York City in a silent movie based on the medieval literary epic *Dante's Inferno*. The film was sixty-nine minutes long and spread out over five different reels that had to be changed periodically. It was directed by Italian filmmakers Francesco Bertolini, Giuseppe de Liguoro, and Adolfo Padovan. The movie was an amazing financial success at the time and convinced movie moguls that depicting Satan and exploring the problem of evil on the big screen could help them sell more movie tickets!

The visual arts media of the medieval world, whether in stone carvings, marble sculptures, stained glass windows, or in frescoes painted on church walls, portrayed biblical scenes that often included images of Lucifer and demons delighting in human temptation and sinfulness. The visual arts media of the modern world provided a forum for the exploration of evil and human violence in highly realistic cinematic representations that traditional literature and the arts could not convey as effectively (Pomerance 2004, 8–10). Scholars in both biblical studies and the history of Christianity have observed that, although depictions of Satan and the forces of evil decreased among popular culture and literature from the 1700s to the early 1900s, the beginnings of the cinema industry had an indirect but noticeable effect on the modern rediscovery of the Prince of Darkness.

Inspired by the work of American inventor Thomas Edison, in 1895 Louis and August Lumiere of France developed the cinematographe, a new camera-projection system that inaugurated the art and industry of cinema. Two years later, the first theater for showing movies opened in Paris, and by 1902 Thomas Talley opened the first American movie theater in Los Angeles. The Lumiere's movie company boasted a catalog of over one-thousand titles before 1900, but it was comprised mostly of short documentary features of people in factories or people engaged in various types of recreational and work-related activities. The success of short films such as Georges Melies's *A Trip to the Moon* (1902), Edwin Porter's *Jack and the Beanstalk* (1902), and Stuart Blackton's *The Life of Moses* (1909) convinced some entrepreneurs among the growing number of directors, writers and producers, and movie companies that the public might respond very well to story films based upon some of the great myths or religious narratives from the past.

Melies is also credited with making the first horror film in 1896, *The House of the Devil*, which, with a running time of only two minutes and with no demonic voices or screaming, offers a stark contrast with more contemporary portrayals. Consider, for example, the agonizing screams and makeup effects of the two-hour-plus-long 1973 classic horror movie, William Peter Blatty's *The Exorcist*, which was based on a distorted "true" story of an alleged 1949 demonic possession of a fourteen-year-old boy from Washington, D.C.[1] The turn-of-the-century pioneers of moviemaking could not have imagined in 1896 or in 1900 how lucrative the rediscovery of Satan and the problem of evil were going to be for the future development of the cinema industry.

The first feature-length silent movie ever shown in a U.S. theater, and the most expensive film ever made at the time with a staggering price-tag of over $180,000, was the 1911 production of *Dante's Inferno*, discussed above. Inspired by the popular artistic illustrations of Gustav Doré and based on Dante's thirteenth-century tale of human depravity and damnation, the movie earned over two million dollars in revenue over the next several months. The damned are portrayed mostly nude and surrounded by pitchfork-wielding demons as the directors use brief episodes to show the audience how the sins and evils of these lost souls brought about their damnation. Near the film's conclusion, Satan is portrayed eating the souls of humans condemned to an eternity in hell for their deadly sins. The film's success convinced marketing executives among film companies that demons, evil and human suffering, and Lucifer's presence would help them sell lots of movie tickets in the years ahead.

Not long afterward, between 1912 and 1915, a group of film companies operating in the general area of Hollywood and Los Angeles, California, gradually joined forces under the leadership of Carl Laemmle and founded Universal Pictures. The new company had great success with adaptations of classic literature and horror stories for the big screen. Over the next few years Universal Pictures released some of the most famous fantasy, thriller, and suspense movies in the early history of the silent cinema, such as *Dr. Jekyll and Mr. Hyde* (1915), *The Phantom of the Opera* (1925), and the hugely successful *Hunchback of Notre Dame* (1923). Like the mythical story of Dr. Faustus, who made a blood-pact with the devil to gain worldly success and magical powers and whose story we will examine in chapter 5, the City of Angels and its neighboring district of Hollywood (literally meaning "Holy Wood") entered into a virtual pact with the Prince of Darkness when it discovered the potential payoff from a type of suspense and fantasy film that would eventually lead to the beginnings of the horror and thriller movie genres.

The movie industry and American moral standards, however, were at odds with each other almost from the very beginnings of filmmaking and the opening of the first movie theaters. In fact, film historians like Tom Gunning and Murray Pomerance point out that America's social and legal doubts about the goodness of filmmakers and the movies dates back to the very origins of the cinema industry. Critics on both the right and left of the political spectrum believed from the outset that the industry was prone to evil and manipulation because of the inherent power of visual images to inspire and seduce human beings into certain behaviors while molding individual opinions with the persuasive power of the visual image. Christians also criticized the cinema industry for its unrestrained depictions of violence, nudity and sexuality, and evil in the form of human cruelty and depravity.

Tom Gunning observed that for "more than half a century movies shown in the United States were not allowed the privilege of free speech guaranteed to print media" (2004, 22). The reason for this denial of free speech to movie makers and writers resulted from the February 1915 U.S. Supreme Court decision set forth in the landmark case of *Mutual Film Corporation vs. Ohio Industrial Commission,* in which Justice Joseph McKenna wrote the opinion for the court's unanimous decision that "the new medium of film was 'capable of evil, having power for it, the greater because of the attractiveness and manner of exhibition'" (2004, 22). McKenna's court opinion represented the prevailing legal notion of the social and moral implications of films from the beginnings of the film industry in the late 1800s to the series of cases before the Supreme Court in the mid-1950s (2004, 23–26). Nonetheless, moral debates and social concerns similar to these continue to the present day as Hollywood continues to capitalize on the public's fascination with on-screen evil and moral depravity.

Early horror films, which probably originated in Germany during the era of silent movies, often had a Gothic twist, being set in mysterious castles or dark manors. In the 1930s Universal Pictures began remaking many of the German horror films. The American public became possessed by the alluring elements of fear, suspense, and evil that characterize the horror genre. Today, movies with a touch of evil and scenes of depraved human violence, or demonic shape-shifting beings that morph on the screen with weird sound effects that make some of us jump out of our seats and others utter scared screams in the theater, account for millions of dollars in movie sales and theater revenues.

In her book *Exploring Evil through the Landscape of Literature* (2002), Gloria Cigman suggests that our fears about "the imagined apotheosis of evil" has much to do with both the disturbing allure and moral disdain we experience when confronted by evil. Although her work focuses on literary portrayals of evil across the annals of English literature, Cigman acknowledges that movies create narrative spaces in which story and symbol can affect human emotions and notions of suffering in much the same way that great works of literature can move our souls and influence our emotions and thoughts (2002, 240–45). She detects a connection between modern literary and cinematic portrayals of the power of evil over good and the increasing nihilism and anxiety of post-modernity in thriller films such as *The Silence of the Lambs* (1991). "We have watched the second half of the twentieth century growing less and less convinced that triumph over evil is a viable option" (2002, 241). Audiences throughout the world were both titillated and disgusted by the character of Hannibal Lecter, a reminder to us all that there is something demonically seductive in the viewing of evil and violence on film, as well as an allusion to the age-old portrayals of the devil as a highly intelligent and sophisticated creature capable of inflicting intense harm on others without remorse.

The possibility that evil might somehow triumph over good was at the root of adverse public and ministerial reactions to *The Omen* movie trilogy of the late 1970s and early 1980s, which is now being remade for a new generation of apocalyptic connoisseurs and horror movie aficionados. Some among the viewing public apparently forgot in 1976 that *The Omen* was such a movie. Directors and producers received stern criticism from concerned Christians among the general public and from the clergy about making a film in which the Prince of Darkness triumphs over Jesus Christ and his holy church. Of course, that is precisely what the medieval myth of the Anti-Christ is all about—Satan's attempt to defeat Christ and his followers by wreaking havoc across the earth and igniting human violence and warfare among all nations while destroying the Christian church.

On the other hand, if we read the book of Revelation carefully, we are reminded that God has promised humanity that personal repentance and God's loving grace through the return of Christ will lead to the defeat of both Satan and the Anti-Christ. Nonetheless, the success of *The Omen* trilogy in North America may also have been related to American paranoia about a communist takeover of the world originating in Europe and to the apocalyptic expectations of Evangelical Christians theorizing about the Soviet Union's meddling in global affairs, along with general fear of the potential side effects of a revitalized Western European military establishment aimed at curbing Soviet expansionism someday being turned against the United States.

In the 1976 gothic thriller and series opener, Katherine Thorn, played by Lee Remick, loses her first child while giving birth at a hospital in Rome, Italy. Her husband, American Ambassador Robert Thorn, played by Gregory Peck, is then offered an allegedly orphaned baby by a Roman Catholic priest.

Ambassador Thorn accepts the bizarre offer but does not realize the evil fate to which he has damned his new family by adopting Damien until it is too late. As the mysterious deaths of anyone who comes close to figuring out the little boy's true identity multiply, Thorn learns that Damien is the infernal offspring of a female jackal and Satan. He also learns that his natural child with Katherine was murdered in order to arrange for him to adopt Damien. His wife, too, is eventually murdered by their nanny while convalescing in a hospital after falling and suffering a miscarriage of what would have been the Thorns' second child. When news of Katherine's death reaches Robert Thorn, he is in Israel to meet with an archaeologist named Bugenhagen, who informs him that the only way to stop the Anti-Christ is to stab him in the heart with the "seven daggers of Meggido," and preferably on hallowed ground such as a Christian church. After returning home and finding the infamous 666 birthmark of the Anti-Christ under Damien's scalp, Robert becomes convinced that he must ritually kill little Damien or risk unleashing the son of the Prince of Darkness upon the world stage. The police catch up with him in a church and shoot him in the act of trying to stab and kill his son.

Damien is then placed under the protection of the President of the United States and is to be raised by his paternal uncle and aunt, who appear in *The Omen II* as the owners of Thorn Industries, a multinational corporation with highly significant military and agricultural contracts. This is just the sort of lucrative family business and access to high-level political and military figures that the Anti-Christ can use to take over the world while turning nations against each other en route to Armageddon. Among the general public's apocalyptic fervor in the late 1970s, there was already the notion that the dreaded Anti-Christ had been born sometime after the Second World War and was slowly growing to maturity somewhere in either Western or Eastern Europe. Damien's character profile was perfectly aligned with these collective visions and fears.

The *Omen* films' director, Richard Donner, and his team of producers, Harvey Bernhard and Mace Neufeld, spent years trying to make sense of all the strange tragedies and near-tragedies that befell them and their production crews while making this movie in the 1970s. The newspapers and entertainment magazines thought these men created their fantastic stories about being cursed for publicity purposes. Among the alleged reports of sinister events, there was the emergency landing of several airline flights the film's production team was aboard, two of which were struck by lightning;

the crash-landing of another airliner carrying members of the film crew that then struck a car at the end of the runway, killing several people (including the pilot's wife and two children); an almost deadly near miss of film crew members by an IRA bombing at a local London restaurant; and the gruesome decapitation in a car accident of special effects engineer John Richardson's girlfriend when the couple was driving through Belgium and collided with another vehicle by a road sign listing "66.6 kilometers" as the distance to the nearest town.

While the publicity department at Twentieth Century Fox surely delighted in reporting on all of these uncanny "omens" of evil, and while the public got very excited about these reports when the film was released in June of 1976, the production team never forgot their feelings of fear and apprehension as these and many other unusual things, too numerous to list here, affected them and their colleagues while making the first installment of the trilogy. Harvey Bernhard believes the pattern of unusual coincidences and strange things happening indicated "an aura of not being welcome. I really sincerely believe that the Devil didn't want the picture to be made."[2] Robert Munger, who worked on the original picture as a religious advisor, maintains that he did not believe in the devil before making the movie. As a devout Christian he had previously believed that faith in Christ as his Savior was all his religious life and soul needed. But he and some of the others working on the movie were advised by theologians and clergy that by the end of the film shooting, they would each be convinced of Satan's existence. Concerned Christians among the general public were equally upset over the making of a movie like *The Omen*, in which the forces of evil were allowed to triumph over the forces of goodness and love signified in the life and mission of Jesus Christ. Nonetheless, the public's appetite for horror movies won out over these nobler spiritual concerns as this particular film series emerged as one of the most financially successful among all of Hollywood's portrayals of Satan and the Anti-Christ.

A slightly different twist on the Hollywood portrayal of Satan was inspired by Mike Mignola's comic book series *Hellboy*, which he pitched to DC Comics in the early 1990s. Originally turned down as a result of the marketing team's uncertainty about promoting a super hero from hell also known as "The Beast of the Apocalypse," the first *Hellboy* movie, written and directed by Guillermo Del Toro, debuted in 2004 and was followed by the release of *Hellboy II: The Golden Army* a few years later. Both films fared well at the box office, and plans are underway for the making of a third picture in the series.

The comic book and movie biography of this character reads as follows: Hellboy, played by Ron Perlman, was brought to earth from hell on December 23, 1944, during a Nazi experiment on a remote island off the coast of Scotland by Rasputin and a host of sinister and violent Nazi occultists from the infamous Thule Society. In the hope of disrupting their diabolical use of technology and machines aimed at unleashing the gods of evil and chaos, the United States Army launches a surprise attack on Rasputin and his Nazi collaborators. From the ensuing explosions and confusion emerges a devil-like child. His skin is red. He also has horns and a tail, as well as a powerful sledgehammer-shaped hand made of what looks like red stone, the hand known in the comic book series as the "Right Hand of Doom."

Hellboy is taken in by Professor Trevor Bruttenholm, who raises him with the help of the U.S. Army and the Bureau for Paranormal Research and Defense (BPRD). His superhero abilities are super human strength, the production of fire and resistance to its harmful effects, and the power to regenerate injured tissue and bones after being beaten, shot, cut, burned, or blasted. He loves cats and, in the movie version, is also somewhat addicted to Baby Ruth bars. In the comic book series, we also learn that Hellboy is the three-hundred-year-old offspring of a demon and a witch whose family ties link her to Morgan le Fay of the famous Arthurian legends, Morgan being King Arthur's sister. Exactly what these medieval and Arthurian family ties are meant to conjure up in the public imagination will have to be left to the creative imaginations of Mignola and Del Toro as each of them develops this fictional character and his marvelous story further.

However, the portrayal of Nazis alongside themes of diabolical scientific plans or black magic is one of the most persistent symbolic images that emerged in the American mythic consciousness after World War II. Satanic and evil characteristics are projected onto persons such as Hitler or Eichmann, or projected onto movements such as the Nazis or institutions like Himmler's S.S. and Gestapo. This leads to Nazis being equated with absolute Evil by Hollywood film writers and movie producers, whose notions of Nazis as evil are then reinforced in the public imagination where these "images" take on a mythic meaning in the culture at large.

For example, in the genre of science fiction fantasy and adventure films, we find the Imperial Storm Troopers of George Lucas' *Star Wars* film sagas

(1975–2005) as an example of the many ways that Satan and evil are imagined and manifested by our pop culture and how these manifestations not only shape our views about evil but also how we have come to define goodness and the Divine. Indeed, the Nazi-styled black helmet worn by Darth Vader, whose cruelty and lust for power rank him as one of the most evil characters in modern film, is another example of these mythologizing tendencies perched somewhere between the idea of cosmic battles against super villains and our collective fear over the moral and existential possibility that we as "the good guys" might not be all that different from the Nazis as "the bad guys." After all, one of the most intriguing elements of Darth Vader's story and character is his youthful and innocent beginning as the former Jedi Knight Anakin Skywalker.

In his informative and insightful essay on images of Nazis in American film, Lester Friedman, humanities scholar and prolific film historian, suggests to his readers:

> Try this experiment during the next week: see how often the words *Hitler*, *Holocaust*, and *Nazi* enter your world. My guess is that you will not be able to go more than one or two days without hearing or seeing some reference to those words. Images taken from and inspired by the Third Reich saturate our culture functioning as concrete representations of that specific historical era, free floating signifiers of universal evil and, for some, emblems of purity, power, and erotic fascination. (Friedman 2004, 256)

Friedman's comments remind us of the alleged racial purity of the Aryan master race juxtaposed with the carnival-like images of Liza Minnelli and Joel Grey in *Cabaret* (1972), which was set in 1931 Berlin where the pair performed night after night at the Kit Kat Klub as National Socialism rose to power and the Nazi reign of terror began unfolding across Germany and Austria before consuming Europe and the world. We can imagine Madonna or Lady Gaga in an alluring grey and black fascist-style uniform intended to make their viewers and listeners imagine the comingling of power and sensuality. We are also reminded of Mel Brooks' movie adaptation of the bawdy, record-breaking smash Broadway hit *The Producers* (2005), in which Nathan Lane and Matthew Broderick played the wacky production duo who set out to make more money with a box office flop than with a record-breaking success by backing a musical titled *Springtime for Hitler*. "The reasons for this cultural obsession with the images, figures, and narratives of the Third Reich mark the starting point for any serious discussion of films containing Nazis. One must explore their power to understand their appeal" (Friedman 2004, 256–57).

The presence of Nazis in the annals and varied spectrum of American movies is so widespread that Friedman identifies five basic components to help students of film history understand the perplexing appeal for the symbols and satanic evils of one of America's and Western civilization's greatest and most destructive enemies: "1) Nazi image power; 2) sympathy for the Devil; 3) the erotic dimension; 4) the Holocaust culture; and 5) the thought that we might be *them*" (2004, 257). While Friedman observes that these component categories are not found among all movies portraying Nazis, most movies dealing with Nazi figures or themes contain a combination of one or more of these elements. The component of "sympathy for the Devil" is an intriguing one for our purposes in the quest for the historical Satan because taking our cues from popular culture usually assume that the rank and file of American society recognize the Nazis as the "bad guys." But what about the percentage of the viewing public for whom the defeat of the Nazis, when juxtaposed with the power and orderliness of an authoritarian state alongside the eroticism of Nazi uniforms, leather boots, polished caps, and sadomasochistic imagery, produces what Friedman very astutely refers to as "sympathy for the Devil" (2004, 257–61)? This is a most perplexing and confounding realization, yet one that explains the bizarre appeal to some people of Darth Vader's persona and dress, as well as the appeal of the evil Sith Lords of the *Star Wars* movie franchise.

The symbolic and mythological dimensions of how Euro-Western and North American culture has been conditioned to think about the Nazi menace and evil legacies since 1945 also explains the portrayal of Nazi themes and images in the American cinema. Nowhere is this more noticeable than in the Indiana Jones movie franchise series where the lead character, played by Harrison Ford, routinely states: "Nazis? I hate those guys!" In *Raiders of the Lost Ark* (1981), the Nazis are mythologized as the archetypal enemies of the Judeo-Christian tradition, for their obsession with obtaining the Ark of the Covenant in order to harness its awesome powers, and as the enemies of the United States, the archetypal "good guys," signified by archaeologist Indiana Jones. Ironically, this mythologizing of a major war has been part of America's geopolitical predicament in the post–World War II era as we have somehow equated the outcome of that particular war and American national identity with absolute Good against the absolute Evil of Adolf Hitler and National Socialism.

This mythic theme and social conception of absolute Evil versus absolute Good is especially true in the third installment of the highly successful Indiana Jones movie series, *The Last Crusade* (1989), wherein Sean Connery and Harrison Ford teamed up to play father and son archeologists fighting the Nazis throughout the world and trying to keep the chalice of Christ's Last Supper, the Holy Grail, from falling into the hands of the evil Nazi empire. Ironically, many among the Nazi high command, such as Adolf Hitler and Heinrich Himmler, were quite fond of the legends of the Holy Grail and the Knights Templar. We now know that Hitler and Himmler, inspired by Otto Rahn's *Crusade against the Grail* (Fribourg, 1933), dispatched a team of S.S. scholars and archeologists in search of the Holy Grail to southern France where local legends said that Mary Magdalene had brought the chalice with her after the crucifixion. Many churches and graveyards were desecrated in order to satisfy the Führer's will to possess this sacred object, and the records of this infamous expedition are still available at the Bibliotheque National in Paris. Thus, the S.S. began its aggressive brand of reformism aimed at bringing about a new world order through seemingly reputable "scholarship," as well as by its much more well-known system of legalized violence and murder across Germany and its conquered territories during World War II.

Hitler's rationale for the archaeological expedition must have had something to do with his own self-image of the Führer as literally meaning "the vessel" of the German spirit, or *Volksgeist*. In 1934 Hitler wondered: "How can we arrest racial decay? Shall we form a select company of the really initiated? An Order, the brotherhood of the Templars round the Holy Grail of pure blood?" (Rauschning 1939, 227). These virtually unknown events found comic expression in American popular culture when Steven Spielberg and George Lucas wrote and directed for the final chapter of the Indiana Jones trilogy. One of the most amazing moments in the entire film occurs when Indiana Jones, while clutching his father's archaeological "grail-diary" to keep it from falling into Nazi hands, stumbles upon a Nazi parade route in Berlin and bumps into Adolf Hitler. Infatuated with his own narcissistic importance and assuming that he is being asked for an autograph, the Führer then extends one hand asking for the diary and, as a bewildered Indiana Jones hands it over to him, proudly autographs the front page and returns it to Jones before resuming his place and role in the Nazi parade rally.

Not so funny about this cinematic moment is the realization that Hitler and the Nazi S.S. and Gestapo really did leave their mark upon the history of the Holy Grail. This intriguing episode from a tiny moment in American film history coincidentally speaks volumes for the ways that notions of Hitler and the Nazis as the personification and embodiment of absolute Evil in league with Satan can be projected and mythologized into a cosmic struggle against Christ and his church. In this scenario American democratic culture and capitalism emerge as the personification and embodiment of absolute Good against Satan and his evil empire of fallen angels.

Hollywood fuels the imagination so that reality can imitate fiction. The cinematic experiment that began in the late 1800s as an attempt by movie-makers to explore new plot content by reinterpreting the familiar stories and symbols from mythology, religion, classic literature such as Dante's *Inferno*, and biblical stories of both goodness and evil has been transformed over the past one hundred years into a visual medium and thriving entertainment industry in which Satan and the problems of evil and human sinfulness become the focus. Satan went to Hollywood in the early 1900s, signed a deal with the cinema industry, and has been in the moviemaking business ever since. Indeed, perhaps the greatest trick the Prince of Darkness offered over the past five hundred years was to fool modern society from the Renaissance to the Enlightenment that the God of Reason had vanquished this fallen angel and that psychoanalysis had cured human beings of the need to perpetuate the myth of Lucifer and the problem of evil. Our quest for the historical Satan would have been incomplete if we had not taken this detour and stopped in Hollywood for a little reflection on how lucrative the power of evil and the image of Satan were during the movie industry's first century in operation. If the surviving representations of ancient and medieval art attest to the presence of Satan in the historical record and in the imaginations of historic Jewish, Christian, and Islamic societies, then surely the extensive presence of satanic images and unspeakable acts of evil on the big screen, and among nearly all related mass media portals, reveal that Satan, as both deceptive trickster and Anti-Christ, will continue to live and prosper in the popular culture of the twenty-first century.

## Satan among Satanists

Representations of Satan are not limited to the movies. For some, Satan is not a being to be feared or rebuked but rather an exemplar to be revered and embraced. Those who seek to be Satan's disciples have created congregations where they can gather to worship Satan, or more accurately, what Satan represents. Probably the first congregation established for this purpose was the Church of Satan, founded in 1966 (*Anno Satanas*—year one of the Age of Satan) by a former circus and carnival showman named Anton Szandor LaVey.[3] Part religion and part capitalist venture, the Church of Satan, led by the high priest LaVey, helped shape, through his many writings, what Satan means today to the Satanists. According to LaVey, "Without a devil to point their figures at, religionists . . . would have nothing with which to threaten their followers" (1969, 55). In spite of some of the theatrics associated with the Church of Satan, the term Satanist might be a bit of a misnomer. "[Satan] merely represents a force of nature—the powers of darkness which have been named just that because no religion has taken these forces *out* of the darkness" (1969, 62).

For LaVey, devotion to Satan is really devotion to the carnal, nonconforming "self," coupled with materialism. It seeks personal power and the gratification of individual desires. "Why not be honest and if you are going to create a god in your image, why not create that god as yourself" (1969, 96). LaVey based the philosophical foundation for his countercultural church more on the writings of Ayn Rand, Aleister Crowley, and Friedrich Nietzsche than on anything supernatural—although he does advocate for choosing a rationally based metaphysical perspective. For LaVey, humanity progressed in the sciences and philosophy when people rebelled against God, the "church," or the acceptable mores of society. What is needed is not a Father God but a rebellious brother. Satan as accuser challenges the status quo, specifically the prevailing and ruling religious concepts (that is, a self-denying Christianity). A Satan that means "opposite," that enables the advancement of human civilization, was created by LaVey to serve as a metaphoric representation of the individual. In short, to hail Satan is to glorify self.

The Church of Satan's Golden Rule is "Do unto others as they do unto you" (1969, 51). As a congregation, it adheres to nine satanic statements written by LaVey to serve as their Ten Commandments. These nine satanic statements denote what Satan signifies for the church. They are: (1) Satan represents indulgence instead of abstinence; (2) Satan represents vital existence instead of spiritual pipe dreams; (3) Satan represents undefiled wisdom instead of hypocritical self-deceit; (4) Satan represents kindness to those who deserve it instead of love wasted on ingrates; (5) Satan represents vengeance instead of turning the other cheek; (6) Satan represents responsibility to the responsible instead of concern for psychic vampires; (7) Satan represents us humans as mere animals, sometimes better, more often worse than those that walk on all-fours, who, because of our "divine spiritual and intellectual development," have become the most vicious animals of all; (8) Satan represents all of the so-called sins, as they all lead to physical, mental, or emotional gratification; and (9) Satan has been the best friend the wider Christian church has ever had, having kept it in business all these years (LaVey 1969, 25).

Sin is also redefined as an attempt to respond to the Christian church's seven deadly sins. The seven deadly sins of the Catholic Church were written by a fourth-century desert monk named Evagrius of Ponticus and reconstituted by Pope Gregory the Great in 590 CE. The final list included: greed, pride, envy, anger, gluttony, lust, and sloth.[4] But for the Satanist, rather than avoiding or repenting from these deadly sins, they advocate indulging in all of them as a path to physical, mental, and emotional gratification (1969, 46). This is not to say that the concept of sin does not exist for Satanists. For them, the nine satanic sins are: (1) stupidity; (2) pretentiousness; (3) solipsism; (4) self-deceit; (5) herd conformity; (6) lack of perspective; (7) forgetfulness of past orthodoxies; (8) counterproductive pride; and (9) lack of aesthetics (Barton 1992, 243–45).

A portion of the Church of Satan splintered in 1975, creating a new sect under the leadership of a Lt. Colonel with the U.S. Army, Michael Aquino. He began the Temple of Set in 1975 with himself as high priest. The reason given for his break with LaVey is due to, according to Aquino, LaVey's "egotistic irresponsibility," with Aquino accusing LaVey of turning the Church of Satan into "a nonfunctional vehicle for his personal expression, exploitation, and financial income."[5] The alleged corruption of the Church of Satan led to Aquino being informed by Satan during a ritual that he wanted Aquino and the Church of Satan leadership to start a new church. In addition, Satan wanted to be known by his true name, Set—a reach back to pre-dynastic Egyptian times. This mandate came from Satan, or better yet, Set, in the form of a book called *The Book of Coming Forth by Night*.

According to the Temple's official website, Satan is understood:

Not [as] the evil scarecrow of Christian myth, but [as] a champion of anti-hypocrisy—a crusader against the corruption and moral bankruptcy of society, which LaVey blamed largely upon Christianity. In another, more private context, the Satan of the Church of Satan was understood to be an authentic metaphysical presence: a being not evil, but rather independent, assertive, and creative—a true Prince of Darkness after the imagery of Milton, Blake, Baudelaire, and Twain.[6]

Like the Church of Satan before it, an attempt is made by the Temple of Set to raise the individual to personal godhood—free from submission to any other god. To worship Set is to worship self—indulging in all legal desires of the ego and the body. Similar to many Eurocentric Christian organized religions, the focus of Satanist organized churches is on the individual. One exception is that while the emphasis for Christians is the quest for individual spiritual gratification, Satanists seek individual physical gratification.

Perhaps the most damning indictment made against modern-day Satanists occurred during the 1980s. Satanists were accused of engaging in crimes, specifically drugging children and forcing them to participate in sexual acts at their day care centers, or offering human sacrifices, usually babies, to Lucifer. Contrary to such anti-Satanic church propaganda, there appears to be no foundation to the claim linking such churches to crimes or violence against individuals. The *Satanic Bible* clearly states that "Under NO circumstances would a Satanist sacrifice any animal or baby! . . . [because] man the animal, is the godhead to the Satanist [and thus sacred]" (1969, 89); nevertheless, such nefarious accusations were usually made by so-called ex-Satanists who claimed to have been eye-witnesses to such activities. Fueled by the news media, specifically the May 16, 1985 ABC *20/20* television show and the Geraldo Rivera 1988 two-hour documentary special, a "Satanic Panic" ignited throughout most of the 1980s and early 1990s among the general public. The book that is probably most responsible for launching the "Satanic Panic" was *The Satan Seller*, written by Christian comedian Mike Warnke in 1972.

Mike Warnke, an alleged former high priest of Satan, one of the three Master Counselors of the Brotherhood with fifteen hundred disciples (Warnke 1972, 57), claimed that Satanists, backed by the Illuminati (1972, 93–95), are responsible for two million human sacrifices a year throughout the United

States (Medway 2001, 199). He appeared as an expert commentator on the 1985 ABC *20/20* report, which bore the title "The Devil Worshippers." Unfortunately for him, his character, and thus his witness, eventually came under question when his testimony was debunked in 1992 by the cover-story of the Christian magazine *Cornerstone*. The exposé refuted his claims of living a drug-addicted life or ever belonging to a satanic cult (see Trott and Hertenstein 1992). Further investigative reporting revealed he was engaged in financial irregularities, collecting funds at evangelical events for preschool children abused by Satanists and diverting said funds for personal use. In 1991 Warnke Ministries paid over $800,000 in salaries to Warnke, his wife, and his brother-in-law and only $900 for charitable purposes (Warnke 1972, 168).[7]

Warnke was eventually forced to "clarify and acknowledge" that his conversion story from Satanism and accusations against Satanists as outlined in his best seller, *The Satan Seller*, contained "some exaggerations and embellishments . . . due to old and perhaps faulty memories as well as deliberate attempts to 'protect the innocent.'" Additionally, he confessed to "the previous ungodliness of [his] personal life, to [his] multiple divorces and unwise decisions" (2002, 169). Also problematic was Warnke's assertion that two million human sacrifices a year were occurring. Two million human sacrifices a year is a statistically significant number; yet there is a total and complete lack of evidence substantiating his claim. If these figures were true, one would expect at least one body would have been found, one arrest would have been made, one conviction would have been on the records. It must be asked if the yearly murders of two million individuals offered up as human sacrifices was an exaggeration or a fabrication. Medway concludes by pointing out, "In alleged cases of criminal Satanism, there are no missing persons, no bodies, no bones, no blood, no temples, no altars, no robes, no rituals, and no Satanists (2001, 199, 329).

## Satan among Fundamentalists

It is ironic that while Satanists see Satan more as a symbol signifying qualities needed for human progress and power, many Christian Fundamentalists see Satan more as an actual being. If Satanists perceive the Devil as a figure needed to spur forward the advancement of civilization as a means by which the individual is centered, then Fundamentalists see Satan as someone to fear, someone bent on destroying God's good creation and the sacred mission

of Christ's church on earth. Fundamentalists' stern support of biblical literature has led to the advocacy of mass media censorship to protect Christ's lost
sheep from the lures of the Evil One. They are not deceived by the satanic
motivations inspiring Rock music or Hollywood's obsession with horror
films and science fiction fantasies like Darth Vader or Hellboy. They recognize that the destruction wrought by the Prince of Evil is usually conducted
by subtle means. Take the example offered in the book *Satan Is Alive and
Well on Planet Earth*, written by famed evangelical author Hal Lindsey. He
argues that the methodologies used at universities and seminaries to study
the sacred text known as higher criticism is part of Satan's plan to discredit
the Bible and lead people away from having a personal relationship with God
(1972, 42–45).

Hal Lindsey is best known for his best-selling 1970 work *The Late Great
Planet Earth*, in which he predicts that the earth would end around 1988
(1970, 43). In his follow-up book, *The 1980's [sic]: Countdown to Armageddon*, he boldly claimed, "The decade of the 1980's [sic] could very well be
the last decade of history as we know it" (1980, 8). For Lindsey and the millions of Christians whose perception of Satan resonates with Lindsey's work,
Satan is the mastermind behind non-Christian religions, specifically Eastern
religions (1972, 44), and the drug culture of the 1960s (1970, 114). He even
credits UFO sightings with the demonic: "I believe these demons will stage a
spacecraft landing on Earth. They will claim to be from an advanced culture
in another galaxy" (1980, 33).

According to the narrative, as advocated by Lindsey and most Fundamentalist proponents, God created an angelic realm to glorify the Creator,
making Lucifer the crowning achievement of creation. Among all the angels,
Lucifer was the most beautiful and the most intelligent, bright as the morning star. Realizing his superiority to the other angels, Lucifer's ego became
overblown, leading him to rebel against God. Inflated with pride, Lucifer
dared to equate himself to God. Attributing a satire on the king of Babylon
(Isa 14:4) to Satan, most Fundamentalists believe that the fall of Daystar, son
of the Morning from the Heavens, refers to the reason for Satan's rebellion.
Isaiah 14:12-15 reads:

> How you have fallen from the heavens, O shining star, son of the morn-
> ing. You who weakened the nations are cut down to the ground. In your
> heart you have said, "I will ascend to the heavens, I will raise my throne

above God's stars, and I will sit on the mount of meeting, on Zaphon's heights. I will rise over the tops of the clouds. I will be likened to the Most High." Yet to Shoel shall you go down, to the depths of the Pit.

Arrogance and self-importance caused Lucifer to become the first created being to sin. To make matters worse, he led an insurrection, backed by a third of the angelic host, against God. This rebellion of angels brought impurity into God's perfect universal order. Although the insurrection was crushed, thanks to the archangel Michael, Lucifer, along with his followers, was cast out of Heaven. With Lucifer's fall from the highest pinnacle came a name change to Satan, an eternal banishment from Heaven, and the start of a cosmic war that could be won only by a wounded God. Hell was created for Satan and all who chose to follow him.

Prior to creating humans, God restored harmony and perfection to the universe in the form of Eden. Other scholars and biblical interpreters have tended to date Satan's rebellion to a time after the six days of creation when everything was still good and before the disobedience of Adam and Eve. Regardless of the timeline, God placed the first man, created in God's image, and the first woman, created in man's image [*sic*], to enjoy perfection. Humans, rather than angels, became God's crowning achievement because they contained the *imago dei*—the image of God. The first couple was to rule over all creation as long as they obeyed one rule: they could not eat from the tree of the knowledge of good and evil planted in the center of this idyllic garden—for if they were to eat its fruit, surely they would die. After providing the warning, God allowed Satan to enter the scene, for Satan is unable to do anything without God's permission. Satan had but one goal, lead this new creature into rebellion against God. Disguised as a serpent with legs, Satan tempted Eve, the more susceptible of the two [*sic*], with the fruit of the forbidden tree, knowing that if she sinned, Adam would follow. Eve ate of the fruit, as did Adam, thus disobeying God and falling from grace.

The disobedience of humans meant that they and all of their descendants became enslaved to Satan. Their only salvation would be a perfect sacrifice that could redeem humanity and break loose the bondage of Satan. But how, if all begotten by man would carry this original sin of disobedience? Only a perfect sacrifice, born of a woman, not man (because the substance of original sin was located in the man's semen), could be sinless and thus an unblemished sacrifice. Through the death of this unblemished sacrifice, humanity could be redeemed and restored to fellowship with God. It should have been us, as humans, who should have died, but Jesus took our place on the cross. He, the perfect sacrifice, the Lamb of God who took away the sins of the world, paid the price for our transgressions. Through Jesus Christ's redemptive suffering in the crucifixion, humanity is healed. Hence, salvation would occur for those who believe that through the incarnation of God in Jesus, Satan's hold on humanity is broken. But for those who reject Jesus/God, they remain in rebellion and thus under the power of Satan. Those who participate in other faiths or are more liberal in their interpretation of the biblical narrative are, in reality, whether they know it or not, still following Satan's lies and thus separated now and for all eternity from God.

Among some Fundamentalists, specifically those who are Pentecostals or charismatic, demons can possess any individual. These demons have names associated with sins. For example, there is the demon of lust or the demon of envy. Demons could also be associated with illnesses, like the demon of cancer or the demon of back pain. Finally, these demons can be named after activities that the overarching group believes to be a sin, as in the case of the demon of homosexuality. Exorcism can become part of the worship service, where the pastor or minister, anointed by God, lays hands upon the one possessed with a certain demon for the purpose of casting the demon out. The minister, speaking in the name and authority of Jesus, commands the demon to identify itself. Because the demons are forced to obey the one anointed by God speaking in Jesus' stead, they must obey truthfully. They respond through the voice of the one possessed, revealing its demonic identity. Once the minister knows the demon or demons' name(s), the minister can cast them out in Jesus' name. Usually a struggle ensues, with the demon yelling it does not want to leave—but eventually, because all authority over demons is given to the believer, the minister wins the spiritual battle, leaving the once demon-possessed individual collapsed on the floor from physical exhaustion.

## Satan among Catholics

Many Catholics, like their Fundamentalists counterparts, have a history of promoting the concept of Satan's existence, contributing to the creation of a Christianity of damnation. The Devil is engaged in a cosmic warfare against the spiritual forces of God, and as punishment the Devil and all those who follow his lies will be damned to Hell and eternally separated from God.

Satan's existence was reaffirmed by Pope Paul VI in an address he gave to a general audience on November 15, 1972 titled, "Confronting the Devil's Power." In his address, Pope Paul VI portrays the Devil as "a dark, hostile agent . . . [who is] an active force, a living being that is perverted and that perverts others. It is a terrible reality, mysterious and frightening."[8]

Like most Protestant belief systems, many Catholic teachings confirm that Satan was at first a good angel made by God who rejected God's reign and authority. He then led the first human parents, Adam and Eve, into rebellion by tempting them to eat from the tree of the knowledge of good and evil, and their subsequent Fall from grace as a result of these temptations and their disobedience to the Will of God. Although powerful, Satan's power is not infinite. Due to the original sin of the first parents, death entered creation and all of humanity is born under the sway of the Evil One.

Only through Jesus freely giving himself up to death can humanity be delivered from the Devil. Thus, baptism becomes an exorcism signifying the candidate's explicit renunciation of Satan and liberation from sin and from sin's instigator. Why God would allow Satan to exist and wreak havoc with creation is chalked up as "a great mystery" (*Catechism of the Catholic Church* 2000, 391–97, 413, 1237, 2853). Like Protestants and Evangelicals, Roman Catholics have also been alarmed at the satanic and evil nature of much that passes for the secularism and pop culture of the modern world, and since the nineteenth century, the Papacy has sought to engage modernity more creatively and more focused on peace and social justice activism than most other denominations. In the wise pastoral words of John Paul II: "The evil of our times consists in the first place in a kind of degradation, indeed in a pulverization, of the fundamental uniqueness of each human person" (de Lubac 1993, 171–72). His own experiences of violence and loss in Poland during the Second World War convinced him of the subtle and persistent power of evil in the world, and in his thoughtful speeches and moving sermons, while traveling around the world during his pontificate, encouraged young men and women to practice true compassion and forgiveness by becoming the "craftsmen of a new humanity" despite the persistent mystery of evil and human violence in the world.

## Satan and the Left Behind Series

Probably no other book series has contributed more to the modern Christian understanding of evil than the twelve-book Left Behind series written by

Tim LaHaye and Jerry Jenkins. When the first book made its début in 1995, it, along with the next seven books of the series, received modest attention among a conservative, evangelical niche market. However, its lack of popularity was reversed shortly after the collapse of the Twin Towers. According to the authors, sales of the series skyrocketed immediately following the events of 9/11 (LaHaye, Jenkins, and Swanson 2005, 13). For the first time, one of the books in the series, the ninth book, *Desecration*, the first to be published after 9/11, made the *New York Times* best-selling fiction list. As of 2006, over sixty million books were sold (Flesher 2006, 7). Although the book is fictional, the authors insist that it is based on the correct and only valid literal interpretation of biblical prophecy. In their version of biblical interpretation, common among most conservative fundamentalists who are mainly Protestant and evangelical, but also Catholics (even though the series is extremely anti-Papal),[9] all believers will be raptured before Jesus returns to earth.

The rapture is based on 1 Thess 4:15-18, where the author of the epistle states that Christ will return and take up into the clouds those who are still alive with those being resurrected from the dead. To be taken or snatched by Christ has come to be called the rapture. Those who are left behind are the enemies of Christ, in league with the Devil, whether they know it or not. They are usually characterized as being anti-family, understood as being pro-feminist, pro-homosexual, and pro-abortion. In effect, a dichotomy is created where everyone who disagrees with how LaHaye and Jenkins interpret the eschaton, that is, the last days, are in cahoots with the Devil. Hebrew Bible scholar Leann Snow Flesher best summarizes who, according to LaHaye and Jenkins, is a true believer and who follows Satan:

> [LaHaye and Jenkins] have used the premillennial agenda to declare what is good and what is evil, who is in and who is out, and how proper Christianity ought to behave. According to these authors, secular humanism is the satanic nemesis of the true Christian church; the Roman Catholic Church is filled with idolaters; the Chinese are pagan humanistic communists plotting to take over the world; the world is quickly moving toward a one-world government, economy, and religion over which the Antichrist will reign; white U.S. males will physically take charge and lead us to the path of salvation; Jewish men will convert to Christianity and teach that Bible prophecy speaks of Jesus;

women play support roles, which includes the priority of bearing and taking care of children; the 'other' is the enemy and is to be evangelized whenever possible; Greek philosophy has polluted Christianity; martyrdom is an honor; and taking arms is part of the call. (2006, 56–57)

Once true believers are raptured, all the world religions (Hinduism, Islam, Buddhism, and so on), except Judaism, can put aside their differences and join forces as one faith system because, after all, they have the common denominator of being inspired by Satan.

After Christians miraculously depart planet earth, those left behind will face seven years of tribulation. Tribulation is the period of time marked by global trial and suffering. Those who advocate, as do the writers of the Left Behind series, that the believers in Christ will be spared this period of earthly destruction and desolation are called pre-tribulationists, because they will be raptured before the start of the tribulation. Those, on the other hand, who believe the church of Christ would also undergo the trials of the tribulation are known as post-tribulationists, while those who claim the church would be spared the last, more brutal part of the tribulation but will endure the first half are known as mid-tribulationists. It is during the tribulation, according to the Left Behind series, that fictional character Nicolae Carpathia, the Anti-Christ, establishes his worldwide government.

Under the Anti-Christ's rule, all Hell literally breaks loose as the world suffers God's merciless judgment. For example, the fifth book of the series, *Apollyon*, which is based on Rev 9:1-12, interprets the blowing of the fifth trumpet by God's angel as the prelude to the release of locust-type creatures with scorpion-type powers. Led by a chief demon named Apollyon, these locust creatures attack those who are without God's seal on their forehead. The pain inflicted by the sting of these demonic insects is so great that people try to kill themselves but are unable to die.

In the Left Behind series, the Anti-Christ is eventually assassinated in the sixth book, *Assassins*. Yet on the third day, according to the seventh book, *The Indwelling*, the Anti-Christ arises from the dead, indwelt by Satan. Halfway through the tribulation, the Anti-Christ demands total allegiance (Carpathianism—the worship of Nicolae Carpathia), and those who refuse are sent to the guillotine in public squares throughout the world. Soon he is forcing the mark of the Beast upon the world. He goes to Jerusalem to desecrate the Temple by declaring himself god. There, he gathers all the world's armies for one last cosmic battle against the Host of Heaven, led by Jesus Christ riding a white horse. With the Anti-Christ defeated, all the people of the world are gathered for the final judgment prior to the start of the millennium. The millennium, based on Rev 20:5, starts with the first resurrection, when those who have been martyred for the cause of Christ come back to life and rule with Christ for a thousand years.

This understanding of a tribulation occurring before Christ returns to earth and establishes his thousand-year reign is known within theological circles as premillennial, the view held by the authors of the Left Behind series. Humanity is beyond reform; hence, the world would become more and more violent, as in the days prior to Noah's flood. Total world destruction is averted through God's intervention; evil is defeated and Christ physically establishes his kingdom on earth. Postmillennialism, on the other hand, believes that as the gospel is preached and people are converted, evil would come to an end, making it possible for Jesus to return and establish his thousand-year reign.[10]

Premillennial thought became part of theological belief known as dispensationalism. U.S. Christians since the Revolutionary War up until the Civil War were mainly postmillennialists. They believed that the only thing preventing God's return was the social issue of slavery. Once slavery was abolished, Christ's second coming would occur. Reading the lyrics of the "Battle Hymn of the Republic" clearly reveals the songwriter's postmillennialist tendencies. The first verse of the song is, "Mine eyes have seen the glory of the coming of the Lord: He is trampling out the vintage where the grapes of wrath are stored; He hath loosed the fateful lightning of His terrible swift sword: His truth is marching on." The verse is a clear reference to the final cosmic battle laid out in the book of Revelation, where an angel of the Lord is found casting grapes into "the great winepress of the wrath of God" (14:19), and where we find a description of how God's Word wields "a sharp sword" that "treads the winepress of the fierceness and wrath of Almighty God" (19:15).

After the carnage of the Civil War and the unrest and chaos during Reconstruction, many Christians lost faith in the optimistic postmillennialist proposition that humans were morally getting better and closer to God's ideal. In fact, the reverse occurred, humans were becoming more reprobate with each passing year—hence the rise in popularity of premillennialism (Marsden 1980, 48–55). Dispensationalism is a modern theological invention, never held by any church scholar, teacher, or minister until it was introduced to the American public in the 1870s by a man named John Nelson Darby. Darby's dispensationalism is a system of interpretation imposed upon the biblical text. Human history, according to Darby, can be divided into seven dispensations, namely: (1) innocence (prior to the Fall); (2) conscience (from the Fall up to the Flood); (3) human government (from the Flood to the call of Abraham); (4) promise (from the call of Abraham to the giving of the law at Mount Sinai); (5) law (from the giving of the law to the death of Christ); (6) grace (from the giving of the Spirit at Pentecost to Christ's second coming); and (7) kingdom (from the second coming of Christ to the establishment of the throne of judgment). Obviously, we are presently living in the sixth dispensation of grace.

Darby's ideas became popular with such conservative evangelicals as D. L. Moody and C. I. Scofield. With the rise of fundamentalism as a response to the spread of secular humanism, liberal Christianity, Darwinism, and the use of biblical higher criticism epitomized in the so-called Scopes Monkey Trial of 1925, Darby's dispensationalism became a major tenet of most conservative-leaning believers. The problem with dispensational thought is the negative contributions it makes to moral reasoning. Followers of dispensational theology, like LaHaye and Jenkins, are suspicious of justice work and humanitarian concerns. Such concerns are not part of true Christianity but rather are expressions of secular humanism. To challenge oppressive social structures or to try to achieve a more just political or economic system are sure signs of apostasy. To work for justice, that is, to try to make the good news of the gospel as expressed in the Sermon on the Mount a reality within human history, is to participate in evil, for such efforts are inspired and directed by Satan. In a perverted form of logic, to feed the hungry, give drink to the thirsty, or clothe the naked is Satanic.

## Satan among Liberals

For liberal Christians, science, the child of the Age of Enlightenment, killed Satan—if not God. An evil being responsible for much of the world's misery was exchanged for the evil that lurks within human hearts and minds. All may wrestle with their "personal demons," but these satanic minions are not metaphysical beings as Fundamentalists might argue. Instead, they are personal addictions that may be caused by chemical imbalances or unfortunate circumstances caused by personal or societal wrong choices. For example, the casting out of the devil by Jesus from a boy who was constantly in a wretched state, always falling into the fire or into water (Matt 17:14-18), is interpreted by most liberals not as a demonic possession but as an epileptic seizure. Not having the benefits of modern scientific knowledge, the Gospel writers used the supernatural to explain physical and emotional ailments.

Some liberals would argue that the Christian's spiritual warfare against demons is, in reality, a psychological attempt to repress the libido. While the term libido is usually linked to sexual energies, the term is here understood in its more general definition, the psychic and emotional energy that is associated with primitive biological urges and drives (that is, self-preservation) expressed in conscious activity. While the Christian teaches sexual self-restraint, putting the needs of others before self-interest, self-sacrifice, and a willingness to seek martyrdom, our libido urges us to do the opposite. The libido, representing the biological, wars against the spiritual ideals humans wish to achieve. We do not wrestle with non-existing demons but with flesh and blood. There is no Satan to blame, there is no exorcism that can cure us; rather, the problem lies with us—individually or as part of human society—and thus the cure lies with us and our repressed drives and biological urges.

This was the gist of the argument behind the theory of psychoanalysis that emerged in 1899 with the landmark publication in Vienna, Austria, of Sigmund Freud's *The Interpretation of Dreams*. As a student of Classical philosophy and modern psychology at the University of Paris, Freud's humanistic convictions theorized that people could be healed from their anxieties, phobias, neuroses, repressed emotions, and behavioral complexes through a series of dialog sessions aimed at uncovering the contents of the patients' unconscious. It was a sort of modern Socratic Method applied to the process of self-discovery by which Freud and his disciples substituted their role as psychological guides for the traditional roles of priest, pastor, or rabbi in the spiritual and mental development of the person.

Sigmund Freud (1856–1939) later published two of the most influential books of the modern world: *The Future of an Illusion* (1927) and *Civilization and Its Discontents* (1930). The latter volume elaborates his psycho-sexual theory on the relation of repressed sexuality to neurotic behaviors and expands on his theory of the "death-drive." Freud, like many others of his generation, was profoundly disturbed by the violence and destruction of World War I and Europe's post-war social problems, which influenced his negative views in *Civilization* and his growing conviction that as a "collective neurosis" religion was the root of many of humanity's problems. Freud was also an intensely passionate supporter and defender of the Enlightenment legacy that scientific rationalism and logical positivism held the potential to emancipate humanity and society from the age-old superstitions, repressions, and childish wish-fulfillments of religion. He and many others from among the generation of intellectuals and sociologists who came of age in Europe and the Americas during the 1890s believed that an ethics and epistemology based on the principles of science might lay the foundation for a new human consciousness by the year 2000 that would be free from the need for a God or a Satan to hold human behavior in check while allegedly struggling against each other for the salvation or control of the human heart and mind.

Religion, Freud maintained, was an illusion with no future. It was as if psychoanalysis had invited Satan into therapy and, there on the psychologist's couch, had tricked Satan into believing he did not have power over the human spirit. Or was this trickery actually the opposite—such that Satan had once again fooled humanity into believing the Prince of Darkness did not exist? Faith seemingly could not stand up to the liberating influences of the new scientific spirit:

> If this belief is an illusion, then we are in the same position as you. But science has given us evidence by its numerous and important successes that it is no illusion. Science has many open enemies, and many more secret ones, among those who cannot forgive her for having weakened religious faith and for threatening to overthrow it. She is reproached for the smallness of the amount she has taught us and for the incomparably greater field she has left in obscurity. But, in this, people forget how young she is, how difficult her beginnings were and how infinitesimally small is the period of time since the human intellect has been strong enough for the tasks she sets. Are we not at fault, in basing our judgments on periods of time that are too short? No, our science is no illusion. But an illusion it would be to suppose that what science cannot give us we can get elsewhere. (Freud 1927, 70–71)

In the end, however, this "scientific spirit" proved to be another modernist ideology masquerading as a meta-narrative that Roman Catholics, Fundamentalists, and Protestant Christians came to view with skepticism and mistrust. Some, disturbed by Freud's atheism and preoccupation with sexuality, went so far as to repudiate all Freudian ideas and applications of psychoanalysis as a demonic derailment of the pastoral care of persons suffering from mental illness and behavioral disorders.

Some therapists from among the ranks of the clergy, including the Swiss Lutheran pastor Oskar Pfister (1873–1956), responded sternly to the Freudian ideology by developing the field of pastoral theology and care as one grounded in the basic teachings of Jesus, Christian humanism, and the early Christian legacy of healing and promoting personal wholeness. A lifelong student and supporter of Freud's theories, Pfister responded to Freud's attack on religion with a highly critical essay in 1928, "Die Illusion einer Zukunft" ("The Illusion of the Future").

Other therapists, such as Freud's most brilliant and favorite disciple, the Swiss psychiatrist Carl G. Jung (1875–1961), responded to Freud's antireligious ideology by investigating the spiritual and symbolic dimensions of the unconscious and the care of the soul in the psychoanalytic process. His approach led the famed teacher and his designated heir to a devastating professional break around 1913 (Donn 1988, 137–85). As Jung's career unfolded in Zurich and he witnessed the horrors that European totalitarianism and Nazism set loose upon the world, he came to despise the naïve and optimistic dreams about scientific emancipation and the "Good Life" that intellectuals and politicians in such modern-day societies as Germany, Russia, Japan, Great Britain, and the United States had promised the world in the late 1890s and early 1900s. In the face of such atrocities and terrors as those caused by two World Wars, Germany's descent into the abyss of Nazism and the Holocaust, and America's development and deployment of atomic weapons, Jung became one of the twentieth century's most ardent protesters against the denial of evil in the cosmos, criticizing modern civilization's obsession with absolute good and its denial of the demonic realities of the dark side of human behavior.

The rift between faith and science grew wider in the first half of the 1900s as a result of such reactions and suspicions to the effectiveness of psychoanalysis in the treatment of mental health. Nonetheless, Freud's convictions regarding the possibility of healing the mentally afflicted by simply "talking-out" their fears, repressions, or anxieties and analyzing the content of patients' dreams proved to be a game-changing moment in the quest for the historical Satan and in the ancient struggle to understand the origins of evil within and among human societies. No area of human knowledge, medicine and education, leadership and ethics, or social relations was immune to the influence of Freudian psychoanalysis and its related movements since 1900. In this sense, Sigmund Freud was a prophetic writer and thinker who perceived the final demise of the old medieval spiritual and religious worldview.

Yet we must pose a major question that we shall have occasion to ponder more deeply later in this volume: Did Freud invite Western Christian civilization into a psychoanalytic therapy session on a comfy, cozy couch in an office surrounded by ancient religious icons and scientific books and then convince men and women that our dreams of Satan and his demons were now irrelevant in the liberated new worldviews of modernity?

## Satan and Ethical Thought

Satan, as a meta-narrative that personifies evil, is a term today's Christian ethicists hesitate to use as a moral category. Nevertheless, the definition of Satan and his host of demons relentlessly tempting humans, coupled with a stern God quick to punish twisted sinners and the wicked, have served as powerful tools for social control. Fear of Satan and the threat of Hell have historically forced large segments of the population toward self-policing while setting high moral standards. Individual guilt has been used by churches, both Catholic and Protestant, throughout the ages to scare parishioners into obedience and compliance. It matters little if Satan actually exists. What is important is that the figure of Satan, and the theme of "satanic" intentions and actions, has become an institutional construct employed to control the masses.

The pursuit of goodness requires the repression of those who fail or refuse to obey. And what better way to justify the silencing of subversives to the authority of the church and/or society than to project evil tendencies upon them? Inquisitions, crusades, the burning of witches, or the genocide of heathens and unbelievers become means by which the good—here defined as the status quo—is maintained. To oppose dissent, by definition, transforms the accuser into the defender of the good, righteousness, and the forces of light. It is as if the defenders project their own lower, base instincts and desires upon the accused to provide an excuse to rid, and in so doing exorcise, the qualities society's defenders possess and detest.

Widespread demonic conspiracies are created to mobilize the public (mob?) in empowering leading spokespersons against the satanic threat. But for the evil of others to be believed, the community must first be made to be afraid. Anxiety over those in league with the Devil must be maintained at a fever pitch. Such an anxiety is usually maintained on half-truths and manufactured facts, as was the case made concerning Iraq's connection to the 9/11 events and its alleged stockpile of weapons of mass destruction. A vested interest exists in keeping Satan and his dominion alive for the "grand inquisitors" who derive their power by maintaining fear among the masses and by having an evil to purge. Because fire must be fought with fire, satanic methodologies, out of necessity, must be adopted. During the first Persian Gulf War (1990–1991), Saddam Hussein and his regime were repeatedly compared to Adolf Hitler and the Nazi Party. Hence, torture was employed by the defenders of the good (liberty) against those they labeled terrorists. To torture publicly Satan's allies and followers assures that others will privately police themselves and submit to the authority of the church and/or society's rulers, lest they, too, be accused and face a similar fate.

Still, the problem with evil may not lie as much with the Satan figure as with the "thoughtlessness" of humans who simply accept and follow those on a crusade against the satanic. In Hannah Arendt's classical discourse on the banality of evil, she reveals that the logistics manager responsible for transporting millions of Jews to the death camps, the individual known as "the architect of the Holocaust," did not carry out his responsibilities due to any personal malice or depravity. S.S. Lieutenant-Colonel Adolf Eichmann was no Shakespearian villain like Macbeth. He was no fanatical anti-Semite but in fact had plenty of "private reasons," including Jews within his own family, for not being a Jew-hater (1977, 26–30). What makes Eichmann frightening, according to Arendt, is the banality of his normalcy. "He *merely*, to put the matter colloquially, *never realized what he was doing. . . .* It was sheer thoughtlessness—something by no means identical with stupidity—that predisposed him to become one of the greatest criminals of the period. . . . [W]ith the best will in the world one cannot extract any diabolical or demonic profundity from Eichmann" (1977, 287–88). The satanic exists not because there are a few villains among humanity, a few who are vicious or cruel, a few who reject God or Christianity. "The trouble with Eichmann," Arendt writes, "was precisely that so many were like him, and that the many were neither perverted nor sadistic, that they were, and still are, terribly and terrifyingly normal . . . this normality was much more terrifying than all the atrocities put together" (1977, 276).

Similarly, the infamous founder of the Nazi Gestapo and leader of the S.S., Heinrich Himmler, was born and raised in a devout Roman Catholic family descended from Bavarian nobility and had access to the finest educational and religious opportunities for German youth of his era. He was also fascinated by mythic tales of the Aryan master race and medieval legends of the Knights Templar who guarded the Holy Grail. In the early 1920s, Himmler's interest in medieval lore and the history of Aryan racial origins known as Ariosophy, led him either to join or at least to examine the teachings of German-Aryan secret societies such as the Thule Society and the Ordo Novi Templi (O.N.T.), which was modeled on the legends of the Templars. In his groundbreaking work on "Ariosophy," *The Occult Roots of Nazism* (1992), Nicholas Goodrick-Clarke describes the ideological delusions and theories of race that led to this strange mixture of childlike attraction to chivalry with ardent nationalism and Anti-Semitic hatred. Membership in groups such as the O.N.T. depended upon the novice's ability to prove his racial purity, adhere to the rules of the order, and assist in the task of founding new chapters and lodges across Austria and Germany.

The ideal of breeding racially pure "god-men," who could act above the laws of humanity by virtue of their exalted spiritual and biological status and who would then advance the mission of the Order, has been documented by Goodrick-Clarke, who suggests a direct link between these romanticized chivalric fantasies and the killing machine that emerged when Himmler assumed increasingly more command over all S.S. operations in the early 1930s. From that moment on, we find Himmler's revitalized S.S., bolstered by the research of Ariosophy, adopting numerous ideals and symbols that formerly characterized Aryan fraternities and cults.

In the years that followed, Himmler directed an amazing number of "culture-preserving" and "culture-creating" activities by annexing medieval castles, villas, and priory lands across Europe. These endeavors were part of the overall design by which he and his administrative staff sought to bolster the prestige of S.S. officers and troops as modern Aryan knights. This elite-guard of the Nazis even had their own departments of culture, prehistory, and archaeology at S.S. headquarters that issued manifestos and publications on the history of Aryan origins. Himmler also hired architects and consultants to design a lavish museum of S.S. history and lore where the *Übermensch* (literally, "Overman" or "Super-Man") of this racialized culture of power and hatred would be honored and glorified well into the next Aryan-Christian millennium (Goodrick-Clarke 1992, 108, 192–204, 209–14, 217–25).

As fate would have it, however, Himmler's chivalric fantasies and murderous reign came to an end in May 1945 when he was captured by a British army unit after trying to negotiate the surrender of all Nazi forces with General Eisenhower's office. He allegedly had also asked to be appointed as the national "police director" of the new German government after the war, which oddly would have been just another "ordinary" and "normal" job for a major Nazi war criminal. He committed suicide a few days after being arrested while awaiting his trial. Himmler's Waffen-S.S. numbered nearly one million members by the close of the war in 1945. Of the surviving S.S. leaders and members investigated by Allied tribunals after the war, the vast majority claimed to be just "ordinary" German citizens and "normal" individuals attracted to the ideals, discipline, and culture of the S.S. and to Himmler's charismatic and patriotic qualities.

After the war, when public knowledge of Nazism's mechanized murder became more widespread, it exacerbated psychiatrist Carl Jung's moral crisis over the problem of absolute Evil versus absolute Good. How did the presumably most intellectually and scientifically sophisticated nation among Western civilization plunge itself into the apocalyptic juggernaut of Nazism? As his patients struggled with these same concerns and other related sentiments of collective guilt, Carl Jung found himself questioning Saint Augustine's conception of the origin of evil as the absence of good (*privatio boni*) and, as the result of disordered love, against something much more sinister and demonic in human nature. Jung's professional efforts to restore an appreciation for the reality of the human soul among psychiatrists and psychoanalysts were juxtaposed with his personal struggle to deal with modern humanity's individual and collective denial of the problem of evil. Before passing away in June 1961, Jung was rumored by some among his inner circle to have been quite disturbed by dream-like visions of continued global violence and environmental destruction throughout the early twenty-first century. In his own words, and as reported by his colleague and close friend, Marie Louise von Franz (1915–1998), on the occasion of her last meeting with him before his death: "I see enormous stretches devastated, enormous stretches of the earth, but thank God it's not the whole planet."[11] One wonders today if it was just another *illusion of the future?*

The satanic ceases to be limited to the intentional infliction of suffering, pain, and/or the forces of death. Evil becomes more than just the absence of the good. The satanic can very easily become complicit with social structures designed to benefit some at the expense of others. Eichmann and Himmler were ordinary individuals complicit with such evil social structures. They were like so many of us are today—normal. And it is those who are "normal" that go to church each Sunday, sing hymns of God's goodness, and through their "thoughtlessness" remain complicit with social structures that bring death to those on the underside of the dominant culture, death to those who are disenfranchised by the status quo. Arendt's critique on evil's banality is that there might be more "little Eichmanns" around us (as Ward Churchill, professor of ethnic studies at the University of Colorado expressed concerning the 9/11 tragedy) than we care to admit. Blaming Satan for the horrors of the Holocaust, or for the terrors of 9/11, has the tendency of acquitting thoughtless "normal" people from responsibility, people who fail to see the everyday immorality of social structures and indifference to human suffering.

To deal with the satanic is to move beyond the metaphysical toward praxis, social actions. We should be less interested in Satan the being than with the satanic. If Satan represents death, then actions and the social structures that sustain oppression—more so than individual people, no matter how evil they may appear—are satanic. It was not Eichmann or Himmler who was the satanic monster but the social structures of Nazism that allowed normal, everyday people like Eichmann and Himmler to participate as a cog in the wheel of death and destruction. For those on the underside of society, there is less interest in answering questions about metaphysical beings than in seeking Christian actions that combat the evil that causes oppression. The struggle is with the historical causes of oppression that forces the vast majority of the world's population to live in want so that a small minority can amass power, possessions, and privilege. The Christian ethical response is not to explain Satan but to explain the satanic and point toward forms of praxis that rebuke such evil.

In the final analysis, regardless of whether one believes or disbelieves in the existence of Satan, the Devil has become a cultural construct. Unfortunately, this construct is responsible for much of human misery, from inquisitions to crusades, from colonialism to genocide. Maybe our conception of Satan as signifying absolute Evil has outlived its usefulness and thus deserves once and for all to be put to death and buried—and let the dead bury the dead. And yet maybe, just maybe, Satan as eternal trickster continues to confound humanity by providing us with the simplistic choice of either the personification of unadulterated evil or simply a figment of humanity's imagination. Maybe Satan can be a more important construct to the development of ethics if we return to a more original understanding of the figure of Satan as a trickster. Our attempt in the present quest for the historical Satan is not to dismiss Satan but to shift our understanding of him so that he can become a better tool for bringing about liberative ethical responses to evil. But before exploring this possibility and how it can change contemporary ethical discourse and the historic dichotomy of absolute Good versus absolute Evil, this book will first explore the textual birth of Satan in the biblical tradition and his influence on human history. ✳

# Chapter 2

## THE BIRTH OF SATAN: A TEXTUAL HISTORY

I n an instant, entire families were crushed to death. The earth shook, buildings collapsed, and the virtuous, along with the villainous, perished together. Those with deep faith and those whose faith was centered on their own life pleasures now occupy the same mass grave for all eternity, as their remains decompose and mingle together as dust. On January 12, 2010, those who put their trust in God met their end alongside those who rebuked all that is holy when a devastating earthquake struck the impoverished island of Haiti. As the dust settled, Christians were left struggling for meaning in the wake of a calamity that destroyed seemingly innocent lives and communities. Those searching for, if not demanding, an answer from an all-loving God are often as befuddled as our prehistoric ancestors were when dealing with something as unpredictable and sudden as a meaningless death, especially one due to a natural disaster.

Less than two days after the horrible earthquake that killed over two-hundred-thousand people hit Haiti, televangelist Pat Robertson announced on the Christian Broadcasting Network's *700 Club* that the Haitian people were cursed as a result of a pact they made with the Devil over two centuries ago. In his own words:

> Something happened a long time ago in Haiti, and people might not want to talk about it, they [Haitians] were under the heel of the French,

and, uh you know, Napoleon III or whatever, and they got together and swore a pact to the Devil and they said, "we will serve you if you get us free from the French." True story. So the Devil said "okay, it's a deal." And they kicked the French out, you know, the Haitians revolted and got themselves free, but ever since they have been cursed by one thing after the other, desperately poor. That island of Hispaniola is one island, cut down the middle, on one side is Haiti and on the other is the Dominican Republic. The Dominican Republic is prosperous, healthy, full of resorts; Haiti is in desperate poverty. Same island. They need to have a great turning to God. (Schapito 2010)

Juxtaposing Robertson's commentary against the unimaginable loss of life and collapse of Haiti's basic infrastructure left both longtime supporters of his ministry and longtime critics of his views with bewildered responses such as "stunned," "speechless," "utterly stupid," and "he must have misspoken." Although he referred to the wrong Napoleon in his initial remarks and mistakenly believes the Dominican Republic is a prosperous nation, Robertson's source for the alleged curse and Haitian pact with the Devil may be traced to the legendary account that in August of 1791 Haitian revolutionary leaders Jean Jacques Dessalines and Georges Biassou used voodoo during a ritual at Bois Caiman to invoke the voodoo spirit Legba—whom Christians like Robertson would readily identify with Satan—for the overthrow of their French colonial oppressors. The comingling of superstition and popular myth led to the belief that their alleged pact with Satan was accomplished when Haiti won its independence from France in 1803.

Regardless of how odd some people may consider Pat Robertson's comments assigning prophetic blame for the Haitian earthquake on the national character of the victims of this enormous tragedy, harsh interpretations of natural disasters by Christian clergy is not new. The query concerning the origin and nature of evil has become a central question asked by all religions, and one of humanity's most ancient preoccupations when wondering about the purpose of life in a world of suffering, tragedy, and death. Non-Western and indigenous religious traditions have tended to observe a cyclical view of nature and humanity's place in the cosmos. The Abrahamic religions of Judaism, Christianity, and Islam have instead observed a linear progression of time as the will of God is revealed in the social and political arenas. In the fullness of time, all of creation, according to these Abrahamic traditions, approaches the unknown yet long-prophesied eschatological end of time. The quest for the historical Satan is a story with deep roots in the formative events of the children of Abraham. This is a story with both direct and indirect influences from the interaction of the Hebrews with adversaries and conquerors, such as the Egyptians, Babylonians, and Persians, whose ideas about evil left a mark on the development of Jewish, Christian, and Islamic conceptions of Satan and the problem of evil.

Our search for the origins of Satan covers over five thousand years of religious and cultural history spanning the three continents on which the story of Adam's descendants and Abraham's children were forged in covenantal relation to their one true God of love and mercy, wisdom and salvation. Any attempt to cover such a vast time period across multiple religious cultures in a single chapter can prove to be problematic. Obviously, our textual search cannot be exhaustive. Nevertheless, no search for the origins of Satan and the problem of Evil will be complete without exploring his historical development in the literary and textual traditions of the ancient Middle Eastern religions in which he first appeared. Although it is not our purpose to provide the reader with a complete account of these historical-textual records (several fine scholarly books have already done this task); we nonetheless wish to explore the textual evidence so as to get a sense of how our present day concept of Satan and the related ethical problem of absolute Good versus absolute Evil developed.

One of the lessons inherent in this vast story is that Satan's historical development is akin to the formative process of a human being's birth, childhood, adolescence, and adulthood. Despite prehistoric and mythological conceptions of disorder as an evil in the universe, such as the ancient Egyptian god of chaos and natural disasters known as Seth, our quest will examine stages in the legendary life of Satan across the pages of the Jewish, Christian, and Muslim sacred scriptures, as well as some of the apocryphal and wisdom literature of each tradition. Hence, a textual and symbolic map of the relationship among God, Satan, and human beings emerges that defies our familiar rational categories or doctrinal explanations of the origins of the Prince of Darkness.

## Before Satan's Conception

One of our most primordial fears is that caused by natural disasters like violent storms and floods, turbulent seas, earthquakes, or exploding volcanoes.

The appearance of such images and episodes in dreams during periods of turmoil or acute stress in our lives indicates the extremely ancient roots of our individual and collective fear of nature's fury. If God signifies cosmic and moral order, then our tendency to equate unexpected natural catastrophes with either some form of evil or divine retribution suggests that chaos and destruction have been equated with evil and disorder since humanity first wondered about the forces of nature. Such ancient civilizations as the Egyptians, Sumerians, and Babylonians had mythological conceptions of deities and demons that in divergent ways signified the forces of chaos and disorder in nature and the universe. The Egyptian god Seth was regarded as the lord of chaos and all forms of unrest or confusion caused when the forces of nature were unbalanced or unleashed. This Egyptian concept may have had a direct and early influence on the development of Hebrew and Christian conceptions of evil and destruction.

The ancient civilizations of the Mediterranean basin regarded Egypt as the oldest and most mysterious among their neighbors. When one considers that by the time of Julius Caesar's arrival in North Africa Egyptian culture and religion was already over three thousand years old, it is not surprising that in nearly all matters of sacred wisdom Egypt's priests regarded their Phoenician, Persian, Greek and Roman, and Hebrew neighbors as still being children. Given the historical association of the Hebrews with Egypt, the mythological stories and relationships among the primary Egyptian gods and goddesses—such as the story of their god of chaos, disorder, and natural disasters, Seth—may have influenced the formation of some of humanity's earliest conceptions of evil.

The Nile river valley emerged from the end of the last Ice Age around 8000 BCE and may have entered the Neolithic Period of agricultural and technological development earlier than any of the river valleys in Europe or the Middle East, a historical feature that may account for the much older status conferred upon Egypt by fellow Mediterranean peoples across North Africa, Southern Europe, and the Middle East. Pyramid-like structures were being built in Egypt as early as 2800 BCE and construction of the Great Pyramid at Giza began around 2570 BCE. Egyptian religion understood the gods and goddesses as the personification of the forces of nature, both on earth as well as in the heavens. Although the Greeks and Romans would later ridicule the Egyptians for their bizarre and exotic half-human, half-animal deities, Egyptian priests at sacred sites including Heliopolis, Memphis, and

Karnak stood firm in their religious convictions and traditions. The eternally recurring cycles of creation and regeneration, birth and death, or growth and decay were explained through the elaborate stories and symbols of the Egyptian gods and their children.

For example, the Egyptian pantheon consisted of a creation myth based on an ennead of nine original gods and goddesses whose stories, myths, and legends were constantly changing and evolving throughout the several millennia of Egyptian history. The Egyptians believed that creation occurred when a mound of earth emerged from the cosmic flood waters and the mighty sun shone forth on this primeval ground from which the god Atum arose by himself. Atum then continued unfolding the whole of life and the cosmos. Atum is the same god later equated in Egypt with the sun-god Re, and hence his varying designations as Re-Atum. He was also equated with the scarab for the manner by which this insect emerges from a ball of dirt. Atum created the god Shu and the goddess Tefnut, who respectively signified "Air" and "Moisture." Shu and Tefnut then gave birth to the goddess Nut and her husband Geb, who respectively signified "Sky" and "Earth." Nut and Geb then gave birth to the other four principal Egyptian deities. They had two daughters, Isis and Nephthys, and they had two sons, Osiris and Seth. As time passed, Egyptian mythology developed stories that personified the eternal struggle among the forces of nature in the legend of the perpetual conflict between Osiris and Seth. Osiris represented cosmic and terrestrial order plus the life-sustaining waters of the Nile while Seth represented chaos, natural disasters, and the dry and lifeless lands of the desert.

The Greek historian Herodotus, who traveled extensively throughout Egypt during the middle of the fifth century BCE, referred to Egypt as "the gift of the Nile," for it was the river's annual cycle of flooding that made the surrounding fields highly fertile and capable of sustaining a large population through agriculture, hunting and fishing, and grazing livestock. Hence Osiris, the god of the Nile, came to symbolize the lord of creation and the afterlife as elaborate narratives about him and his divine family offered meaning and comforting explanations to the Egyptian people about the ebb and flow of the river's annual cycle. Throughout the regions of Upper and Lower Egypt, popular local narratives and legends emerged over three millennia about the majesty and power of Osiris.

While it is not advisable to generalize too much, nor too concisely, across the several millennia spanning Egyptian religious history, the sun god was eventually regarded in New Kingdom times as the highest ranking among the primordial deities of Egypt. His life-sustaining rays and cosmic powers stood at the center of creation and the agricultural bounty that made life along the Nile a reality. Yet for life to thrive in abundance, the sun's life-giving energy could not be separated from the life-giving nourishment of water, and that always led the Egyptians back to the myth of Osiris.

Osiris was the most well-known and revered figure in the Egyptian pantheon. As god of the Nile, grain, and the afterlife, Osiris signified the interrelated life-giving attributes of natural order, fertility, and abundance. By 1500 BCE Osiris had become as important to the religious beliefs, culture, and political symbolism of Egypt as the sun god Amun-Re. He was believed to have been the first king of Egypt. Osiris's wife and sister, Isis, was also regarded as a fertility goddess and was often portrayed with a throne or lunar symbol above her head that presumably signified her status as consort of Osiris and queen of the Egyptian pantheon. Their son, Horus, was a sky god with both solar and lunar attributes and was eventually equated with the temporal authority of the Egyptian Pharaohs.

Osiris's brother Seth was the god of chaos and confusion, the desert and foreign lands, storms and turbulent seas. He was also the god of earthquakes and other natural catastrophes. He signified disorder and darkness, the opposite attributes of his life-giving and life-affirming brother Osiris. Seth was identified with a variety of sacred animals, most of them considered either dangerous or undesirable by the ancient Egyptians, such as the hippopotamus, crocodile, donkey, and scorpion. During certain periods of Egyptian history, Seth was revered as a protective god of strength who fought the evil Apophis snake from the bow of the solar god's sacred barge. The story of how Seth became jealous of his brother Osiris and then plotted to kill him, along with Seth's association with chaos and disaster, are the main reasons that by 700 BCE during the Nubian dynasties Seth emerged as the personification of evil in the Egyptian pantheon.

The often dynamic yet turbulent relationship between these two brothers is echoed in what the Egyptians called their land: "the Black Land" (*Kmt*) and "the Red Land" (*Dšrt*). The name "Black Land" was a direct allusion to the fertile black soil that was the result of the Nile's annual flooding, which deposited organic matter rich in nitrogen and other vital minerals along Egypt's farmlands. This fertile land was regarded as sacred to the god Osiris. The imagery of the "red land" was a direct allusion to the dry and barren lands of the Egyptian desert and its association with death and the unknown as a place where nothing grows and one thirsts for the sustenance and the abundance of the Nile. Hence, this infertile land, from which the very word for "desert" originates, was a realm sacred to Seth (Lurker 1980, 13). It is interesting that according to the Gospels of Matthew and Luke, before Jesus Christ set out on his public ministry he went into the desert for forty days and forty nights of trial; there he struggled mightily with Satan. It is also noteworthy that some Egyptian legends describe Seth as having red hair and white skin, which gave him an almost demonic, corpse-like appearance. Christian imagery would later associate the color red with the Devil and his demonic kingdom in hell.

Egyptian legends describe how Seth murdered his brother Osiris and then attempted to kill his nephew Horus. Seth cut up the body of Osiris and scattered the pieces throughout Egypt. An image of murder that, despite our modern disdain for serial killers who dismember the bodies of their victims, needs to be understood against the meaning of key Egyptian beliefs about the afterlife. The Egyptians believed that in order for a person's *ka*, meaning "other self" or "soul," to gain immortality, the body and its vital organs had to be preserved through the embalming process known as mummification. Isis's profound love for her brother and husband would not give in to the suffering and disorder provoked by Seth's jealousy. With the assistance of Anubis, god of the dead and lord of the mummification process, she recovered the pieces of his body from all over Egypt and helped secure eternal life for him in the underworld. Horus later succeeded his father as King of Egypt, while in death Osiris became the King of the Underworld. After Horus avenged his father's murder, he exiled Seth to the desert for all eternity with the advice and assistance of other gods who were appalled at Seth's deceitful and violent actions. The desert became metaphorically synonymous with evil and death and with Egypt's foreign enemies, whether from the east or from the west, who usually had to traverse the desert in order to attack the capital cities of Thebes or Memphis. Over the centuries, however, Seth came to represent the principle of evil in the Egyptian pantheon, especially for the act of killing his brother Osiris and plotting to murder Horus.

It is important to realize that the Egyptians had a dualistic view of human life and nature: the world of the living as contrasted with the underworld of the dead; the fertile green land along the Nile as contrasted with the dry reddish land of the desert just beyond the Nile's flood zone. Another form of dualism that affected the development and identity of this civilization was the division of ancient Egypt into two rival kingdoms, known as Upper and Lower Egypt, which sometimes were united under the leadership of powerful pharaohs while at other times fought against the other for control of the Nile valley and its people. The capital of Upper Egypt for most of its history was Thebes, while the capital of Lower Egypt for most of its history was Memphis. The patron god of Upper Egypt was Horus, while the patron god of Lower Egypt was Seth.

The period from 3500 BCE to 2500 BCE witnessed the greatest political and cultural expansion across the regions of Upper and Lower Egypt, an expansion phase that also generated increased military tensions between the two kingdoms. For a long time after the unification of the two Egyptian kingdoms, Horus and Seth were portrayed in balance with each other, jointly crowning the next "pharaoh of the two lands," but eventually the pharaohs of Lower Egypt, who resented their overlords, began describing Seth in terms of evil and tyranny. Given the various stories of family betrayal and violence among Osiris and his divine kinsmen, it should come as no surprise that warfare and competition over natural resources was often commonplace between the dynastic clans of Upper and Lower Egypt. Sometimes the two kingdoms were united under powerful ruling factions, while at other times one region was dominant over the other. The divergent conceptions of Seth that ranged across Egyptian history show us that he was never fully equated with absolute Evil. Rather, he was perceived as the personification of chaos, disorder, and infertility—undesirable states of existence and imbalance as each causes the loss of balance, *maat*, in nature and society.

Many scholars have seen echoes of the story of Cain and Abel in the conflict between Osiris and Seth. One must be careful when suggesting that mythological similarities like these are the result of universalizing tendencies that trump cultural differences, or that such similarities are the result of direct cultural contact or religious influences among different cultures and peoples.[1] Our point is that the Egyptian conception of Seth as a god of evil and chaos offers us a vision of how evil and destruction were personified by an ancient civilization long before the Hebrew Bible was composed and long before Judaism's unique conception of Satan and his demonic powers was developed.

## Satan's Conception: The Hebrew Bible

Before there was Satan, there was the "*satan*." The Hebrew verb *śṭn* appears, in different forms, six times in the Hebrew Bible with the meaning "to bear a grudge against," "harbor animosity toward," "accuse," "oppose," or "slander." The noun *ha-śāṭān* appears six times with the generic meaning "the accuser" or "adversary." For example, King David, a man after God's own heart, is referred to as a *śāṭān*. When the Philistines were preparing to attack Israel, they became concerned about bringing David along "lest he become a [*śāṭān*] in the battle" (1 Sam 29:4). It is interesting to note that this is the first biblical occurrence where a human is called a [*śāṭān*]. We also read about King Solomon's message to Hiram, king of Tyre, where he makes a comment about the absence of warfare, a time when "there is neither adversary [*śāṭān*] nor evil happenings" (1 Kgs 5:4). Even God can be described using the same verb. In the story concerning the prophet Balaam, who incurred God's wrath for undertaking a journey, we read that "the angel of Yahweh set itself on the road to oppose [*leśāṭān*] him" (Num 22:22): the NRSV translates, "as his adversary." This text presents us with two curious features, because the "angel," as the NRSV translates the word, is in Hebrew a *mal'ak*, which is elsewhere translated "messenger." We are left wondering if the text is telling us that this "messenger"/"angel" of God opposing Balaam was a heavenly creature; but the use of the verb *leśāṭān* should be taken in its ordinary sense—that is, there is no hint here that this "messenger"/"angel" was Satan. Satan opposes Balaam per God's instructions.

In the Hebrew Bible, anyone or any creature can be a *śāṭān*, an adversary. But at some point, the concept illustrated by the word *śāṭān* in the Bible began to be personified into the being we have come to know as Satan. This being is mentioned eighteen times in three books in the Hebrew Bible: once in 1 Chronicles (21:1), three times across two verses in Zechariah (3:11-12), and fourteen times within the first two chapters of the book of Job.[2] In reality, both in Zechariah and Job, the definitive article is used, literally "the *satan*." Still, these two books personify "the *satan*," introducing us to a being with agency, and so the NRSV translates these occurrences with the proper name, Satan. (The definite article in Hebrew can sometimes introduce proper names.) Even if it is not referring to the proper name Satan, they are referring to an office or role occupied by a heavenly being. For the purposes of this book, we will take these references to a heavenly being, occupying an adversarial role against God, as references to Satan. It is important to note that all three of these books—1 Chronicles, Zechariah, and Job—are post-exilic (after 597 BCE, when some of the Israelites returned from the Babylonian Captivity). Before exploring these biblical passages to mine the significance of this spiritual being we call Satan, it behooves us to have a more general exploration of spiritual beings as they appear in the Hebrew Bible.

Prior to the appearance of Satan, the biblical reader is introduced to angels, celestial beings called *mal'akîm* (sg. *mal'āk*), the Hebrew word for "messenger." Of the 213 occurrences of *mal'āk* in the Hebrew Bible, the vast majority of the time the word refers to human messengers, as in the case of the individual who came to King Saul with a message that the Philistines invaded his realm (1 Sam 23:27). Less frequently, *mal'āk* refers to a heavenly being or supernatural emissary, as in the case of the angel summoned to lead and guide Moses to the Promised Land (Exod 23:23). Still, in other passages, the identity of the *mal'āk* (human? angelic?) remains in dispute, as in the case of the messenger who traveled to Bethel to proclaim a word from God (Judg 2:1). Our English word *angel* comes from the Greek word *angelos,* which has the same meaning—(divine or human?) "messenger." We will use the word "angel" when the biblical reference is apparently to a heavenly being.

As heavenly beings, the *mal'ākîm* perform a wide variety of functions and tasks. They can bring the word of God to God's prophets (1 Kgs 1:3); commission a person for a special task (Judg 6:11-24); announce births (Gen 18:9-15); guide persons in the correct path (Ezek 40:1-4); provide salvation from oppression (Num 20:16); administer punishment (Ps 35:5); or offer comfort (Gen 31:11-13). At times, these heavenly beings form the army of God (Josh 5:13-15), an army that numbers in the thousands (Ps 68:17). God appoints these warrior angels to guard over each nation (Deut 32:8) and holds them accountable if they fail to maintain justice (Ps 82). Finally, an ambiguity exists in how these angels relate to God. On several occasions, the "angel of Yahweh" (*mal'āk YHWH*) at the beginning of a passage morphs into God by the time the passage ends (Exod 3:2-6).

Generally speaking, these angels are faithful to Yahweh. Still, cases exist when heavenly beings participate in evil acts. Prior to Noah's Flood, "sons of God" seduced human women (Gen 6:1-4). These figures, not otherwise identified, may have been understood as angels from God's divine council.

(Centuries later, the apostle Paul may have this episode in mind when he commands women to cover their heads "because of the angels" [1 Cor 11:10]. Does he blame the women for sexually seducing these "sons of God" with their long hair?) Their sexual union disrupted the natural order between celestial and mortal beings, resulting in the introduction to the world of a mighty race known as the Nephilim (believed to mean literally "the fallen ones"), offspring who became the source of malignant powers. The rebellion of these angels with human women provides a rationale and justification for the worldwide cataclysm that is to follow. Some scholars see this passage as the beginning of the flood story, connecting the deluge with the need to wash away these half-celestial, half-human offspring.

Passages such as these suggest to the reader the Hebrew Bible images of both good angels and bad angels. Still, there appears to be no distinct Hebrew word for these "bad angels"—no word equivalent to the later designation *demon*. Indeed, the Hebrew Bible lacks a comprehensive understanding of the later Christian concept of demons. Probably the term coming closest to the concept of demons is "evil spirit(s)" (*ruah ra'ah*). These evil spirits, which appear in a few passages, lived in the wastelands and were usually held responsible either for causing or somehow being present in cases of illness or natural disasters.

Although, as we shall soon see, the full concept of demons developed only later in the Christian faith tradition, the term does appear in the Greek translation of the Hebrew Bible, the Septuagint. The Hebrew word *šēd*, which appears twice, was translated by the Septuagint[3] with the Greek term *daimonion*, which entered English as "demon." (The term *daimonion* is a diminutive of the Greek *daimōn*, which simply means "god.") In both cases, they refer to new or false gods—in other words, the idols or gods of the non-Israelites became demons (Deut 32:17; Ps 106:37; in both places the King James Version translated "devils"). Another Hebrew word, *śā'iyr*, has also been translated as "devil"; still, a more literal translation might be "goat idol" or "satyr" (KJV, NRSV: Lev 17:2; 2 Chr 11:15; Isa 13:21; 34:14).

Three other possible "demons" appear in the Hebrew Bible by name. The first is Azazel, who appears once (Lev 16:8, 10). Azazel is often understood to be the name of a demon to which a sacrifice must be made. According to the text, "And Aaron shall cast lots over two goats, one lot for Yahweh, and one lot for Azazel. . . . And the goat on which the lot fell for Azazel shall be made to stand alive before Yahweh to atone over it, so it can be sent away into the desert to Azazel." The King James Version translates the Hebrew *le'aza'zēl* with "for the scapegoat"; the NRSV renders it with the proper name, however, "to Azazel," and Azazel has come to be imagined by some as a demon in goat form, because of the goats used in the ritual and probably because of comparison with the goat idol or satyrs (*śā'iyr*) referred to above as well.[4]

Still, a biblical mandate to offer a sacrifice to a desert demon is quite problematic in a monotheistic faith. Are we to make offerings to God and a demon? It should not be surprising that some have argued that Azazel represents a geographical location, while others insist that Azazel refers to the scapegoat sent into the wilderness. Nevertheless, Jewish literature written during the postbiblical period[5] understood Azazel to be a demon who taught humans how to make swords, knives, and shields (*1 En.* 8:1), taught them all forms of oppression upon the earth, and revealed the eternal secrets of heaven (*1 En.* 9:6). Most revealing is Azazel's transformation in apocalyptic literature[6] to a serpent so as to tempt Adam and Eve in the garden (*Apoc. Ab.* 23:5-12).

The second demon, Lilith, appears once (Isa 34:14) in the Hebrew Bible. In this passage that describes God's prophetic judgment upon Edom, she is found in the company of unclean animals in what will become a wasteland. According to a much later Jewish legend, Lilith was the first wife of Adam, but she left him after a quarrel, refusing to submit to his authority. She has wandered the earth until meeting Sammael, head of the fallen angels, whom she married. Since then, she labored to get Adam and Eve expelled from the Garden. Some traditions have even said she was the tempting serpent of Genesis. Since the expulsion of Adam and Eve from the garden, she has continued her attacks on humanity, being blamed for the death of small children.[7]

The third demon, Belial, appears ambiguously in the Hebrew Bible. Although Belial is Hebrew for "wickedness," the passages in which the term appears can be interpreted as a personification of this concept. For example, in the song recorded in 2 Samuel 22, David refers to the torrents of Belial bursting upon him (22:5). In post-biblical times, Belial emerged as a common name for the principal evil spirit—what we would call the Devil—leading the forces of malevolence. In the apocalyptic writings found at Qumran, Belial's name is mainly associated with the Ruler of evil and darkness. By the time we get to the New Testament, even Paul is apparently referring to Belial as a person: "What agreement has Christ with Belial, or has a believer to share with an unbeliever? Can light associate with darkness?" (2 Cor 6:15-16).

It is important to note that nowhere in the Hebrew Bible does a connection exist between the personhood of Satan and these evil spirits or demonic forces. In fact, one should exercise caution in making any overarching claims concerning demons based on such limited references within the Hebrew Bible. This scarcity of demonic figures might help explain why the early writers of the Hebrew Bible had no difficulty in associating evil elements or events with God. The reader of the Hebrew Bible does not find a clear dichotomy between who is responsible for evil, Satan or God? Instead, the God of the Hebrew Bible is routinely described as responsible for creating evil. We are told, for example, that God sent an evil spirit to Abimelech and the leaders of Shechem (Judg 9:23), and to King Saul (1 Sam 16:14-16). The prophet Isaiah has God admitting that "I form light, and create darkness. Make peace, and create evil. I, Yahweh, do all these things" (Isa 45:7). Over time, however, as the idea that evil comes from God became more problematic and theologically unacceptable, the belief in an independent, personified source of evil developed. For example, in the Hebrew Bible it is God who tempts Abraham to sacrifice his son Isaac (Gen 22:1). Centuries later, however, in the collection of rabbinic traditions known as the Talmud, this aspect of the story had apparently become theologically questionable and we read that it was Satan who made the suggestion to God (*Sanhedrin* 89b).

If Satan is not connected to evil spirits or demonic forces in the Hebrew Bible, what then is his role there? As we have seen, we are first introduced to a being who occupies the position of "the *satan*," the Accuser. This being is part of God's council, serving God, apparently at God's request, as a judicial adversary to humans. This role for the *satan* is best illustrated in the book of Job, where "the *satan*" appears most often. There we read that the "Children of God" attended to Yahweh and that the being we will identify as Satan (taking the Hebrew phrase as a proper name) is among them (1:6).

The concept of a divine council imagined a heavenly court analogous to an earthly royal court, with God taking the place of the king and celestial beings functioning as warriors, counselors, emissaries, and servants. Elsewhere we find the prophet Micaiah describing how this divine council provided advice to God on how to trick King Ahab into marching to his death. One member of the council came up with the solution: putting a lying spirit into the mouths of the King's prophets (1 Kgs 22:20-23). The prophets Isaiah (Isa 6) and Jeremiah (Jer 23:18, 22) also receive God's word while present before the divine council.

Of interest for our purposes is that the book of Job has Satan as a member of this divine council. He does not reside in some "Hell" but "roams the earth" and stands before God's throne as one of the celestial counselors, filling the role of the Accuser—specifically impugning Job's motive for faithfulness. He does not appear to be intruding on council business; rather, Satan appears to be part of the procedures. In this role he asks a legitimate question: Does Job (or in fact, any of us) honor God because we benefit from God's protection? Is piety linked to prosperity? Or do we continue to trust in God in times of adversity (Job 1:9-11)? Satan proposes that the real test of righteousness is continued faithfulness to God during adversity with no promise of retributive justice or hope for any reward.

God takes Satan's advice and tests Job. It bears notice that God is responsible for Job's misfortunes, including the loss of his possessions, the loss of health, and, more tragic, the loss of all his children. God sends this evil through Satan (1:12; 2:7), for the text shows us that Satan is unable to act independently from God. The disturbing conclusion the book of Job elucidates is that the evil Satan causes can occur only with permission from the Almighty. In other words, God sends the evil through God's agent Satan.

The concept of "the *satan*" as a member of the divine council is reinforced in the book of Zechariah. The prophet Zechariah sees a being occupying the role of the *satan*, whom we will call Satan, standing at the right hand of the high priest Joshua accusing and slandering him (Zech 3:1-2). Again, Satan stands before God as the Accuser, having no power over Joshua, impotent to destroy him. All he can do is bring accusations and rely on God to bring about Joshua's punishment and downfall.

The final appearance of Satan occurs in 1 Chr 21:1, which retells the story found in 2 Sam 24—with one major difference. This is the only time that the word Satan appears without the definite article, making it clear that this *satan* represents the name of a personal being, Satan, not just the title of a role or office, that is, "the Accuser." Furthermore, the question arises whether the Satan of Chronicles is depicted in the same way as the *satan* of Job and Zechariah. In the 2 Samuel story, David is incited by God to conduct a census. In the Chronicles story, however, it is Satan who is responsible for tempting David. Here Satan is described as tempting and tricking, apart from God's permission. If we were to try to harmonize the Samuel and Chronicle accounts following the pattern established in the books of Job and

Zechariah, might we argue that God incited David by using Satan as the instrument by which God sends evil?

We see, at any rate, that the appearance of Satan in the Hebrew Bible is highly problematic. We are left with the following observations: (1) the infrequency of Satan's appearance as a personified celestial being in the biblical writings; (2) the ambiguity surrounding the word *satan* and its usage as a proper name; (3) the confusion existing between the role or office of "the Accuser" who participates in God's divine council and the word *satan*; (4) Satan portrayed as an obedient servant of God; (5) God depicted as sending evil and lying spirits and in sending misfortune and tragedy to the unfaithful (Saul) and faithful (Job) alike; (6) a total absence of the Western Christian imagery of Satan as the ruler of Hell, in charge of an army of demons, waging war against God and humans; and (7) the inability of Satan to inflict any malevolence without the blessings of God, who remains the primary cause of evil. The last observations apparently disturbed early readers of the Hebrew Bible. In effect, Yahweh's relationship to evil came to be seen as problematic, requiring remedy: hence the increasing need for a Satan who was more than just God's messenger. The representation of Satan as God's archenemy was further developed in the post-exilic period, rooted in the religious cross-fertilization of the Babylonian Captivity and subsequent Israelite encounter with Persian culture.

## Satan's Childhood: Babylonian Captivity and Persian Influence

The conquest of the northern kingdom of Israel and the deportation of its inhabitants by the Assyrian King Sargon occurred in 722 BCE. What remained was the southern kingdom of Judah. But with the rise of the reorganized Neo-Babylonian Empire of the Chaldeans, Judah became one of its vassal states. By 597 BCE, the Babylonian King Nebuchadnezzar II (605–562) had despoiled the Temple of Yahweh and carried King Jehoiachin, who reigned over Judah for only three months, along with the Judean nobility and leading citizens, back to Babylon. Nebuchadnezzar installed King Jehoiachin's uncle, Zedekiah, as governor of Jerusalem. But within a decade, Zedekiah rebelled. In the year 586 BCE, Nebuchadnezzar laid siege to Jerusalem, destroying the Temple and carrying the remnant of the population back to Babylon, thus commencing what has come to be known as the Babylonian Captivity.

While in Babylon, the Jewish community thrived economically and intellectually but mistrusted their autocratic rulers and the injustices of the Neo-Babylonian culture of that time. Religious and intellectual challenges arose as the exiles attempted to understand why Yahweh would allow the destruction of their sacred temple and the loss of their homeland. Theologically, they began to wonder if Yahweh was just a local deity tied to their old homeland or if Yahweh's reign and power extended to Babylon and beyond. Ironically, as a result of this period of exile in Babylon, the Jews not only developed a more global understanding of Yahweh, but they were influenced by the religious concepts of Persian theism and other evil beings prevalent among the peoples and cultures of the exile. These new ideas influenced the further development of Satan.

Although the Babylonian exile was a major traumatic event affecting the social and political identity of the Jewish people and their religious beliefs, the rise of Cyrus the Great, around 560 BCE, as the brilliant Persian king and military strategist intent on freeing Mesopotamia from the yoke and tyranny of the Neo-Babylonian Empire, soon renewed the Hebrew nation's hopes for returning to the native soil of their Judean ancestors. In the autumn of 539 or 538 BCE, Cyrus and his armies surrounded the fabled city of Babylon and deposed the last of its Neo-Babylonian rulers, King Nabunaid. An empire focused on protecting its people from foreign invaders, promoting trade and commerce, and not interfering with its subjects' diverse religious beliefs and practices has proven over the centuries to be a recipe for imperial success and popular support, and that was exactly what the Persians had in mind for their multicultural and multireligious subjects. The vast empire that Cyrus, his son Cambyses II, and their successors established at this time enjoyed widespread support based on toleration and economic prosperity (Ezek 1:1-9).

The empire relished in the new propaganda of its Achaemenid rulers as "saviors" for having liberated many of the nations and tribes of Mesopotamia who had been conquered by the Assyrians and Babylonians. Even the biblical text refers to Cyrus as a messiah, anointed by God (Isa 45:1). As suggested in the book of Ezra, some scholars estimate that about forty thousand Jews returned to Judah and Palestine after Babylon fell to a combined military force of Persians, Medes, and Elamites commanded by Cyrus the Great (Ezek 2:1-64). Yet other historical assessments and biblical accounts, such as the book of Esther, suggest that a sizable population of Jews remained as loyal and productive subjects in the heart of the Persian Empire (Cook 1983, 25–43).

The period of the Babylonian Captivity, and the subsequent years when the Hebrews lived as one of the most successful subjects of the Persian Empire, had a profound cultural and religious impact on the development of Jewish theological concepts. Judaism's understanding of monotheism re-emerges in a much firmer position after the Babylonian Exile. Eschatological speculation about end-time events and rulers became much more common in Judaism, and ideas about a cosmic struggle between good and evil took on a renewed urgency in Hebraic thought, as well as in the scriptural themes recorded in the Bible. Scholars have attributed some of these changes to the trauma of losing the Temple and then relying on the essential teachings contained in the Torah during the several generations of the exile in Babylon. Crises sometimes bring people together and sharpen their sense of identity as a cohesive group. Displacement and exile, however, also open people's thought patterns and sensibilities to new and foreign ways of thinking or imagining their ultimate truths and religious traditions.

After the fall of Babylon, the Jews came into contact with the Persian way of life. It was at this stage of his life cycle that Satan's historical development in Judaism came under the influence of the Persian tradition, represented in the visionary teachings of Zarathustra, who flourished around 630 BCE. Zarathustra's apocalyptic religion was based on individual moral choices that determined whether the souls of believers either rose to heaven or tumbled down to hell after death (Stausberg 2008, 101–12; Neusner 1993, 1–27; Carter 1970, 28–68).

Bearing the Persian name Zarathustra Spitmata, Zoroaster—to use his more familiar Greek name—is today regarded as the founder of the religion of the Persian Empire, whose much more ancient regional and ethnic identity is Iranian. This Iranian religious tradition, known as Zoroastrianism to the Western world, is also known as Mazdaism throughout the region of modern-day Iran, Iraq, Tajikistan, western India, and Pakistan. Some scholars argue that Zarathustra may have lived as early as 1000 BCE, but most experts today place the active part of his public ministry at just before the rise of the Persian Empire (Mehr 2003, 64–66). The three Magi from the east who visited Jesus at Epiphany are widely regarded as Zoroastrian priests, who by their esoteric knowledge of the stars were able to find the location of the nation whose "savior" (*soter*) and god-king had been recently born.

Not much about Zarathustra's early life and public ministry is known with certainty. His teachings are preserved in the three major Zoroastrian texts: the *Gathas*; the series of dialogical hymns between the prophet and the supreme deity, known as the *Zend-Avesta*; and the allegedly posthumous *Liturgy of the Seven Chapters*. Legendary and mythological accounts suggest that he was born of a virgin, while others suggest that he was a messianic figure who knew how to command the element of fire. Other more reliable legends tell us that Zarathustra regarded himself as no more than a poet and teacher of righteousness and that he gave away a hefty portion of his father's wealth and food supplies to feed the poor. Another story recounts how, after his death, he ascended to heaven by the miracle of a flash of lighting that carried off his body for protection in the afterlife.

The more reliable account describes Zarathustra as a young man who became a devotee of a benevolent god, whom he called Ahura Mazda, and whose names literally signify the "Supremely Wise Lord Creator," or more precisely the "Creator Lord of Wisdom." Among Ahura Mazda's attributes we find the powers and characteristics of fire, goodness, light, truth, and mercy. In one of the visions, the god commanded Zarathustra to denounce lies and liars, the bloody animal sacrifices his people had been practicing for centuries, and to care for the poor by feeding and clothing them. Ahura Mazda taught Zarathustra that the human heart and mind was a perpetual battle ground between the forces of good and the forces of evil. In the *Gathas*, we read that: "In the beginning, there were two Spirits, Twins spontaneously active; these were the Good and the Evil, in thought, and in word, and in deed. Between these two, let the wise choose right; be good, not base" (Mehr, 2003, 89). Thus, we see how and why this ancient Iranian religion has been described as one of dualism.

Ahura Mazda is also known as the "Spirit of spirits." The good spirit, identified as Spenta Mainyu, was a manifestation of the essence of Ahura Mazda and can be likened to Jewish notions of the Spirit of God or to Christian notions of the Holy Spirit, especially given the power of fire and light as characteristics of this good spirit's presence among humanity. Spenta Mainyu promoted truth, unity, goodness, and balance in the cosmos. On the other hand, this comforting spirit of light and goodness, Spenta Mainyu, was locked in an eternal cosmic battle against Angra Mainyu, the spirit of evil, darkness, and lies who promoted falsehood, disunity, wickedness, and imbalance in the cosmos [see Figure 2]. In later Hellenistic-Roman times, Angra Mainyu also came to be known as the "Demon of demons" (Mehr 2003, 102).

In a manner nearly equivalent to later Christian and Muslim conceptions of human free-will, Ahura Mazda informed Zarathustra that he had created humanity with the right to choose which of these contrasting paths to follow but firmly warned that the law of cause and effect (*Asha*) always favors good over evil, for both nature and the universe incline toward balance, justice, and harmonious existence. Hence, one's moral choices and uncontrollable passions had long-term spiritual impact beyond the here and now. Indeed, according to Zarathustra, the character of one's moral choices and subsequent actions determine whether upon death the soul ascends to Heaven or descends to Hell, a now familiar and almost universally well-known Jewish, Christian, and Islamic ethical notion.

Despite the dualistic nature of Zarathustra's moral conceptions and view of the spirit realm, he was firm in his teachings that Ahura Mazda was the supreme creator of the cosmos and of humanity, as well as the life-sustaining force throughout the universe whose sacred presence emanated all around us as "fire" or "light." Scattered throughout modern Iran, we find the ruins of numerous Zoroastrian Fire Temples attesting to these aspects of this faith tradition's ancient beliefs and practices. Zarathustra's stance on living a life of ethical responsibility and recognition of the supremacy of Ahura Mazda's call to human decency is best summarized in his urging all men and women to take up the causes of: "Good words; Good thoughts; and Good deeds." From a historical standpoint this sets Zarathustra apart as one of the earliest advocates of monotheism and personal salvation through moral action in the history of religions.

A number of Zarathustra's apocalyptic ideas are detectable in various aspects of Judaism, Christianity, and Islam. For example, as the Zoroastrian tradition developed, many of its priests and adherents came to believe that at the end of time a final battle would be fought between the forces of light and goodness, represented by Spenta Mainyu and Ahura Mazda, and the forces of darkness and evil, represented by Ahriman and Angra Mainyu. As the story goes, it was prophesied that those who had chosen moral righteousness over sinfulness would ascend to heaven and join with Ahura Mazda and the good spirits in Paradise (*pairidaēza*). Yet those who had chosen evil and lies over goodness and truth by siding with Ahriman and Angra Mainyu against the sons and daughters of light would be cast into a fiery pit for all eternity.

In the ancient Iranian language known as Avestan, the noun used to denote an "enclosed garden" and the concept of "heaven" is *pairidaēza*. Since the Greeks, Hebrews, and Persians interacted with each other culturally, it is not surprising that in the Septuagint the notion of "paradise" is synonymous with both the "Garden of Eden" and "Heaven." Similarly, over the next several centuries of cultural diffusion between Europe and the Near East, the Zoroastrian concept of Ahriman's final fiery dwelling place as being in the bowels of the earth, and outside of this *pairidaēza*, influenced the notion of the place that Christians, Jews, and Muslims eventually came to know of as Satan's kingdom in "Hell."

Whatever happens in history always leaves a trail in the language of a people and their culture. So profound was the Persian influence on Judaism at the time of the Babylonian Captivity, and the Israelites' subsequent release by Cyrus the Great, that the Persian conception of a heavenly garden, *pairidaēza*, made its way into our language as Paradise. It also stands to reason that the fiery pit described by Zarathustra's followers as the opposite of this paradisiacal land of milk and honey indirectly influenced the symbols and attributes of the hellfire associated with "Satan's Hell" in Jewish and Christian lore.

In summary, it would be a mistake to equate completely the Zoroastrian spirits Angra Mainyu, or the demon Ahriman, with the Satan of the Hebrew biblical tradition or with the satanic Devil of the New Testament. Nonetheless, the influence of Zarathustra's emphasis on goodness and justice in enduring opposition to evil, together with the eschatological ideas of a cosmic battle between the principalities of Good and Evil on the Day of Judgment, and the promise of salvation in Paradise, were all major influences in the textual and cultural history of Satan's early development in the cauldron of Middle Eastern civilization.

## Satan's Adolescence: The Apocrypha and Pseudepigrapha

While it is obvious that Satan plays a minor role in the Hebrew Bible, by the time we get to the New Testament, Satan's presence is very noticeable. One intriguing episode occurs in Mark 3:22-27 (compare Matt 12:22-42 and Luke 11:14-15, 29-32). In all three accounts, a demon-possessed man is brought to Jesus. The multitudes who witness Jesus casting the demons out of this person are amazed; but the Pharisees attribute the exorcism to the power of Beelzebub, the ruler of evil spirits. Who is this Beelzebub?

The pseudepigraphical work[8] the *Testament of Solomon* introduces us to Beelzebub and offers us a virtual catalog of demons (6:1-4). According to this testament (which is usually dated to the third century CE but may include much older traditions), King Solomon has power over the demons through a ring in his possession and forces them to build the Temple. We may compare this tale with the report in the Gospels that the Pharisees attributed Jesus' power to cast out demons to Beelzebub. Did the Pharisees know a tradition similar to that later included in the *Testament of Solomon* and accept it as authentic? Did Jesus? Note that in Matthew and Luke, he ends his rebuttal to the Pharisees by explaining that one greater than Solomon is present (Matt 12:42; Luke 11:31); might this saying be a suggestion that he had greater power over demons than Solomon had?[9] In order to understand fully the role of demons in the New Testament, we must first understand how traditions concerning demons developed in the post-biblical period.

During the period between the composition of the last of the Hebrew scriptures and Jesus' day, the personification of Satan, along with an increasingly sophisticated demonology, began to develop. It was during these roughly three hundred years that Satan came of age, so to speak—along with a mythological army of demons and fallen archangels that encompassed an entire celestial cosmology that would have been strictly superfluous to orthodox monotheism.

The reason for the rise in interest in heavenly creatures is difficult to ascertain; there was probably no single cause. No doubt, one contributing factor was the earlier Babylonian Captivity (586–538 BCE), when the inhabitants of Judah were exiled. Contact with Babylonian mythology and Persian-Zoroastrian religious practices and beliefs about benevolent and malevolent deities struggling for supremacy influenced the development of Judaism. Still, it would be a mistake to argue too forcefully for a direct linear sequence of cause and effect. After all, we have already noticed that the notion of demonic figures, though not elaborately developed, already existed in the biblical writings. Nevertheless, it is after the Babylonian Captivity that the popular religion of the Israelites came to find literary expression (Collins 1977, 101–4). Rather than angels simply being messengers of God in texts where the emphasis was on the message and the one who sent it, these celestial beings began to develop names and personalities. According to *Tobit* 12:15, an Apocryphal book,[10] there are seven distinctive angels who stand ever ready to enter the presence of God. Of the seven, only two are mentioned in the Hebrew Bible, both appearing in the book of Daniel: Michael (10:14) and Gabriel (9:21). Two other angels who are frequently mentioned in other literature are Raphael (*Tob.* 12:15) and Uriel (*4 Ezra* 4:1).[11]

As religious writers began to imagine a more and more elaborate heavenly world, they provided a thicker description of angels. The Pseudepigrapha would claim that angels were created on the first day of Creation (*Jub.* 2:2) with penises that were already circumcised (*Jub.* 15:25-27). These angels were arranged hierarchically, with Michael usually identified as the head angel (Dan 12:1). These heavenly figures can be divided into cherubim,[12] seraphim,[13] and ophanim,[14] angels with authority over governments,[15] over faithful individuals,[16] and over natural forces[17] (*1 En.* 61:10).[18]

As the Hebrew narratives were retold, angels were added to the story. For example, it is an angel that makes a covenant with Abram (*Jub.* 14:20) rather than God (Gen 15:18). Or it is the angels who are commended to afflict the Hebrews (*Pseudo-Phocylides* 15.5) as opposed to God striking them down with pestilence (Num 14:12). During this time, angels were depicted not only protecting the faithful—"[God] will set a guard of holy angels over all the righteous and holy ones" (*1 En.* 100:5)—but also punishing the wicked—"Then I saw there an army of the angels of punishment marching, holding nets of iron and bronze" (*1 En.* 56:1).

In these writings, the Hebrew Bible's concept of a divine court, as discussed above, with God filling the role of king and judge surrounded by heavenly beings as counselors, is diminished. In fact, we are told "[God] need[s] no council" (*1 En.* 14:23). Instead, heaven becomes a place of judgment, praise, and revelation. *First Enoch* witnesses a heavenly court that is the locus of "power, punishment, and judgment" (60:6); a place where all present "lift up in one voice, blessings, glorifying, and extolling (61:11); and a place where the mysteries of the cosmos are revealed (61:15-16).

But all is not well among the angelic host. A predominant notion that developed in the pseudepigrapha is the dichotomy of absolute good as represented by God and the host of angels and absolute evil as represented by a dominion of evil angels. The origin of these evil spirits occurred when angels have sexual intercourse with women (cf. Gen 6), as already mentioned. *First Enoch* 6–19 details how angels, referred to here as Watchers, took human wives, causing their subsequent expulsion from Heaven. Besides "defiling themselves with women" (a phrased used six times in the Enoch narrative at *1 En.* 7:1; 9:8; 10:11; 12:4; 15:2-7), these fallen angels also taught humanity idolatry, magical medicine, and sorcery.

Semihazah, the leader of the angels whose task was to watch over the universe (hence the term "Watchers"), persuaded two hundred fellow angels to engage in sexual intercourse with human women. According to *1 En.* 15:8, "But now the giants who are born from the (union of) the spirits and the flesh shall be called evil spirits upon the earth because their dwelling shall be upon the earth and inside the earth." When these semi-divine offspring died, their spirits constituted a race of demons. The flood to come became divine punishment on both humans and "unclean spirits" for their sexual interaction and the evil spirits unleashed as a consequence. The book of *Jubilees* (10:7-11) informs us that when retribution did come, nine-tenths of the "malignant evil ones" were bound and punished "in the place of condemnation" while one-tenth were left behind where they would remain "subject before Satan on the earth." To this day, they continue to tempt and torment humanity.

Enoch's tale of sexual intercourse between spiritual and fleshly beings becomes one of the bases for the duality created between the angelic ruler representing God and the angelic ruler of the rebellious angels. This spiritual battle between ultimate goodness and ultimate evil soon found manifestations on earth, specifically between nations. We can detect echoes of both direct and indirect influence from the Persian belief in the cosmic struggle between good and evil spirits, or *spentas*, represented by Spenta Mainyu and Angra Mainyu, whose battlefield was not always in a far way cosmic place but in the very center of each person's soul.

It was during the post-biblical period that the Greek term *daimon*, which simply means "god" or "spirit," began to take on negative connotations among Jews, who used the diminutive form *daimonion* ("god-let"). Within the Jewish cosmology, these demons (or "god-lets") were identified with the gods of other nations, along with their servant deities. These gods, now demons, were viewed as being in league with a supreme archenemy of the true God, assigned to entice humans away from the true faith. Demons became responsible for tempting humans and providing them with false doctrines. In the Septuagint, the Greek translation of the Hebrew Bible, the Hebrew word used for the wooden and stone deities of foreign people, already regarded as "worthless idols," came to be described as demons. For example, the pun found in the Hebrew of Psalm 96:5, "All the gods [*elohim*] of the peoples are idols [*elilim*]," was translated into Greek to read, "All the gods of the people are demons [*daimonia*]." What started as a pun became a theology. Translations such as this contributed to a biblical theology where the gods of all other nations were transformed from lifeless and spiritless idols made of wood and stone into real spiritual beings, united in warfare against the one true God of Israel. Who set up this dichotomy between good and evil? According to the book of *Jubilees*, it is God who assigned these spirits over every nation "to rule so that they might lead them astray" (15:31).

Seeing the gods of other nations as demons was not limited to Israel. Indeed, the Egyptian god of chaos and disaster, Seth, was also regarded as the evil lord of foreigners and invaders who crossed the desert to attack Egypt. The Persians detested the religious beliefs of the Assyrian and Neo-Babylonians whom Cyrus the Great overthrew and conquered. This way of seeing other religions and faiths eventually became a characteristic of Christianity, as we will explore in future chapters. Both early Christian and Jewish faith developed the conception of a spiritual war that mirrored physical and ideological conflicts on earth. Nevertheless, this spiritual warfare was expected to find resolution in the eschatological victory during the last days when all evil faces its final judgment.

Over time, these demons came to be associated with specific misfortunes or with a particular habitat that each occupied. As we have seen, for example, in the *Testament of Solomon*, Solomon was given a magic ring by God to gain control over a host of demons. Solomon forced the demons to tell him what their particular domains were and which angel in Heaven or protective ritual would serve as a counterforce to their influence. With this ring, Solomon was able to get the demons to construct various parts of the Temple.[19] Important for our discussion is the development of the thought that demons specialized in tormenting humans through particular vices, such as lust, anger, deception, sloth, and so on. The *Testament of Solomon* was a foundational document in the development of the connections between demons and specific vices and of the rites by which humans could conduct exorcisms.

But where does Satan fit into this cosmology? According to *2 Enoch*, these fallen angels or demons number two hundred (18:3) and have their own ruler. But the name of the ruler varies. The ruler of these evil forces was called Belial in the Qumran texts (for example, 1QM 1:1; 13:11) and in the book of *Jubilees* (1:21),[20] Mastema in *Jubilees* (10:8),[21] Asmodeus in the book of *Tobit* (3:8),[22] Sammael in the book of the *Martyrdom and Ascension of Isaiah* (1:8),[23] Semyaz in *1 Enoch* (6:3),[24] Beelzebub in the *Testament of Solomon* (6:1-3),[25] and of course, Satan or Satanail.

Satan appears numerous times throughout the Pseudepigrapha. He is credited with tempting Adam and Eve to fall from Paradise (*2 En.* 31), writing down the sins of Israel so as to urge God to destroy the nation (*3 En.* 12), and refusing to serve or worship Adam on the grounds that he, Satan, was older and greater than any human creature (*Life of Adam and Eve* 12–15). Salvation comes to be understood as the absence of Satan (*Jub.* 23:29).

As we have seen, the proper name, Satan, is the transliteration of the Hebrew *śāṭān*. When the Hebrew Bible was translated into Greek, *śāṭān* was translated with the Greek word *diabolos*. In Greek, *diabolos* denoted someone who was defamatory or slanderous, but over time, especially in the Christian usage, the term came to mean a specific superhuman being who was the main adversary of God. Even later, in Christian and Latin usage, the loanword *diabolus* also signified the idea of someone who had either "turned away from" or "fallen away from" God, just as Satan had been expelled from heaven for disobeying God's order that the angels serve humanity. With time, the various names used for the ruler of demons found in the Apocrypha, the Pseudepigrapha, and other apocalyptic literature came to be synonymous with Satan, who by then was also known in Christianity as the *diabolos* in Greek and as the *diabolus* in Latin, or simply as the Devil.

The Qumran community gave Belial a specific domain and purpose. According to them, "From of old you [that is, God] appointed the Prince of light to assist us . . . You created Belial for the pit, angel of enmity; his [dom]ain is in darkness, his counsel is for evil and wickedness" (1QM 13:10-11).

Here we see a dualism, reminiscent of Zoroastrian beliefs, between the children of light and the children of darkness in which the children of light will be united to God while the children of darkness will be cast into the pit. These notions of an evil figure leading a host of fallen angels and having his domain in a realm of darkness were applied to Satan as the mythology around him developed. Appearing sixty-six times in the Hebrew Bible, Sheol was originally understood to be an underworld of shadows to which all humans descended upon death—a place that lacked the hope of return, rewards, or resurrection. Sheol was not the Christian concept of Hell complete with fire and everlasting torment; rather, it was simply a gloomy netherworld where departed spirits went (Prov 9:18).

By the time we get to later apocalyptic literature, this underworld has become the place where sinning angels go. The angel Ura'el calls this place "a prison house of the angels; [where] they are detained . . . forever" (*1 En.* 21:10), and where "wicked [humans . . . are] destroyed forever and their spirits . . . perish and die, they shall cry and lament in a place that is an invisible wilderness and burn in the fire" (*1 En.* 108:2-3). It is described as "a deep pit with heavenly fire on its pillars . . . a desolate and terrible place" (*1 En.* 18:11-12).

Today, when we think of Satan and Hell, many Christians assume a narrative in which Satan rebelled against God during creation and was banished from Heaven, along with a third of the angels. Since then, Satan and his minions have been tormenting humans in an attempt to sever their relationship with God. If asked, most Christians would probably state that this understanding of Satan and Hell is derived from the biblical text. Yet if pushed to point to the actual chapter and verse in the Bible upon which they base their views, they would be hard-pressed to find any reference. In fact, most of what we know about Satan is not rooted in the Bible but rather in postbiblical pseudepigrapha and apocalyptic writings that are not given any authoritative or revelatory status by Christians. Nevertheless, as we have seen, it is within these books that today's Satan matured and moved beyond adolescence.

## Satan's Early Adulthood

### The New Testament

By the time we get to the New Testament, the *satan* of Job and Zechariah who served as a faithful servant in God's divine council has become God's rival. Satan—the cosmic arch enemy of God and all that is true and holy—is alive and well as the Almighty's antagonist. The oldest Gospel, Mark, introduces readers to Satan in the very first chapter (1:13). This Satan has his own kingdom (3:23-27) and is engaged in a cosmic struggle against God's purposes. Thus began the Christian practice of dividing the supernatural world into two opposing forces: the one true God along with God's angels versus Satan and his hordes of demons and fallen angels. On the human side of this combative arrangement, individuals either belonged in one camp or the other. Refusing to worship Caesar as a god, or denying homage to the gods of non-Christian neighbors, was a rejection of the forces of Satan signified by these symbols.

Satan as a malicious being is mentioned by name (in contrast to simply being called an adversary) in the New Testament at least thirty-five times. The book of Revelation refers to him as that "great dragon . . . the serpent of old called Devil and Satan, the deceiver of the whole world" (12:9). In this passage, Satan and the Devil become interchangeable words connected with the image of Leviathan, the sea dragon whom God will punish (cf. Isa 27:1), and the serpent that deceived Eve in the Garden of Eden (Gen 3:1-15). Elsewhere we read that Satan's children are all those humans, starting with Cain, who failed to live a holy life by showing love for their fellow humans (1 John 3:10-12). The New Testament reveals that angels will be judged by humans (1 Cor 6:3), and those found wanting will be cast into Hell, an actual place where all demons and all humans who oppose God's will are tormented with eternal fire (Rev 20:10-15, see Figure 4).

The concept of a place of eternal punishment, especially by fire, was developed in the apocalyptic literature, for example *1 Enoch*, which describes Hell as "a deep pit with heavenly fire on its pillars" (18:11-16) and a place where the wicked who are blotted out of the Book of Life are sent (108:3). English Bibles use "hell" to translate Jesus' references to Gehenna, from the Hebrew phrase for the Valley of Hinnom, *ge ben Hinnom,* which is located southwest of Jerusalem. The Valley of Hinnom was the ancient site where some of the kings of Judah sacrificed children, through fire, to the god Moloch (2 Chr 28:3). Gehenna is described by Jesus as a "blazing furnace, where there will be weeping and the gnashing of teeth" (Matt 13:42), "an eternal fire prepared for the devil and his angels" (Matt 25:41), and a place where "the worms never die nor the fire goes out" (Mark 9:49).

Although Gehenna can be considered as Satan's abode, other New Testament writings suggest that he is not yet confined there, for he prowls the earth "like a roaring lion looking for someone to devour" (1 Pet 5:8). Satan can be described as having established his throne on the earth, in the city of Pergamum, and it is there that he lives (Rev 2:12-13). Pergamum was an ancient Greek city in Mysia, where the modern town of Bergama is located. During the time John was writing the Revelations, Pergamum provided Rome with wealth in the form of silver and excess agricultural products. Finally, even though the realm of the dead is considered the official abode of Satan, some interpret two passages in the New Testament to argue that Jesus made an appearance there between the time of his death on the cross and his resurrection. First Peter 3:18-19 declares that by the Spirit Jesus "went and made a proclamation to the spirits in prison"; Eph. 4:8-9 declares that Jesus "descended into the lower parts of the earth" so as to make "captivity itself a captive." As we have seen, concepts of Satan, like Hell, were developed in the pseudepigraphic books of Enoch and *Jubilees*. But how did these concepts make their way into the New Testament? It is important to remember that when Jesus was ministering, and later, when the New Testament authors were writing their testimonies and letters, writings beyond the Torah and Prophets were regarded as having authority and possibly even revelatory significance.[26] Because of this, Jesus and his contemporaries could read and draw from Enoch and *Jubilees*, as if they were authoritative.[27] For example, Jude 14–15 directly quotes *1 En.* 1:9. The mind-set of those fashioning the New Testament was to assume as true what we now regard as noncanonical accounts of fallen angels and evil demons set on destroying the faithful.

This being the case, the New Testament, like the earlier apocalyptic and pseudepigraphic writings and oral traditions, takes for granted the existence of demons. In fact, individuals can "have a demon" or "have an unclean spirit." Unlike the Hollywood version of demon possession (for example, *The Exorcist*), the New Testament describes the concept more as a matter of being influenced or controlled by the interior presence of a demon. This presence is usually manifested as muteness (Matt 9:32-34), blindness (Matt 12:22), sickness (Matt 8:16-17), or what we might diagnose as insanity (Mark 5:1-5) or epilepsy (Luke 9:37-43). This is not to say that all illnesses and diseases are caused by demons, for there are examples, such as Peter's mother-in-law, where healing occurs without any reference being made to casting out demons (Matt 8:14-15). Still, there is some ambiguity when at times physical ailments are attributed to demons while at other times they are not. For example, while Matthew attributes blindness to demonic activity in 12:22, he does not do so in 9:27-31. In the former, sight is restored by casting out the demon, while in the latter, two blind men regain their sight because of their faith. On the other hand, Acts has Peter say that Jesus went about "healing all who were oppressed by the devil" (10:38), making the connection between illness and demonic forces more normative for the early church.

Not only is Satan described in the New Testament as able to cause physical ailments, he is also able to invade the thoughts of humans and influence them to work against God. Jesus accuses Peter of allowing him to be influenced by the Devil when he provides a boastful response to a query (Mark 8:33); we are told that Judas Iscariot's betrayal of Jesus was due to Satan putting the thought in his mind (John 13:2); and Peter accuses Ananias of fraud due to Satan's possession (Acts 5:3). Satan is also responsible for preventing Paul from visiting the Thessalonians (1 Thess 2:18) and instigating those in authority to imprison the faithful (Rev 2:10). At times, Satan may cause a physical illness, "a thorn in the flesh," to slow down the work of the faithful (2 Cor 12:7).

Jesus' activity of casting out demons is recorded only in the Synoptic Gospels.[28] It is interesting to note that the Gospel of John makes no mention of Jesus casting out demons. In the other three Gospels, however, this activity becomes a major aspect of Jesus' ministry, signifying the cosmic battle between the kingdom of God that is at hand and the kingdom of Satan (Matt 12:26-27). Until Christ appeared, Satan was believed to have power over death, but through Jesus' death and resurrection, this power was wrested away from him (Heb 2:14); Christ was needed "to undo all the works that the Devil has done" (1 John 3:8).

New Testament scriptures hint that some angels have sinned by leaving their proper dwelling place. As a result, they have been placed in everlasting chains to be released on the Last Day for judgment; therefore they are no longer a threat to humanity (Jude 6). Nevertheless, other wicked angels or demons continue to cause havoc among humans. Jesus' earthly battles against Satan and his demons hint at the coming eschatological victory over Satan and his dominion. But this victory is not limited to Jesus' time, for all future disciples are also given authority over demons. According to Mark, one of the signs associated with true believers is their ability to cast out demons (16:17). If believers "resist the Devil, he will flee" (James 4:7). After Jesus appointed the seventy-two to go and heal the sick, they return rejoicing that the demons submitted to them whenever they used the name of Jesus (Luke 10:9-20). Still, one needs to be careful when casting out demons, for Jesus reminds believers that once the demon is exorcised, it wanders through the desert unable to find a resting place, so it returns to the human host with seven additional demons that are more wicked than the one cast out (Luke 11:24-26).

Unlike other non-Christian accounts of casting out demons through some magical practice or secret knowledge, Christians were simply empowered by Christ's authority to do so without any particular formula, ritual, or procedure. The ability to cast out demons was not the result of sorcery or witchcraft. In fact, Christians were prohibited from participating in such magical feats. Paul condemns the use of witchcraft (Gal 5:20) and calls the Jewish sorcerer Bar-jesus "son of the devil" (Acts 13:4-10). The New Testament makes it clear that power over demonic forces was not the result of anything an individual could do nor a power achieved through merit or status of the individual; rather, power over demons came only from God. Acts recounts the story of a professional exorcist who attempted to cast out demons by using Jesus' name but was unable to do so because he was using Jesus' name as an incantation as opposed to simply believing in the message and person of the risen Christ (19:13-16).

When we turn to the epistles, instead of following the formula evident in the Synoptic Gospels of connecting demonic activity to physical ailments, the epistles represent demonic activity as humans rebelling against God and opposing believers. In advice on the qualification of a bishop (*episkopos*), the author of 1 Timothy warns against choosing a new convert and ensuring the person's reputation among nonbelievers lest the candidate "falls into the Devil's snare" (1 Tim 3:6-7).

Demons become the source of the persecution of believers. When the persecution is carried out by Jews, they are said to belong to the "synagogue of Satan" (Rev 2:9). Jesus refers to the crowd of unbelieving Jews as the children of the Devil (John 8:44). It is interesting—and, given the long history of Christian anti-Judaism, dismaying—to note that with the exception of the book of Revelation, which associates Satan with Rome, the rest of the New Testament usually identifies Satan's activities with those who oppose the good news of the gospel, often specifically Jews. Throughout the four Gospels, Jesus' antagonists, mainly the Pharisees (Matt 23:15) and the chief priests and scribes (Luke 22:52-53), are the ones usually identified with Satan. The conflict between Jesus and his followers with the Jewish religious leaders is interpreted as a physical manifestation of an ongoing spiritual warfare. Still, persecution or conflict need not be present to view the faith and actions of others as Satanic, nor must those influenced by Satan be Jewish. Those Gentiles who converted to Christianity were said to be turning "from darkness to light, from the dominion of Satan to God" (Acts 26:18). And what of those who fail to see the light of the gospel and become believers in Christ? They remain "blinded by the god of this world" (2 Cor 4:4).

Probably the most disturbing role given to demons is the influence they are said to have within all non-Christian religions. Just as they were introduced in the Hebrew Bible, demons are recognized in the gods of other religions in the New Testament as well (1 Cor 10:20).[29] For example, one of the names for Satan, Beelzebub (Matt 12:24), is believed by scholars to be a corruption of the name Baal Zebul, or literally "lord of the flies," who was believed to cause or cure illnesses across ancient Mesopotamia (note that the Hebrew Bible recounts the story of King Ahaziah of Israel who attempts to consult the oracles of the god Baal Zebub from the city of Ekron: 2 Kgs 1:2).

In short, early Christians regarded all other gods as being in fact demons in league with the prince of lies, Satan.

The epistles set up a very dangerous dichotomy between the emerging Christian faith and the faith of others across the vast provinces and colonies of the Hellenistic-Roman world. Either one has citizenship in God's kingdom (Heb 12:22-24) or one remains under the dominion of the Prince of this Satanic world (Heb 13:14). As Paul reminds us, "We wrestle not against flesh and blood but against the sovereignties, against the authorities, against the world's rulers of the darkness of this age, against the spiritual powers of evil in the heavens" (Eph 6:12). The gods of other nations, of other cultures, of other peoples are basically demons. Over the next two thousand years, this exclusive understanding, coupled with the historical process of conquest and colonization, will lead to much suffering, misery, and death between Christians and the people of other faiths and cultures. Because the gods of the conquered were seen as demons and their followers as demon worshipers, the Christian colonizers were emboldened to eliminate non-Christian cultures and murder those who chose to defend these "demon" gods and goddesses. The dichotomizing language we find in Paul often prevented the possibility of learning how to disagree without destroying, for in the minds of those who followed Paul, there can never be any coexistence between the God of truth and purity and the demons of darkness that supposedly are masked as the heads of all other faith traditions. We will return to this unfortunate legacy of exclusion and violence in the next chapter as we examine how the church fathers used the imagery of Satan and demonology to discredit the truth claims of Christian heretics, along with Greco-Roman mythology and philosophy.

In the New Testament, Satan, as the leader of these demonic forces, is referred to as "the prince of demons" (Matt 9:34); "the prince (or god) of this world" (John 12:31; 2 Cor 4:4); "the prince of the power of the air" (Eph 2:2); and "the ruler of the darkness of this age" (Eph 6:12). He is a tempter (Matt 4:3), the Evil One (Matt 6:13), the Enemy (Matt 13:39), a thief (Mark 4:15), the father of lies (John 8:44), a murderer (John 8:44), the Destroyer (1 Cor 10:10), a tormentor (2 Cor 12:7), an adversary (1 Pet 5:8), the primordial sinner (1 John 3:8), a deceiver (Rev 10:9), and an accuser (Rev 10:10). He stands before God "night and day," persecuting the brothers and sisters of the faith (Rev 12:10). Still, his major function is to rule the kingdom of darkness, even though he is able to appear as an angel of light (2 Cor 11:14).

Nevertheless, his judgment has already been sealed (John 16:11) even though the world remains in his power (1 John 5:19). His power over the world is attested by his ability to offer Jesus dominion over all the kingdoms of the earth (Matt 4:8-9).

According to the New Testament writings, Satan can be used by Christians as a way of punishing errant and wayward believers who reject the authority of the church. The latter are to be handed over to Satan in the hopes that their repentance may insure their eventual salvation (1 Cor 5:5). Not only can the church use Satan, but Satan can invade the church with false teachers (2 Tim 2:24-26) and false apostles (2 Cor 11:13-15). But the good news is that Satan's cosmic struggles against God will come to an end with an apocalyptic battle that is supposedly recorded in the book of Revelation, a battle in which war breaks out in Heaven (12:7). We can hear faint echoes in Revelation of the Zoroastrian prediction of an apocalyptic battle at the end of time between Ahura Mazda and Ahriman. According to some late ancient and early medieval interpretations, Christ, God's representative on earth, is matched against an Anti-Christ who serves as Satan's representative.[30] But Christ will prove victorious. Satan will be bound for a thousand years, released for one last battle, defeated, and thrown into a lake of fire to be eternally tortured (Rev 20:7-10).

### The Early Church Fathers

Two of the best known manifestations of Satan within Christendom were developed by the early Christian church: the identification of Satan with the serpent in the Garden of Eden and with Satan as Lucifer, the fallen angel. Although normatively accepted by most Christians as true, these biblical interpretations of Satan are based on a certain reading of the Scriptures that would have been considered foreign to the ears of earlier Jewish biblical commentators.

Justin Martyr, a second-century apologist for the Christian faith, connects the first transgression committed by angels leading to their fall with a sexual desire for women (Genesis 6). This sin placed the entire human race under God's curse. The sexual union of celestial beings with mortal women begat children in the form of demons—demons who now continuously swarm about, obsessed with inflicting vice and corruption upon human souls and bodies.[31] But this was not how the prince of demons, Satan, participated in the fall of humanity. Satan, in the form of a serpent, deceived Eve in the

Garden of Eden, and through her Adam falls in the same way that Satan fell.[32] Tertullian, an apologist of the third century, would argue similarly that because of Satan's deception of Adam, the entire human race, through Adam's seed, becomes infected with damnation.[33]

According to Irenaeus of Lyons, the second-century Roman apologist and heretic hunter, "For as by the disobedience of the one man who was originally molded from virgin soil, the many were made sinners, and forfeited life; so was it necessary that, by the obedience of one man, who was originally born from a virgin, many should be justified and receive salvation."[34] Only through a new Adam who did not contain Adam's seed could the Devil's hold on humanity be broken. Christ's death, according to the second-century apologist Origen, was "not only an example of death endured for the sake of piety, but also the first blow in the conflict which is to overthrow the power of that evil spirit the Devil, who had obtained dominion over the whole world."[35] Although death is identified with the Devil, the Devil was self-deluded in thinking that through Christ's death Christ, too, would fall under Satan's domain. Satan's victory at the cross turned into defeat at the resurrection.[36] Jesus offers his life not to God but to Satan, in substitution for the souls of humanity that belong to Satan because of their sinfulness. Satan accepts the bargain, but Jesus conquers death, and in so doing cannot be held in the Devil's clutches.[37] Through the first Adam, all humans inherited death; through the second Adam, humanity inherited the promise of everlasting life. As taught by Athanasius of Alexandria (c. 298–373 CE), the resurrection fulfilled the promise of the incarnation, for by God's self-sacrifice in Jesus Christ, human beings might restore the *Imago Dei*, the image of God, in their souls and reclaim their divine relationship with God. Hence the serpent in the Garden, responsible for leading humanity astray in their fall, is conquered through the death and resurrection of Christ, with the serpent losing in the transaction his hold upon the souls of Adam and Eve's descendants.

The second image of Satan, as a fallen angel, is derived by the early Church Fathers through a unique interpretation of an Isaiah passage. The prophet Isaiah proclaims to his contemporaries that the kings of Babylon will eventually face their downfall. Specifically, he writes, "O shining one, son of the dawn, how you have fallen from the heavens. You who have weakened the nations are cut down to the ground" (Isa 14:12). No Jewish writing had ever made the connection of fallen angels with this Isaiah passage; Origen was the first to do so among the early Christians. He rejected the notion that the passage could be a reference to the Babylonian king Nebuchadnezzar. Connecting the Isaiah passage with a comment made by Jesus about seeing Satan fall like lightening from Heaven (Luke 10:18), the early church fathers, beginning with Origen, developed the notion that Satan, among the most beautiful of angels, once lived in Heaven with God. Possessing free-will, he resisted God, leading to his being cast out of God's presence prior to the creation of the earth in a pre-cosmic Fall.[38] This led Origen to conclude, "In this manner, then, did that being once exist as light before he went astray, and fell to this place, and had his glory turned into dust."[39] Nevertheless, by the end of human history, because Satan is part of God's divine plan, he, too, will be saved and evil will cease to exist.[40]

The Hebrew word for "shining one," as used in the passage by Isaiah, is *hellel*, which was translated with the Greek word *phosphoros*, literally "light-bearer," the word that is also used for the "morning star." When Jerome translated the "shining one" into Latin for the Vulgate,[41] he purposely chose the Latin word *lucifer*. Hence lucifer, "the shining one," becomes Lucifer the king of Hell, reinterpreting the Isaiah passage to refer to Satan's expulsion from Heaven. Even though today we associate Satan with the powers of darkness, the word "Lucifer" means "the light bringer," a positive image when used in the Scriptures. For example, the book of Revelation ends with Jesus referring to himself as the bright star of the morning (22:16); and in the Latin translation of 2 Peter, the author suggests that the prophets of old are a lamp for lighting the way until Jesus as *lucifer* rises within our minds (1:19).

Being cast to the earth from Heaven makes Satan the prince of this world, a concept illustrated in the account of Jesus' temptation by Satan, when the Devil showed Jesus, in an instant, all the kingdoms of the world, saying, "I will give you power and glory over these kingdoms, because they have been delivered to me and whomever I wish to give them to, if only you worship me" (Luke 4:6). The same concept is confirmed prior to the crucifixion when Christ, referring to Satan, called him "the ruler of this world" (John 14:30). Although it may appear that a certain dualism exists in Christian imagery and belief whenever it seems God's will is being thwarted at every turn by the prince of this world, it is more consistent with Christian belief to suppose that God's all-powerful and all-knowing will allows evil to operate while accomplishing God's ultimate goal of redemption.

The theology of the full Christian "story" of Satan described here is that Satan, as a fallen angel, simply becomes a corruption of good. For the angel Satan once belonged in Heaven, but what was once created as good became perverted. In the same way, all that is evil is in reality a tainted distortion of good. Evil cannot exist in and of itself. It, like Satan, requires the ideal of the ultimate good (*Summum Bonum*) in relation to which it falls short of realizing its ultimate potential. Augustine of Hippo is among those church fathers who developed this concept while debating against those who claimed that if God had created all things out of nothing (*creatio ex nihilo*), then Evil, too, must have originated with God. After all, as an archangel, Satan, too, was one of God's creatures.

Despite Satan's deceitful and wicked role in the early Church Fathers' interpretation of the New Testament, monotheism remained secure because Satan is not equal to God, for he cannot exist on his own accord. Created by God for good but wicked by his own will, Satan remains dependent on the good. The doctrine of *privatio boni* (deprivation of the good) argues that only the highest good has substance and that all that exists is good because God's will decreed it to be so. Evil has no substance. It is simply the negation or privation of that highest Good, existing as attenuation. Even though Satan may will evil, God is able to use Satan to accomplish his divine plan. In a universe structured by sin, Augustine argued, for those who have God's grace, these structures are benign because they can lead to conversion and redemption. God can use Satan as a means to correcting the shortcomings of humans.[42]

## Gnosticism

The Gnostic movement, rooted in Hellenistic Judaism, is a generic term used to describe several religious perspectives that developed during the first centuries of the Christian church. These movements theologically differ from each other yet are held in common by the promise of providing salvation from the material world through *gnōsis*—a special or secret "knowledge" received through revelation, illumination, or initiation based on an intimate relationship with a transcendent source. One of the common beliefs is that all which is material (that is, the world and the cosmos) was created as an act of blasphemy by the Demiurge (a Latinized form of a Greek term that has come to mean "craftsman"). The Demiurge was understood to be an ignorant inferior angel or some malevolent junior deity responsible for creating the physical world of suffering, sin, and illusion. This premise contributes to a fundamental dualism between the physical and spiritual, with the former being corrupt and evil (the world of the Devil) and the latter being good and pure (the world of God). In short, the creator of the world is not the God of Genesis but some demonic being.

The Gnostic movement, in its various manifestations (that is, Manichaeism, the Marcionites, or the Valentinians), was considered heretical by the early Christian church. Most of what we know about the Gnostic movement is derived from the early Church Fathers who wrote against what they perceived to be a heresy. For our purposes, the Gnostic understanding of the spiritual forced Christians to sharpen their own understandings so that they could effectively counter Gnostic teachings and provide a unified witness of Christian beliefs and identity against the persecution of the Roman Empire.

Salvation for the Gnostics was understood as escaping the material world, including one's physical body, so as to ascend to the spiritual realm. Humans were trapped both in a material world of evil and darkness and in a body that is corrupt and ravaged by sin and suffering. Salvation means liberation from the body through right *gnōsis*, a right "knowledge" obtained by rejecting all that is material and attached to the physical world of the senses and passions.

Evil, according to the Gnostic *Gospel of Philip*, is understood apart from Satan. It is found within us, and only knowledge can deliver us from the bondage of sin. According to the text:

> Let each one of us dig down after the root of evil which is within one, and let one pluck it out of one's heart from the root. It will be plucked out if we recognize it. But if we are ignorant of it, it takes root in us and produces its fruit in our heart. It masters us. We are its slaves. It takes us captive, to make us do what we do not want; and what we do want, we do not do. It is powerful because we have not recognized it. While it exists it is active. Ignorance is the mother of all evil. Ignorance will result in death. . . . For truth is like ignorance: while it is hidden, it rests in itself, but when it is revealed and is recognized, it is praised, inasmuch as it is stronger than ignorance and error. It gives freedom. . . . Ignorance is a slave. Knowledge (*gnōsis*) is freedom. If we know the truth, we shall find the fruits of the truth within us. If we are joined to it, it will bring our fulfillment. (*Gos. Phil.* 133)

To recognize the evil rooted within one's self is an essential precursor to knowledge, to salvation. Christian Gnostics believed that the experience of this divine *gnosis* was superior to faith and argued against the claims to apostolic leadership and authority by the early Church Fathers, which led to their persecution as the battle between orthodoxy and heresy gained momentum in the first three centuries of the Christian church.

The Gnostics called themselves the "children of the knowledge of the heart" and believed that when they encountered the living Jesus within their own hearts and minds, a profound transformation would come over them and free them from the bondage of sin and matter. Although the early church fought Gnosticism, one can still find the influences of the dualism it advocated with the popular religiosity of Christians. The denial of the flesh and the pursuit of the spiritual, although a familiar concept in the writings of Paul, were reinforced by the Gnostic movements. Indeed, the age old Christian dichotomy of a fallen material world versus the exalted spiritual realm of heaven, or the tug-of-war between absolute Good as personified in Christ versus absolute Evil as personified in Satan, are vestiges of Christianity's persistent *gnostic* tendencies. Gnosticism was not just an early Christian movement that the Church Fathers silenced and defeated long ago. Gnosticism is also a characteristic of historical and contemporary Christian piety and religious experience with an aversion to structures of authority that undermine the liberation of the gospel message, as well as an aversion to the materialism and suffering of our embodied natures in a world of sin and death.

### The Talmud

Even after the destruction of Jerusalem and its Temple in 70 CE, Judaism survived. This was due in part to the writing and collection of rabbinic laws that covered agricultural tithes, public feasts, marriage, torts, sacrifices, and ritual purity. Fashioned around 200 CE under the guidance of Rabbi Judah the Prince, and known as the Mishnah, these teachings were eventually interpreted and modified through two different collections of religious literature known as the Palestinian and Babylonian Talmuds, with the latter becoming more authoritative to Jewish life. Within this Jewish literature, Satan is further developed. Before exploring the post-biblical development of Satan within Christianity, it behooves us first to explore the continuous contributions made by post-biblical Jewish thought.[43]

Demons, along with the opening of the earth's mouth to swallow up the wicked, are believed to have been created at twilight on the eve of the first Sabbath (*Pesahim* 54a). These demons that cause injuries, harm, and destruction are believed to be the souls that were unfinished prior to the start of that first Sabbath (*Aboth* 5:7). Another view put forth by R. Jeremiah b. Eleazar is that ghosts and demons (male and females) were begotten by Adam during the first one hundred and thirty years after his expulsion from Eden (*'Erubin* 18b). Regardless of how they came into being, demons can haunt houses (*Kiddushin* 29b), ruins (*Berakoth* 3a), areas under drain pipes (*Hullin* 105b), and outhouses (*Berakoth* 62b). They are known to cause stupidity and nervous prostration (*Bekoroth* 44b). Demons lie in wait to bring destruction to anyone who takes his shirt from the hand of his attendant when dressing in the morning, anyone who allows water to be poured upon his hands by someone who did not first wash his own hands, or anyone who returns a cup of asparagus brew to anyone save the one who originally provided it (*Berakoth* 51a).

These demons can turn people's faces backward (*Baba Mezi'a* 86a) or turn themselves into people-swallowing trees (*Sanhedrin* 101a). They can possess those who spend the night in cemeteries seeking to become fortune-tellers (*Sanhedrin* 65b). Demons are also able to provide false dreams, in opposition to God who speaks to humans through dreams (*Berakoth* 55b). They can empower sorcerers to work their magic, although some sorcerers perform their feats through pure enchantments (*Sanhedrin* 67b). The Talmud provides advice on how to protect one's self from night demons, specifically through the reciting of the *shema*[44] upon one's bed (*Berakoth* 5a).

The king of the demons is Ashmedai, who is appointed over those who drink alcohol in pairs (*Pesahim* 110a). The queen of the demons is Mahalath. Jews are warned not to go out alone at night (specifically on Wednesdays and the Sabbath) because the queen's daughter, Igrath, is out and about with 180,000 destroying angels with permission to wreak destruction (*Pesahim* 112b). Some women who lose their children during pregnancy might discover that the stillborn might look like Lilith, the night demon. Their similar appearance occurs if the fetus possesses wings, or looks like a serpent. (*Niddah* 24b).

Demons are numerous. According to R. Huma, "Every one among us has a thousand on his left hand and ten thousand on his right hand" (*Berakoth* 6a). These demons have wings allowing them to fly from one end of the earth to the other, though they are like humans in that they eat, drink, propagate, and die (*Hagigah* 16a). And yet, humans have been able to rule over demons, as did King Solomon who sat on the throne of the Lord (*Megillah* 11b). Reminiscent of the pseudepigrapha book, the *Testament of Solomon*, King Solomon is able to bind Ashmedai, king of the demons, with a chain that is engraved with the divine name. Once bound, Solomon is able to acquire the *shamir*, a worm that could cut through the sharpest stone. This worm was needed in order to construct the Temple (*Gittin* 68a-68b).

Although Satan appears some thirty-three times throughout the Talmud, he does not seem to play a prominent role among the demons. He is seldom mentioned in the older Talmudic literature, and when mentioned, he is simply another demon, at times reminiscent of when the Hebrew Bible referred to him as the *satan*, or the Accuser (*Berakoth* 60a). In one instance, the evil inclinations of people, referred to as the "Evil Urge," is identified as Satan (*Nedarim* 32b). In other places in the Talmud he is referred to as the Prince of Gehenna (*Shabbath* 104a), the Angel of Evil (*Sotah* 10b), the Angel of Death, and the Evil Prompter (*Baba Bathra* 16a). Gradually, belief in Satan as a being began to spread among the people. Originally he was unable to act independently, requiring God's permission, reminiscent of the book of Job where Satan is unable to inflict any torment without God's permission. Only later does he appear as an independent agent. When the Talmud refers to the personhood of Satan, it comments on Satan's limited powers. For example, he is unable simultaneously to have power over two nations (*Shabbath* 32a). Nor does he have God's permission to act as accuser on the Day of Atonement (*Yoma* 20a).

Satan is portrayed as some type of shape-shifter. At times he has appeared as a deer (*Sanhedrin* 95a), a bird (*Sanhedrin* 107a), a woman or a poor man (*Kiddushin* 81a). He can be found dancing between the horns of a black ox in April (*Pesahim* 112b). He is, however, responsible for killing Vashti[45] (*Megillah* 11b) and attempting to slay Moses' child (*Nedarim* 32a). The faithful can confuse Satan by blowing the *shofar*[46] at the start of a new year (*Rosh Hashanah* 16b), or they can be tempted by Satan if they provoke him with their arrogance (*Sukkah* 38a). Satan should never be provoked with arrogant boasts like "an arrow in the eye of Satan."

The Talmud also speaks of a place where the wicked are punished—a place call Gehenna.[47] Although R. Simeon b. Lakish argues that there is no Gehenna (*Nedarim* 8b), the majority of the Talmudic references understand

Gehenna to be the opposite of Paradise. God is credited with creating Paradise and Gehenna, the righteous and the wicked, evil inclinations and the Torah[48] to serve as evil's antidote (*Baba Bathra* 16a). Again, we find within Hebrew thought the concept that evil and temptation, like all that is good, comes from God.

Gehenna covers a large domain—a domain that consists of seven divisions (*Sotah* 10b). Historically, its gates were believed to be centered in the Valley of Hinnon. Yet some say it is located above the firmament, while others say that it is behind the Mountains of Darkness (*Tamid* 32b). Gehenna is larger than the entire earth. While the entire world was but one sixtieth of the Garden, and the Garden is but one sixtieth of Eden, Eden is one sixtieth of Gehenna. Hence, "the whole world is like a pot lid [in relation] to Gehenna" (*Pesahim* 94a). Gehenna is said to be composed of one-sixteenth part fire (*Berakoth* 57b). Although Gehenna was created prior to the creation of the world, its fire was created on the eve of the first Sabbath (*Pesahim* 54a).[49]

Those who will go to Gehenna receive a double portion of punishment (*Hagigah* 15a). Among them are: (1) those making derogatory comments about scholars (*Shabbath* 33a); (2) those who ogle women when counting money into their hands (*'Erubin* 18b); (3) those who cause their community to sin;[50] (4) the rich men of Babylon (*Bezah* 21b); (4) those who sin with their bodies (*Rosh Hashanah* 17a); (5) those who have sex with a married woman (*Sotah* 4b); (6) those whose iniquities are more numerous than their good deeds (*Rosh Hashanah* 17a); (7) idol worshippers (*Ta'anith* 5a); (8) those who lose their temper (*Nedarim* 22a); (8) flatterers (*Sotah* 41b); (9) the haughty, which includes all heathens (*Baba Bathra* 10b); (10) the best doctors whose haughtiness makes them fearless of sickness (*Kiddushin* 82a); (11) judges that render unfair decisions (*Sanhedrin* 111b); (12) idleness from studying the Torah (*Aboth* 1:5); (13) disciples of Balaam (*Aboth* 5:19); (14) those who follow their wife's counsel (*Baba Mezi'a* 59a); and finally (15) those who are informers and scoffers, those who reject the Torah, those who deny the resurrection of the dead, those who abandoned the community's ways, and those who spread their terror among the living (*Rosh Hashanah* 17a).

But those who give charity to the poor (*Gittin* 7a), or those who fast (*Baba Mezi'a* 85a), are protected from Gehenna's punishment. Elsewhere in the Talmud it states that even the righteous descend into the fiery furnace only later to ascend from it (*Pesahim* 118a). The wicked also get to ascend from Gehenna because punishment is neither continuous nor eternal. Even the wicked get a day of rest from their torment on the Sabbath (*Sanhedrin* 65b). Also, the punishment of the wicked is limited to a twelve-month sentence in Gehenna (*'Eduyyoth* 2:10). Eternal punishment is rejected for being vindictive. In its stead, the temporal punishment of a limited sentence promotes regeneration (*Shabbath* 33b).

Still elsewhere in the Talmud, Gehenna's punishment for the wicked is seen as eternal, specifically for those who commit adultery with a married woman, publicly shame their neighbor, or give their neighbor an evil nickname (*Baba Mezi'a*). Those who are intermediate between righteousness and wickedness descend into Gehenna to "squeal" while being refined by fire, and only after their purification do they get to ascend from the Pit (*Rosh Hashanah* 16b-17a).

## The Holy Qur'an

With the rise of Islam in the seventh century of the Common Era, Satan was once again reimagined and reinterpreted. Islam's close association with Judaism and Christianity means that our exploration of Satan's origins and development would be incomplete if we did not consider Muslim contributions to the discussion. Generally, demons or dark spirits are believed by Muslims to represent the opposite of good. They say the opposite of what is true, blame others for their faults, call good evil and evil good, and argue against God and the faithful for the sole purpose of subverting humanity's relationship with Allah. Nevertheless, they are powerless to bring any significant mischievous action. All they can do is lead humans astray. This is also true of the demonic beings who wander the realms of air and spirit in the universe.

According to the Qur'an, Allah created three different types of spirits: angels, jinn, and demons. Angels are the protectors of humans and often communicate the will of God to men and women. Jinn and demons are not necessarily evil in the Islamic conception of these spirits. The Arabic language refers to the demons as *shayāṭīn*, meaning "adversary." The Islamic tradition refers to the most powerful of these demons as Iblīs, a name derived from the Greek *diabolos*, which is also the source of the word Devil. The Arabic term *shayāṭīn* bears a striking etymological resemblance to the term *satan*. Sura 15:28-42 of the Holy Qur'an[51] describes Iblīs as the only angel who refused to bow down before Adam. He disobeyed Allah supposedly because of his conviction in the superiority of angels over humans. After all, Allah made the angels out of fire and humans out of clay (Q18:50). Thus, God's benevolence and mercy to humanity is always being threatened by Iblīs and his demonic legions of *shayātīn*. For his disobedience, Iblīs was cast out of Heaven and now awaits annihilation on the Day of Judgment (Q15:35). The personification of evil as Iblīs, rather than Satan, appears as a stronger link in the Qur'an, but in the Qur'anic tradition, Iblīs (as Satan) does not have the same power or influence as the Satan who confronts Jesus in the New Testament and later appears as the Anti-Christ of medieval Christianity.

Still, it is interesting to note that the Meccan suras frequently use the plural form "*satans*," probably an allusion to other fallen angels with Iblīs as their head. Unlike humans, angels lack good or evil tendencies; they are automatically good. On the other hand, because angels do not have free will, there really can be no fallen angels in Islamic tradition. By the time we get to the Medinan suras, "*satans*" in plural, along with Iblīs, disappear; only Satan in the singular remains. He is credited with tempting Adam and Eve in the Garden, as well as leading armies of *shayātīn* and jinn. Yet contrary to the Christian thought that blames humanity for eating the forbidden fruit, the concept of "original sin," Islam holds the Devil responsible, even though humanity still suffers the consequences of that first disobedience and must repent before the almighty and merciful Allah. Since that first encounter with humanity, Iblīs, or Satan, has been tempting and misleading humans to sin (Q2:36).

Unlike the other two Abrahamic faiths, the Islamic Satan is anemic. Satan is the rival of humans (Q12:5), not of Allah, for Satan does not even come close to having the ability to challenge Allah or to have any influence or sway with Allah. And even though humans were created weak (Q4:28), Satan also has no sway over or power against humans that are on their moral guard and faithful to Allah's way (Q15:42). All Satan can do is confuse and tempt (Q14:22), but such temptations are in vain for those who constantly turn to Allah for guidance and to the Holy Qur'an for moral wisdom (Q7:200-201). Satan does not possess humans but rather whispers his temptations into the ears of humans (Q50:16). Satan only appears powerful because humans choose to be weak and allow themselves to be seduced.

Within Islam there exists the concept of *jinn* (from which the English word "genie" is derived). Some jinn are formless creatures created of "smokeless fire" (Q55:15), while others take on substance in order to appear to humans. Unlike angels, jinn have free will. Like humans, they have intelligence and are capable of salvation (Q46:29-31), although the jinn do appear to be more prone to stupidity and evil than humans. Jinn are understood to be a genre of creation that parallels humans, even though it seems that prior to Islam Arabs worshipped them (Q34:41). It is interesting to note the lesson of the Qur'an: the former gods of the Arabs are but formless, powerless creatures when contrasted with the mercy, majesty, and power of Allah. Some jinn are friendly to humans, others are hostile. Some are lovely to gaze upon; others are repugnant, referred to as *ghūl* (from which the English word "ghoul" is derived). According to some Arabic and Islamic traditions, Satan is considered to be a jinn who originally was an angel (Q18:50).[52]

Like Christianity, there is an eternal and physical Hell in Islamic tradition, also known in Arabic as "Jahannam." The Islamic vision of an afterlife consists of the Garden where the faithful experience joy and pleasure and a Hell that serves as a place for punishment. Unlike Christianity, there are no intercessory beings, like the two other persons of the Holy Trinity, or an intermediate location for repentance, such as Purgatory. All humans stand helplessly before their All-Merciful Creator, Allah, relying on nothing but Allah's compassion, mercy, and forgiveness. The early and middle Meccan periods of the Qur'an provide detailed accounts of the horrors faced by those who are banished to Hell. Hell is a fiery furnace (Q25:11-12) where the fire first burns its victims from within before consuming their outer self (Q104:6-7). As soon as their skin is consumed, they grow fresh skin so that the consumption by fire can reoccur (Q4:56)—a process that lasts an eternity (Q25:65). It is a place of constant death without dying (Q14:17). The only liquid made available to drink is festering boiling water (Q14:16). Those going there are unbelievers (Q3:131) who have bowed their knees before false gods. They and their seducers will join Iblīs and his host of misguided jinn and sinful humans (Q11:119).

According to Adnan Aslan, the Islamic account of the episode in the Garden of Eden and its conception of Iblīs's greatly diminished power and influence in the universe, leads to a healthier theodicy. Islam, he argues, has a distinctive perception of evil that "de-emphasizes the pessimistic elements in the Biblical narration . . . such as the serpent, the alienation of human beings from God, and the original sin" (Aslan 2001, 35). Adam and Eve's act of disobedience in the Garden is simultaneously humanity's first act of free will, which, when not corrupted by the essence of original sin in the soul, renders the story of the Fall of Man in the Garden in a very different context than either the Jewish account in Genesis or the traditional Christian interpretation of this primordial story. This is another way of saying that the will of God cannot be limited by any of the creatures or spirits that God created. The fundamental unity of God (*tawhid*), along with Adam's and Eve's absolute trust in the power and mercy of God (*tawakkul*), completely trumps the power and influence of Satan over the bodies and souls, hearts and minds of all true believers.

## Clearing through the Muddle

When did Satan become the embodiment of evil and an enemy of God? Some scholars would look to the intertestamental period while others might argue that this concept did not emerge until post-biblical times. This may be an interesting debate; nevertheless, we are less concerned with when this transition happened than with its ethical implications. Although we attempted in this chapter to provide clear historical brackets to show when the different developments and transformation of Satan occurred, we are well aware that history is much more fluid, seldom neatly fitting into clearly distinct time periods.

It is somewhat problematic to point toward a textual source during a particular historical period and claim that a certain understanding of Satan occurred at the point when such a text was produced or written. Not only are we millennia away from the formation of the ancient texts this chapter examined, but some of the texts took centuries to develop into the manuscripts and books we hold today. We must consider the transmission of a possible oral tradition that probably existed for some time, possibly centuries, before the stories were actually written down. Whatever value we place on the insights of modern scholars, we must humbly deal with the stark reality that as historians, ethicists, and biblical scholars we can know the past only "approximately," and perhaps even more so when relying on ancient or premodern texts as our windows into a dimly remembered "past," a past whose cultural or social world of people, places, and events—centuries or millennia old—we are attempting to reconstruct in the "present."

Our picture of the past, history, is indeed muddled. However, there are several excellent resources in print that attempt to clear up the confusion by providing a historical analysis of ancient texts; but such an analysis is beyond the scope or intent of this book. Our concern remains the ethical ramifications of the historical development of Satan as the symbol for absolute Evil; and it is with that concern in mind that we close this chapter.

## Ethical Concerns

God's portrayal as a character of absolute goodness is the result of a theology that is read into the Christian Scriptures yet not necessarily supported by a close reading of the texts. Not only is this theology challenged by the Bible, it is challenged also by existentially and morally comparing such a theology of absolute Good versus absolute Evil with the realities of life. All have faced, or will face, tragedy, misery, illness, and death. Events will occur that appear unfair, leading most of us to question if any sense of cosmic justice and mercy truly exists. Natural disasters will claim thousands of lives, as with the Haitian earthquake of 2010, and the victims will include innocent men, women, and children. Many have referred to this dilemma as the theodicy question. How can an all-loving, all-powerful God allow evil to occur? What type of parent would allow a child to suffer if they had the power to prevent evil from touching or hurting their child?

Jesus asks, "What person among you, if asked by their child for a loaf would give a stone? Or if asked for a fish will give a snake? If, then, you, who are evil, know to give good gifts to your children, how much more will your Father in Heaven give good things to those that ask?" (Matt 7:9-11). Yet reading the morning paper, one finds stories about tornadoes that have wiped out good Christian families while they slept peacefully in the middle of the night, or innocent children who perished at the hands of child molesters and murderers, good decent individuals who die in freak accidents, and many others who suffer under moral evils (those actions caused by humans) and natural evils (those actions caused by nature). When we consider the billions of senseless deaths, tragedies, and atrocities that define human history, it would seem that history denies more than it confirms the paternal love of a caring and merciful father God. One is forced to ask: Where is God? Comparing Jesus' words with the reality of evil in our global economy seems to indicate that earthly parents, rather than God, know better about how to care for their children. It is God who appears to be giving the tens of thousands who die each day of hunger and preventable diseases a stone when they are begging for bread, or hands them a snake when they are praying for fish.

In a very real way, the search for the historical Satan is an attempt to justify God's grace while legitimizing the reality and presence of evil in human history. At least this seems to be what was occurring with the birth and development of Satan in the legends of pre-Christian mythology and across the pages of the Jewish, Christian, and Islamic sacred texts and Scriptures. It appears that the development of Satan was, to a certain extent, trying to save God from appearing as the source of evil that is so much a part of the reality of human suffering and death. The Scriptures attempt to convince us that God is still worthy of our worship despite the presence of evil, even though the most troubling conclusion derived from the Judeo-Christian biblical text is the discovery of a God who is the cause and author of all that is good—*and all that is evil*. As the prophet Amos reminds us, "If there is evil in a city, has Yahweh not done it?" (Amos 3:6). The prophet Isaiah understands God to say, "I form light and create darkness, make peace and create evil, I Yahweh do all these things" (45:7). This is a God who sends evil spirits to torment, as in the case of Saul (1 Sam 18:10) or Jeroboam (1 Kgs 14:10). Contrary to popular opinion, the biblical text does not begin by introducing its readers to Satan as the Prince of Darkness and enemy of God whose primordial spiritual warfare continues to manifest itself in our times. Rather, this concept developed over centuries as religious ideals comingled with popular culture and the flow of history.

What if we were to answer the theodicy question by simply reducing evil to a punishment for sins? If evil befalls you, you deserve it for some offense committed. Unfortunately, the book of Job deals with the theodicy question by illustrating that evil befalling an individual is not necessarily caused by sins that individuals have engaged in or committed. Rather, evil may befall a person like Job because God directs it to be so. We are left with the troubling answer from God as to why evil befell such a faithful person like Job: "Because I can" is the heavenly response we hear. The early shapers of sacred texts and religious traditions found themselves in the position of having to protect God from accusations of being the source of evil. As it became less acceptable to have aspects of God represented in evil elements or events, independent evil figures had to be birthed. If Satan did not exist, then perhaps he would have had to be created to serve as an adversary so as to vindicate God.

Evil had to be personified and given a name. As we have seen, the names and characteristics have varied over the last five thousand years, although the name Satan seems to have risen to the top. Satan's physical existence ceases to be our concern; for what is important is the end result that evil became a historical entity we now call Satan. Still, the problem exists that radical monotheism makes it difficult simply to develop a demonology. As troublesome as it may be to conceive of God as being the author of malevolent acts, more bothersome yet is the creation of another supernatural being in competition with God within a strictly monotheistic religion.

In later chapters, we will return to how the theodicy question has been addressed once Satan is eliminated from religious belief and scholarship under the influence of modernism and the scientific rationalism of the Enlightenment. But for now, what would happen if we were to take Satan and his demons seriously? Not so much as a symbol of absolute Evil, but, returning to the Hebrew Bible, as the means of discerning God's will. What if instead our understanding of Satan was influenced by the concept of the "trickster" figure that seems to be present in the Hebrew Bible? Could the concept of the "trickster" perhaps be more in line with the biblical text than the way Satan developed as the personification of absolute Evil? And if so, how does such an understanding of Satan feature in our appreciation of evil? And more importantly, how would Satan as trickster shape our morality? Before turning to these and other such questions later in the book, we will explore how the personification of evil in the figure of Satan was further developed throughout the early Christian struggle against heresy, the formation of the Medieval Church, and the cultural clashes of the Reformation and Colonial periods. ✳

# Chapter 3

# SATAN THROUGH THE AGES

I n the summer of 2010, as people across the nation were preparing to mark the ninth anniversary of the September 11th terrorist attacks on New York City and Washington, controversy erupted in Gainesville, Florida, when leaders and members of the Dove World Outreach Center vowed they would burn as many copies of the Holy Qur'an as they could get their hands on by early September. This conservative, non-denominational, and independent church decreed that each year on the eleventh day of September it would hold an "International Burn the Koran Day." After local officials in Gainesville refused to issue the church a burn permit, the church leadership decided to proceed anyway with the planned burning of the highly venerated Islamic holy book. Followers of Islam believe the Holy Qur'an was transmitted in the seventh century CE to the Prophet Muhammad by the angel Gabriel in a miraculous form of communication. Muslims believe the Qur'an was given by God as an act of mercy to the Arab tribes and to all humankind, an act of compassion from the same loving God who forged the ancient covenantal and monotheistic traditions with the other Children of Abraham, the Jews and the Christians.

The Rev. Dr. Terry Jones, senior pastor at Dove World Outreach Center, is apparently satisfied with comments such as "Islam is a lie based upon lies and deceptions and fear."[1] This was just one of the comments posted on the church's official website in response to public concerns over a hateful sign erected in 2009 on the front lawn of its property, which read: "Islam is of the Devil." The church website also featured such blogs as "Ten Reasons to Burn a Koran," while another blog described the holy text revered by Muslims all over the world as "The Sorcerer's Scroll." One could even buy a t-shirt for under twenty dollars, the front of which bore the slogan "I stand in truth with Dove World Outreach Center. 'Jesus answered: I am the way, and the truth and the life; no one goes to the Father except through me,' John 14:6."[2] The back of the shirt had emblazoned on it the words "Islam is of the Devil," which also happens to be the title of Dr. Jones's inflammatory book exposing what he considers the historic violence and deception of Islam. The book's back cover emphatically maintains that contemporary Christian leaders and church membership have lost their way in these modern times: "God has given the body of Christ everything it needs to become an apostolic, over-coming church in America and around the world. But instead of mobilizing for the battle for truth, many Christians today are bowing to society. Mired in political correctness, the church remains ignorant about one of Satan's most successful, and most accepted attempts to counteract the truth of the gospel—Islam" (2010).

To the great relief of millions of Americans and Muslims around the globe, Dove World Outreach Center's senior pastoral leadership team eventually cancelled its plans to burn the Holy Qur'an on September 11th, 2010. Their mission statement described the center as that of a "New Testament Church based on the Bible and the Word of God," solidly committed to the universal truth of apostolic leadership and anointing by the power of the Holy Spirit in majesty with the Father and the Son—historic phrasing not unlike that used by the apostolic Fathers of the Church when Christianity emerged from Judaism and sought to differentiate itself from other ancient Greek or Roman religions by claiming that their political rivals and theological opponents worshipped Satan and his legions of demons and devils from Hell.

In her own significant contribution to the quest for understanding the Prince of Darkness, *The Origin of Satan*, Elaine Pagels invited her readers "to consider Satan as a reflection of how we perceive ourselves and those we call others" (1996, xviii). She admitted that researching Satan's origins in relation to the New Testament and to early Christian discourse about the enemies of the church stirred up aspects of Christianity that disturbed her. Pagels was one of the first modern scholars effectively to shine a light on this dark side of early Christian ways of portraying and discrediting opposing factions or rival religious traditions. She recognized how much of Christian belief and practice derives from its own origins in Judaism and Greco-Roman culture, but she also correctly identified how the Christian movement had to construct its self-definition while dealing with its opposition. One of Christianity's most novel ploys was in demonstrating "how the use of Satan to represent one's enemies lends to conflict a specific kind of moral and religious interpretation, in which 'we' are God's people and 'they' are God's enemies, and ours as well" (1996, xix). Of course, when one's opponents or rivals are determined to exterminate you, your family, and your followers completely, it becomes much easier to demonize nearly everything one knows and fears about ones' opponents, especially their gods and goddesses. Such extensive demonization was certainly a feature of the Roman Empire's persecution of the early Christians from the time of the execution of Jesus under Governor Pontius Pilate to the reign of the Emperor Diocletian.

For early Christian thinkers such as the North African scholar Origen of Alexandria (c. 185–c. 254 CE), all laws and persons who are hostile to Christianity are by definition demon-inspired. Satan accomplishes these effects on those of weak and malleable faith by tempting and manipulating them, as he has done for millennia along with a legion of loyal demonic servants that is responsible for the evil faced. But more importantly, it also identifies those who are called "others," who come to serve as scapegoats, as enemies of the faith. This was as true in the past for those Christians who demonized the Roman Empire, as it is today for those Christians, like Terry Jones, who demonize Islam. Christians, according to Origen, when "tyrannized by the devil" and the "barbaric and despotic" earthly government he leads, should form "associations contrary to the devil's laws" so as to pursue revolt. After all, Jesus died to destroy the great "spirit" (*daimōn*) who holds in subjugation the souls of humanity.[3]

The rise of Christianity in the Hellenistic-Roman Empire of the ancient Mediterranean world witnessed one of the most profound and far-reaching reinterpretations of the problem of evil in the history of humanity. And since the Roman Empire spanned three continents, it should come as no surprise that the struggle for religious identity and political power between the early Christian movement and the empire left its mark upon nearly every one of Rome's subject peoples and nations. In the previous chapter we examined textual and literary concepts of Satan and the problem of evil ranging from prehistoric Egyptian myths to biblical understandings of evil among the Hebrews, Persians, and Christians. Our quest for the historical Satan in this chapter focuses on the relationship of the early Christian community and the Fathers of the Church to the abundant and highly contested presence of angels and demons, elemental powers, and ethereal beings in the wider culture of ancient Hellenistic-Roman civilization. This is a contentious relationship that we contend became the breaking point for any possibility that Satan's role as a "trickster" figure working in tandem with God might potentially flourish and reduce the dichotomy between absolute Good and absolute Evil.

Early Christian evangelists, writers, and leaders held a moral world-view and relational theology centered on a caring and loving God who intervened in history on behalf of either God's chosen people, the Israelites, or on behalf of those who accepted God's only begotten Son as their personal Lord and Savior. Jesus Christ was portrayed by the Church Fathers as the long-awaited redeemer, or *messiah*, of the Hebrew religious tradition who was destined from the beginning of time as the savior of humanity. Christianity inherited many ideas and symbols, beliefs and practices, and doctrines from Judaism and from the small Hebraic community of "Christians" led by James in Jerusalem after the crucifixion. However, this relational theology about a benevolent, loving, and moral creator who cared about the personal lives and ethical choices of his earthly human creatures set the stage for a contradictory relationship with the diverse religions and philosophical schools the Church Fathers inherited from their Hellenistic-Roman social identities and pagan cultural surroundings. Among the Greek and Roman educated elites, the idea of a loving, parent-like deity must have seemed strange and incomprehensible! Among the masses of peoples and cultures scattered across the vast regions of the Hellenistic-Roman Empire, this unusual Hebrew and Christian idea of a loving and moral God was at odds with their classical understanding of the many gods and goddesses who personified the forces of nature and controlled the ebb and flow of chaos versus harmony in the cosmos.

Among these "pagan" religions we find such male deities as the Greek father of the gods, Zeus, or the Egyptian solar god of creation, Amun-Re, or the Roman lord of the heavens and planets, Jupiter. There were also female deities, such as the Egyptian Isis, or Artemis, the Greek goddess of animals and virginity, who was also known to the Romans as Diana, or the numerous Celtic female goddesses associated with fertility, sacred rivers or streams, and the natural cycles of plants and animal life.

As Christians grew in numbers and social influence throughout the empire, potential converts and opponents began wondering more carefully who this Jesus of Nazareth really was. How could he be the Son of the Highest God? And if he really could be so identified, then what power did Jesus, as the Son of the Most High, and as the Risen Christ, possess over the entire host of angels and demons and elemental spirits? To put the matter in the simplest of terms: If Jesus was indeed the Son of God, then how did his rise from the grave and ascension to heaven offer human beings liberation from both sin and death? How could such sweet deliverance from sin and death be real when most ancient peoples believed themselves to be in the invincible grip and at the mercy of powerful elemental spirits like those portrayed among the Zodiac signs, or like the earth-bound demons that people believed were responsible for all manner of illness, disaster, and death?

Reconciling men and women with the idea of an active and merciful God, as perceived in the biblical portrayal of *Yahweh*, or of a rational and transcendent god as perceived in the Greco-Roman concept of the *Logos*, proved to be one of the great challenges of early Christian theology and evangelization. The economic, political, and social structures of the ancient world were embedded in a harmonious conception of cosmic order as well as celestial and terrestrial correspondences. Despite the plurality of religions and beliefs that characterized antiquity, the arrival of monotheism from Palestine in either its Jewish or early Christian versions posed serious threats to established social norms, especially after several millennia of polytheistic beliefs and worship practices passed down from generation to generation.

Developments in ancient astronomy, philosophy, and Stoic metaphysics eventually began changing the hearts and minds of many people among the educated elites of the ancient Hellenistic-Roman world. Astronomical speculation that the stars and the planets, which were once believed to be gods and goddesses, were actually moving relative to the possible motion of the earth and the sun, fueled speculation about an unseen or Highest God who governed the movements of the heavenly bodies and the fate of human beings. If this was so, then perhaps there was one ultimate and true deity behind all of the manifestations of matter and spirit across the universe.

On the other hand, if all of this astronomical and philosophical speculation was true, then what about Christian claims to the exclusive position of their Savior (*Soter*), Jesus Christ, among all of the other deities and spirits of the ancient religious pantheons? How did the manifestation of the highest divinity in the birth, life, and ministry of Jesus Christ change the influence and power of the *elemental spirits* (or *daemōnēs*) of earth, air, water, and fire over the bodies, hearts, minds, and souls of individual men and women? How could an all-powerful, all-knowing, loving, and merciful Creator God allow his creation and beloved creatures to wallow in the depravity of sin or in the suffering of evil? How can the human heart and mind discern whether one's dream visions, insights, or spiritual revelations are benevolently angelic or malevolently demonic? After all, Satan tempted the first humans in the Garden of Eden with uncanny trickery and promises of god-like knowledge. If God is truly the caring and forgiving Lord of all Creation, then where does evil come from? And why does God allow Satan and his legions of demonic spirits to wreak havoc and discord by tempting men and women into committing acts of sin and then falling away from their providential relationship with God? Although in the wake of the European Enlightenment and the Age of Reason such questions may seem irrelevant to many of us living in the technologically advanced societies of the twenty-first century, during the first four hundred years of Christianity such questions had profound and far-reaching implications for defining the problem of evil in human history. To be sure, the search for answers to these questions brought about a reinterpretation of evil that generated important and culture-changing repercussions for the life and times of Satan.

## From Hellenistic Syncretism to Christian Exclusivity

Every tribe, nation, or civilization that ever existed has had its own unique ways of "knowing" and relating new knowledge to cherished narratives about its origins and its cultural traditions, ways of testing new or emergent "truths" against old and proven forms of "Truth." The answers early Christianity offered for the kinds of existential, religious, and moral questions cited above, together with its persistent rhetorical and theological demonization of other people's gods and goddesses, would eventually bring about the end of paganism and the rise of a new Christianized society in late ancient times. Such was the social situation in the fifth and sixth century CE as the divine beings and elemental spirits of the ancient world were replaced by the Holy Trinity of Father, Son, and Holy Ghost, or by the holy men and holy women whose spiritual lives became the raw material for the Christian cult of the saints.

Indeed, many of the heroic attributes and intermediary roles of the former avatars and demigods of Greek or Roman mythology were inherited by the cult of the saints that emerged in late Roman times. An invisible world-view developed populated by terrifying demons and sympathetic saints, by roaming dead souls and malicious monsters. Conversion to Christianity and the sacrament of baptism, according to *Clementine Recognitions*, which supposedly was penned by Clement of Rome (first century CE), was to rid the body of whatever demons were infecting it (Kelly 1974, 39). This all serves to illustrate further that for ancient societies and their intellectuals or visionaries, there was a "way of knowing" and relating knowledge across cultural boundaries based upon a theory of "correspondences" that focused on the harmony (*harmonia*) that existed between different ideas and symbols, philosophies and beliefs, wisdom traditions, or the stars and planets in the night sky. In this way the truth claims of other civilizations or religions could be evaluated and judged true or false not merely on ideological grounds but primarily with regard to the practical application of ideas or wisdom borrowed from other cultures or worldviews.

The term most often associated with these practices is *syncretism*, which in the special case of the ancients signifies the blending or union of different beliefs and ideas from across the varied cultures of the Mediterranean into a more complex and unified worldview. Syncretistic associations and correspondences became quite common after the conquests and death of Alexander the Great in the period known to historians as the Hellenistic Age (323–c. 31 BCE). As the power of Rome expanded and as Rome conquered most of the former Hellenistic states set up by Alexander's generals and successors, the Roman Empire also developed a syncretistic culture among its major urban centers of commerce and cultural vitality. The early Christian movement became quite adept at the process of syncretism as evidenced by the large number of symbols and influences it picked up from the Hebrews, Egyptians, Persians, Greeks, Romans, and later from the Celtic peoples of Europe. Ironically, Christianity transitioned from being itself just another one of the many religious cults and philosophical movements of the Hellenistic-Roman world into being the premier religious movement whose exclusive claims to truth and power superseded all other religions and schools of thought that contradicted the apostolic teachings and supreme spirit of Jesus Christ.

The role of agricultural cosmologies on the ability of ancient people to compare notes and ponder their similarities and differences each night by simply gazing at the stars and constellations cannot be underestimated. The older a particular society or nation was, the more prestige, or religious clout, it had among its neighbors across the ancient Mediterranean basin and the Middle East. The Egyptians and Babylonians were often perceived as possessing this type of sacred ancient wisdom by the Persians, Greeks, and Romans. What modern scholars often refer to as *syncretism* was partly also the result of astronomical speculation for the purpose of measuring and predicting the agricultural seasons, or the result of intercultural conversations about the stars and planets as related to farming and navigation. Since everyone possessed a creation myth, questions about the origin of life, or about the gods and the afterlife, also generated theories, ideas, and symbols of harmony, which functioned as signifiers of mutual correspondences based on existential and cosmological observation upon whose foundation any claims of universal wisdom or truth eventually found a rock or an anchor.

As a point of mutual dialogue and meaning, the visible stars and planets mattered very much to the application of this theory of correspondences because, at the end of the day, when someone went to sleep or woke up in the early morning hours, they saw essentially the same heavenly bodies in the night sky whether one was in Rome or Alexandria, Cairo or Baghdad. These cosmological notions of order and wisdom were grounded in polytheism, the belief in multiple gods and goddesses, many of whom were associated with their own special star or planet. Notable examples are the worship of the sun, which is attested to by the many different conceptions of the solar gods, or the veneration of the planet Venus, who signified for many people the various conceptions of love, beauty, and fertility that abounded in the ancient world. On the other hand, while the starry heavens and planets were the acknowledged realm of the gods and goddesses, as well as the final resting place of the souls of great kings, demigods, and heroes who had come and gone over millennia among the living, the physical world and the interior regions of the earth were seen as the realm of the spirits. In the natural and moral understanding of most ancient men and women, nearly everything in the world *possessed a spirit* or *was possessed by a spirit*. The word for an ethereal being or spiritual, force-like presence in ancient Greek culture, art, and literature was *daimōn*, which most closely approximates the meaning of the English word "spirit." However, the term "spirit" actually derives from the ancient

Latin word *spiritus*, which often was used to signify "breath" or "soul" or the "life force." Our examination of these ancient religious belief systems begins with some of the basic ideas and definitions about "spirits" scattered across the literary, philosophical, and artistic landscape of Hebrew, Egypto-Greek, Hellenistic, and Roman culture.

In previous chapters we pointed out how Egyptian and Persian beliefs about natural catastrophes, or about the forces of chaos and destruction in the natural world, led to some of humanity's earliest ideas about destructive forces being associated with "evil" and personified by a deity like the Egyptian Seth, or represented among a group of deities such as Angra Mainyu, the Persian-Zoroastrian spirit responsible for disorder and suffering in the world. We also observed how the Greek term for demon (*daimōn*), which simply means "spirit," began taking on negative connotations among the Hebrews during the intertestamental period from the writing of Malachi to the writing of the Gospel of Matthew. Jewish cosmology and social ethics associated these demons with the gods of other nations, along with the lesser or servant deities of these gods and goddesses. Thus, as Christianity emerged from its Jewish historical and biblical background and from the Jerusalem-based Christian community led by James, it was predisposed to equating and discrediting the gods and goddesses of others as malevolent spirits or demons inspired and led by Satan.

However, capturing the Hellenistic and Roman centers of power and making disciples of all nations under the aegis of the Christian Holy Spirit, while waiting for the promised return of Jesus Christ as the "King of kings," was not going to be an easy task, especially with the Romans and most of their allies honoring the emperor as their divinized version of the "King of kings" on earth. Roman provincial governors and judges came to view the Christians as an antisocial and fanatical cult whose continued existence threatened the survival of the new Roman imperial state and its cult of emperor worship instituted by Octavius Caesar in honor of his murdered uncle and first emperor Julius Caesar. Here we have occasion for examining examples of ancient pagan spiritual beliefs that, although similar, were not identical to the rising exclusivist beliefs of the Christian community. Long before Jesus preached in Galilee, some of the legends about the Persian sage Zoroaster suggested that he was of semi-divine origins. There were also legends surrounding the birth of Alexander the Great, legends that claimed that he was the son of Zeus-Amun or that a bright star appeared in the heavens on the night of his birth. Such legends were designed to secure Alexander's divine status among the kings and emperors of the ancient world.

The ancients believed that the gods could have intercourse with mortal women and give birth to half-human, half-divine demigods or avatars. Some of these unique and heroic persons were also destined to serve as highly successful and seemingly invincible "god-kings." Indeed, this is how many came to understand the apparent divine favor behind the political exploits and military successes of both Alexander the Great and Julius Caesar, whose souls were understood by their contemporaries and successors as something more than ordinary, mortal souls. It was often believed that such remarkable persons possessed a *genius* in their souls, as if they were literally "incarnated" with a very special deity or powerful guardian-spirit on the day of their birth. The symbol of a "halo," a thin veil worn lightly over the head, or the use of heavy white make-up was a means of depicting the special *genius* or divinized aura of sacred heroes or of semi-divine political and spiritual leaders.

Some ancient writers and cosmologists believed that when a new star appeared in the heavens, it was a signal from the gods that a new god-king, savior (*soter*), or avatar was being born on earth. The story of Jesus also possessed very similar divine attributes, including the Star of Bethlehem, his lineage from the house of King David, and the miracles and healings he performed across Palestine during his three-year public ministry. As the Roman cult of emperor worship was growing in popularity across the empire about the same time the Apostles were spreading the good news of the Gospels, this incarnational political theology of the expanding Roman Empire collided with the incarnational religious theology of the growing Christian movement. Hence Roman imperial protocols and symbolism about the Emperor as a semi-divine *genius* clashed with Christian notions of Jesus as Lord and Savior of humanity, or as King of the Jews and the Son of God.

The persecution of Christ's followers as enemies of the Roman state began quite early, and Jesus' followers were often under suspicion of treason for refusing to swear the oath of citizenship, which consisted of an oath of allegiance to the *genius* in the emperor's veins before a statue of the emperor. As thousands of Christians were arrested, tortured, or executed from the middle of the first century CE until about the autumn of 394 CE, when Christianity was declared the official religion of the Roman Empire by Theodosius the Great, the Roman Emperors came to be viewed by many among the ranks of Christian clergy and laity as the agents of Anti-Christ in league with

Satan and his legions of demons. Ironically, Christianity's widespread and steadily growing appeal to the societies of the ancient Mediterranean basin from the first Pentecost to the fall of the Western Roman Empire nearly five centuries later rested on the remarkable similarities between the existential and moral themes of Hellenistic culture with the merciful and communal themes that Christian evangelists and missionaries preached while ministering to the needs of the poor and the sick. Today, most of us tend to possess a slightly inaccurate historical assumption that the early Christian movement was a grassroots coalition of the poor and dispossessed from all over the ancient world. However, Christianity's ability to express itself in the international language of Koine Greek, along with its ability to give eloquent witness in front of Roman emperors, governors, and judges by drawing allusions and comparisons with its teachings and beliefs and those of the more popular Greco-Roman culture, collectively attests to Christianity's high appeal among both the uneducated masses and the educated intellectual and political elites of these ancient societies. In this context, the role of Christian apologists, who sought to give witness to the truth and relevance of their faith to the Caesars and the imperial system of magistrates and law courts, played a vital role in the process of early Christian syncretism.

The rhetorical techniques of the Christian Apologists were aimed at defending the faith while informing the wider world of the Roman Empire about the basic ideas of their movement as well as promoting conversions to Christianity. Many of their letters and treatises were addressed to Roman Emperors, but we do not know if these were ever answered. Mark Ellingsen summarizes the objectives of these Fathers of the Church: "The core question for them in arguing for the credibility of Christian faith was to address the classical pagan culture and the Hellenistic philosophical commitments that surrounded them. The Church needed to address the question of whether the work of Plato, Aristotle, and the Stoics revealed any truth and, if so, how this could be reconciled with the Gospel" (1999, 48).

The apologists were divided into two camps. On the one hand, the *orthodox* faction was highly critical of distorting the gospel message by allowing too much syncretistic blending of beliefs or ideas from pagan culture and Hellenistic thought with Christianity. Tertullian (c. 160–c. 225 CE) is perhaps the best example of and most influential advocate of orthodoxy among the Apologists of the second century. On the other hand, the *correlationist* faction followed the example of Saint Paul by drawing correlations from

Christian ideas, doctrines, and practices to those of Greco-Roman culture and Hellenistic thought and religions. Arguing from historical, moral, and literary evidence, this camp hoped to stem the tide of Roman hatred and discrimination against Christians for being perceived as a bizarre and anti-social religious cult. Among this faction were such figures as Clement of Alexandria, Justin Martyr, Athenagoras, and Tatian.

Perhaps the best-known and most influential of the Christian Apologists was Justin Martyr (c. 100–c. 165 CE). He was also one the earliest of the second-century *correlationists* who sought to blend the teachings of Jesus, the Gospels, and the Hebrew Bible with the philosophical truths of Greco-Roman thought and culture. Justin was born into a Greek family in Palestine, where he received a pagan upbringing and education. He was well versed in Platonic and Stoic philosophy. His attempt to reconcile his Christian faith with certain elements of pagan philosophy and culture is perhaps the most important of these types of efforts among the Apologists of the Christian cause. He eventually opened the first Christian school in Rome. In the process of offering a defense of Christian teachings and beliefs before the empire, however, Justin also helped pave the way for the reinterpretation of Satan and the problem of evil that is the central focus of this chapter. His writings and ideas had the effect of giving the early church a vision of human history that was more complete and unified than any before his time, save for that promulgated throughout the Hebrew Scriptures as Yahweh and the Israelites nurtured their relationship with each other through the medium of biblical memory and sacred covenants.

Connecting the incarnation of Christ as the Son of God to the Stoic idea of the divine Logos ("word") as infused in the human heart and thereby uniting all of humanity, Justin reasoned that Christianity was the only exclusively valid religious and moral doctrine that existed since the beginning of time. In his *First Apology* Justin writes to the Emperor Hadrian, explaining the "irrationality of paganism" in the following section:

> And when we say also that the Word, who is the First-begotten of God, was born for us without sexual union, Jesus Christ our teacher, and that He was crucified and died and rose again and ascended into heaven, we propound nothing new beyond [what you believe] concerning those whom you call sons of Zeus. For you know of how many sons of Zeus your esteemed writers speak: Hermes, the interpreting word and

teacher of all; Asclepius, who, though he was a great healer, after being struck by a thunderbolt ascended into heaven; and Dionysus too who was torn to pieces; and Heracles, when he had committed himself to the flames to escape his pains; and the Dioscuri, the sons of Leda; and Perseus, son of Danae; and Bellerophon, who, though of mortal origin, rose to heaven on the horse Pegasus. For what shall I say of Ariadne, and those who, like her, have been said to have been placed among the stars? And what of your deceased emperors, whom you think it right to deify, and on whose behalf you produce someone who swears that he has seen the burning Caesar ascend to heaven from the funeral pyre? And, what kind of deeds are related of each of these reputed sons of Zeus, it is needless to tell those who already know. This only shall be said, that they are written for the benefit and instruction of students; for all consider it an honorable thing to imitate the gods. But far be it for every sound mind to entertain such a thought concerning the deities as to believe that Zeus himself, the governor and begetter of all things, was both a parricide and the son of a parricide, and that being overcome by the love of evil and shameful pleasures he came into Ganymede and to those many women whom he seduced, and that his sons did like actions. But, as we have said above, wicked devils perpetrated these things. And we are taught that only those are deified who have lived near to God in holiness and virtue; and we believe that those who live unjustly and do not change their ways are punished in eternal fire. (1997, 37–38)

Justin's experience of Christian faith and the Gospels convinced him that the cosmological, existential, and moral truths of Platonism and Stoicism had their most complete expression in the unifying and redemptive birth of Christ. This he further augmented with his profound faith in the mission of the apostolic community of teachers and evangelists who succeeded Jesus after his crucifixion at the hands of the Roman Empire, and Jesus Christ's subsequent resurrection and ascent to heaven. Justin explains this even more emphatically in his *Second Apology*: "What we have then appears to be greater than all human teaching, because the whole rational principle became Christ, who appeared for our sake, body, and reason, and soul" (1997, 80). He goes on to explain that the great contemplative truths and moral precepts of Greek and Roman civilization, such as the teachings of Socrates, Plato, and Stoicism were anonymously attuned to the power and wisdom of the Logos even though these pagan sages did not yet know Christ in their hearts and minds.

Throughout the first and second parts of his *Apology,* Justin alludes to the power of Satan and his evil demons and devils (1997, 42) and portrays Satan as the master of deception and lies to lead humanity astray from the reality and truth of the Logos:

> For I myself, perceiving the wicked disguise which the evil demons had cast over the divine doctrines of the Christians, in order to avert others from joining them, laughed both at those who framed these falsehoods, and at the disguise itself, and at popular opinion. And I confess that I both pray and with all my strength strive to be found a Christian; not because the teachings of Plato are different from those of Christ, but because they are not in every respect equal, as neither are those of the others, Stoics, and poets, and historians. For each person spoke well, according to the part present in him of divine logos, the Sower, whenever he saw what was related to him [as a person]. But they who contradict themselves on the more important points appear not to have possessed the hidden understanding and the irrefutable knowledge. Therefore, whatever things were rightly said among all people are the property of us Christians. For next to God, we worship and love the Logos who is from the unbegotten and ineffable God, since also He became man for our sakes, that becoming a partaker of our sufferings, He might also bring us healing. (1997, 83–84)

Hence, the Incarnation and Resurrection of Jesus Christ took on a universally powerful connotation as the Church Fathers consolidated their apostolic claims to rightful leadership and ecclesiastical authority among the early Christian communities that spanned the vast provinces and territories of the Hellenistic-Roman world.

Justin Martyr was executed by the Romans during the reign of Marcus Aurelius (c. 163–167 CE) for refusing to pay homage to the gods. In the final years of his life he worked as a teacher in Rome, and it was through his pupils that his ideas became quite significant for the future of Christian doctrine and theology. His writings offered the next generation of Church Fathers a comprehensive vision of salvation history stretching from God's act of creation in Genesis, through Moses and the Hebrew prophets, and culminating in the unifying revelation of the Logos in Jesus Christ, who, despite being executed by the Roman Empire, conquered death by rising from the grave and ascending to heaven. Thus, it became possible for Christians to speak of truth and wisdom as exclusively pertaining to this sacred trajectory, attested to by the numerous accounts of God's love and mercy in the Hebrew Scriptures and in the growing canon of the Christian New Testament and perpetuated after the miracle of Pentecost in the succession of Apostolic teachers and evangelists recognized as the rightful leaders and vicars of Christ on earth. This had the effect of co-opting the wisdom of the ancients through the rhetorical and methodological ploy of the anonymous existence of Christ as the Logos since the beginning of time while simultaneously dismissing the truth claims of pagan religious culture and Hellenistic philosophy as incomplete and originating in the realm of Satan.

Any alleged truth or wisdom traditions outside of this sacred and exclusivist biblical and apostolic path came to be regarded among the Church Fathers as perverted fragments of the truth derived from Satan and his devils, who are also the source of all lies, deception, and evil in the physical and earthly realms of existence. In this way the practical *syncretism* of ancient Mediterranean beliefs and traditions that characterized the different ways of knowing the unknowable, or relating the realm of the living to the realm of the *daimōnes* (spirits), was gradually discredited by the rising discourse of Christian missionaries and heretic hunters. The Church Fathers developed their version of Christian exclusivity by casting out devils, healing the sick, and liberating both the poor and the elite from the demoniacal grip of the Zodiac's elemental spirits as well as from the gods and goddesses of their Roman imperial oppressors.

An ancient Gnostic sect known as the Nassenes, a sect discussed in the *Elenchos* of Hippolytus, may have summarized these perceptions best by describing the incarnated Christ as a magnet (*magnesia*) capable of attracting the fragmented religious and philosophical truths of ancient civilization into a unified whole known as the *aqua doctrinae*, or as the "living waters" of Christ's divine "teachings" and wisdom (Jung 1978, 184–201). As Carl Jung noted when studying the same section of the *Elenchos:* "Christ is the magnet that draws to itself those parts or substances in man that are of divine origin . . . and carries them back to their heavenly birthplace" (1978, 185–86). So, for better or for worse, in their evangelistic advocacy for the Jewish monotheism of Jesus, the Fathers of the Christian church drove out the polytheistic beliefs of the other nations and rival religions of the ancient Mediterranean world and dismissed all of these other gods and goddesses, elemental spirits and ethereal beings, as either demons or devils in the service of Satan, entities locked in perpetual struggle against the angelic hosts of heaven commanded by Jesus Christ.

## Satan's Army versus the Sword of the Spirit

The Christian discourse on healing, spiritual happiness, and wholeness was one of its most powerful messages to the people and nations of the Hellenistic-Roman world. Jesus walked with sinners and offered bread and healing to the poor. He was a calming presence among the disenfranchised and marginalized members of Hellenized-Jewish society throughout Galilee. He was generous and comfortable in the company of others, whether rich or poor, righteous or sinners. He dared to touch individuals who society identified as unclean or unworthy of being touched and shared his loving presence with them. Nonetheless, the early Christian movement was also aware that the struggle for salvation was no mere philosophical debate on the question of "What is the good life?"—such as those sometimes famous public dialogues that took place at the Agora in Athens or at the Roman Forum.

There is a passage in Ephesians that uses metaphors of armor and weaponry to describe the struggle of good versus evil: "Put on the full armor of God that you may be able to take a stand against the tricks of the devil. We do not struggle against flesh and blood, but against the principalities, against the powers, against the rulers of this present darkness, and against the spiritual forces of evil in the heavenly realm. Therefore put on the full armor of God so that you may be able to withstand the day of evil and stand your ground" (6:11-13). The Church Fathers and their followers increasingly adopted the attitude of being locked in a cosmic battle against Satan and the forces of evil, a war of annihilation whose final battle was prophesied as far back as Zoroaster and the Hebrew prophets. Considering the Roman Empire's relentless persecution of Jesus' followers and its gruesome executions of Christians in the public arenas of the empire, battle and armor metaphors must have seemed all the more real. Ephesians continues by stating: "Stand firm having girded your loins with the belt of truth, and having put on the breastplate of righteousness, and having fitted your feet with the gospel of peace. Besides all this, take up the shield of faith, with which you can quench all the flaming arrows of the evil one. And take the helmet of salvation, and the sword of the Spirit, which is God's Word" (6:14-18).

Ironically, pagan philosophy and popular religious culture also had its own beliefs and practices about healing, spiritual happiness, and wholeness. Near the end of his life and career, Aristotle returned to the legacy of Socrates, who repeatedly asked his students to think long and hard about the most fundamental human question: "What is the good life?" In other words: What does it take to lead a fully rational and happy life in which one's highest human aspirations and potentiality might be realized in an ethical way? Aristotle was pondering the problem of *eudaimonia* as his Classical Athenian world lay vulnerable and threatened in the wake of Alexander's remarkable military conquests. This remarkable word from the common everyday jargon of Hellenistic times literally derived from the Greek prefix *eu*, meaning "well," and from the term *daimōn*, meaning "spirit." Thus, in mundane terms the word literally meant "being in good spirits," "well-blessed," or "good fortune." In the hands of Aristotle's ethics, and the profound crisis of meaning that swept through Hellenistic philosophy after the death of Alexander the Great, the word became a key moral term among the Stoic, Epicurean, Cynic, and Skeptic schools of thought that existed until the fall of the Roman Empire. Although the word is often mistranslated by modern researchers as meaning "happiness," philosophers from each of these schools transformed the meaning of the word to signify "human flourishing." It was also an allusion to the notion of being "well-blessed" with a favorable or good "divinity implanted in one's chest," or, more precisely, in one's heart as the seat of the Logos, as was the belief of the Stoic persuasion like the Emperor Marcus Aurelius.

Such lofty Greco-Roman ideas about human dignity and potential intersected rather nicely with pagan themes of healing or salvation. The Greek word for "salvation" was *soteria*, while the Latin word for "salvation" used among the Romans derived directly from ancient medical terminology was *salve* or *salvus*, which was a direct allusion to notions such as "mending," "healing," or restoring "wholeness." The prevalence of such images among pagan vocabulary and practices associated with healing and medicine demonstrates the persistence of the *daimōnes*, and of the ancient gods and goddesses throughout the entire ancient discourse on personal salvation and religious identity. Despite local differences and variations, these characteristics also were found in trans-local ways from Rome to Egypt, or from Greece along the coasts of

Asia Minor and Palestine, and were especially noticeable at urban centers such as the *asclepieons* found at Pergamum, Heliopolis, and Epidauros, or at more remote centers such as the Isle of Kos. An *asclepieon* was an ancient center of healing named after the god of medicine and health, Asclepius, which functioned much like a modern holistic clinic though adorned with statues of the god and goddesses and attended by priests and priestesses.

Details and anecdotes provided by ancient writers suggest that traveling to these and other healing centers created the world's first known tourist industry as men and women who could afford this luxury journeyed across the Mediterranean on a quest for physical and spiritual health. Although Christianity adopted much of this ancient terminology about healing and salvation, the pagan nature of each *asclepieon*, with its emphasis on the therapeutic interaction of *daimōnes* on patients, led Christians to dismiss most aspects of this medical tradition on the grounds that it subjected human beings to the perverse influence of demons, devils, and evil spirits. Among the Church Fathers, *salvation* as spiritual *wholeness* and moral *healing* came through the power of the Holy Spirit and by following the teachings of Jesus Christ.

The gods and goddesses of the diverse peoples and nations who made up the cultures of ancient Egypt, Greece, Carthage, and Rome were eventually cancelled out by the new worldview of the Christians based on the biblical event of their one, true God incarnated in Jesus Christ, who later rose from the dead, walked among the living for forty days, and then ascended to heaven nine days before the miracle of Pentecost, which saw the Holy Ghost poured into the hearts and minds of the Jerusalem Christian community. Indeed, early Christians were both inspired and empowered by this Holy Spirit, who infused them with various spiritual gifts for leading and serving the church of Christ and for battling the Prince of Darkness whenever necessary. In the Gospel of Luke, when Jesus commissioned the seventy to spread the word and deeds of God, they returned to him and the other disciples exclaiming, "Lord, even the demons submit to us in your name!" (10:17). Jesus then emphatically adds the following lesson for them to ponder: "I saw Satan fall like lightning from heaven. I have given you power to tread upon serpents and scorpions, and over the power of the enemy—nothing will hurt you. Nevertheless, do not rejoice that the spirits submit to you; rather rejoice that your names are written in heaven" (10:18-20).

In John 14, just before we learn of the promise of the Holy Spirit, Jesus offers one of his most empowering statements, one that the Church Fathers later recited in times of persecution as they spread the gospel message all through the Hellenistic-Roman Empire: "Surely I tell you, whoever believes in me will also do the works that I have been doing; and greater works than these they will do, because I am going to the Father. Whatever you ask in my name, I will do, so that the Father may be glorified in the Son. You may ask anything in my name, and I will do it" (14:12-14). Romans, Greeks, Egyptians, and Syrians wondered how this humble teacher, called Jesus, could be so powerful, since the Christians and Hebrews worshipped an unseen and thereby inferior god.

The miraculous and fiery outpouring of the Holy Spirit on Pentecost, just as Jesus had promised, created the conception and reality of an intermediary Comforter or Intercessor "spirit" among early Christians capable of advocating between their finite earthly existence and the infinite heavenly realm of the Father and the Son. In contrast, the gods of other nations and peoples, now dismissed as demons, were viewed as being in league with Satan and as the supreme archenemies of God, enemies hell-bent on enticing humans away from the true faith and healing message of Jesus Christ. Demons became responsible for tempting humans and providing them with false doctrines. Christianity became a spiritual movement with a plan to overturn the social order of ancient society, which Christians considered oppressive and unjust, by unleashing the miraculous powers of the "sword of the Spirit" (Eph 6:17).

However, in addition to the social and political agendas their followers promoted, the Church Fathers also transformed what their opponents believed about "spirits" and "demons" by preaching that all pagan and non-Christian religious beliefs and philosophies that did not correspond with the truth of the Christian revelation were the product of Satan. In other words, the Incarnation, Resurrection, and Ascension of Jesus unified all truth through the person and spirit of Christ: "Therefore God has exalted him high and bestowed on him a name which is above every name, so that at the name of Jesus every knee should bow, in heaven, on earth, and beneath the earth, and every tongue shall confess that Jesus Christ is Lord to the glory of God the Father" (Phil 2:9-11). And so the early Christians let it be known unto the ends of the Roman Empire that their exclusive Savior (*soter*), Jesus Christ, superseded the power of the lights and planets in the starry heavens. He had dominion over the demigods and nature spirits of the earth, and through the Holy Spirit each of them could tread on all manner of demonic spirits from above, from the earth below, or from the underworld of the Devil. It mattered little to them that those "spirits" from above were worshipped and revered among ancient religions as divine, angelic, or benevolent—all such pagan "spirits" were evil demons who represented a perverted fragment of the wholesome truth incarnated in Jesus Christ.

## Jesus Saves!

Jesus as the incarnated Savior became the only means by which this entire world could be wrestled back from the hands of Satan. Throughout the Gospel of John, Satan is repeatedly referred to as "the prince of this world" (John 12:31; 14:30; 16:11). During the temptation of Jesus in the desert story in the Gospel of Matthew, Satan has the authority to offer Jesus the splendor of all the kingdoms of the world if only he would fall at the feet of the devil and worship him (Matt 4:8-10). Early Christian Fathers, like Origen, Irenaeus of Lyons, Augustine, and Pope Gregory the Great, advocated for the "ransom theory" of atonement: Jesus Christ had to die on the cross and shed his blood so as to ransom humanity back from the authority of Satan and humanity's bondage to evil. Satan, according to this theory, gained power over humanity in the Garden of Eden. Appearing there as a serpent, he tempted Adam and Eve, whose sin of disobeying God's command against eating from the tree of knowledge condemned all of their descendants to be prisoners of Satan. God eventually offered God's only begotten son as a ransom for humanity's fall. Although Satan accepts the exchange, he cannot hold Christ in Hell when Jesus descends there after his crucifixion and death (Eph 4:9) because, unlike humans, he is born without sin (original sin was transmitted as a genetic spiritual substance in the male semen—*fomes peccatum*) and lived a perfect and blameless life as the incarnated Son of God.

Christ becomes the ransom paid, a debt paid to Satan that saves humanity from their enslavement to the prince of this world. Once the debt is paid, anyone who believes in the name that is above all names, Jesus Christ, can accept the blessed assurance of their salvation. The early Christian Church claimed that Jesus saves—but saves from what? To be saved is, at the very least, to be liberated from sin—the sin of spiritual

Fig. 1. *President Obama is more than simply demonized, he is Satan—the Anti-Christ.* PUBLIC DOMAIN.

Fig. 2. *Persian King Darius Slaying Ahriman depicted as a Lion, a destructive spirit or Angra Mainyu.* COPYRIGHT © SEF / ART RESOURCE, NY.

Fig. 3. *Our modern image of Satan is similar to representations of the Greek god Pan who also possesses hindquarters, cloven hooves, goatee, wrinkled skin, and the horns of a goat.* PUBLIC DOMAIN IMAGE (COURTESY WIKIMEDIA COMMONS).

Fig. 4. *Hell is the place where Satan devours and defecates the souls of those opposed to God's will.* COPYRIGHT © SCALA / ART RESOURCE, NY.

Fig. 5. *Relief sculpture shows souls being judged and condemned to Hell by demons.* COPYRIGHT © VANNI / ART RESOURCE, NY.

Fig. 6. *Vergil guides Dante to the depths of Hell where Satan is consuming the soul of traitors Judas Iscariot, Brutus, and Cassius.* PUBLIC DOMAIN IMAGE (COURTESY WIKIMEDIA COMMONS).

Quáto noi fiúno latoue lacosfeia fuolgr apúto i fulgrossovelláche lotuca cófatica er cónágosfeia

Volfe latesta ouesli auea legancbe er agrassosi alpelo comuom hefale fi cbonunferno credia cónaz anelx

Fig. 7. *Reality was infested with demons who tempted humans, even holy saints like St. Anthony.* PUBLIC DOMAIN IMAGE (COURTESY WIKIMEDIA COMMONS).

Fig. 8. *Witches gather around a he-goat in monk's attire.* PUBLIC DOMAIN IMAGE (COURTESY WIKIMEDIA COMMONS).

Fig. 9. *Those who succumbed in life to the Devil's temptation find themselves reaping the rotted fruits of eternal damnation.* PUBLIC DOMAIN IMAGE (COURTESY WIKIMEDIA COMMONS).

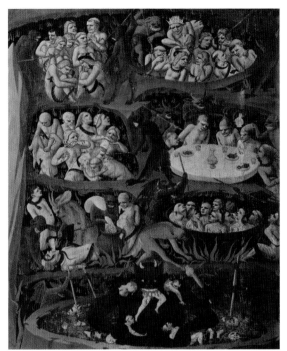

Fig. 10. *An eternity of sadistic punishment awaits those who failed to walk the "straight and narrow" while alive.* PUBLIC DOMAIN IMAGE (COURTESY WIKIMEDIA COMMONS).

Fig. 11. *No hope exists for those ferried to Hell for living a life that failed to resist the Devil.* PUBLIC DOMAIN IMAGE (COURTESY WIKIMEDIA COMMONS).

Fig. 12. *More than 150 individuals were imprisoned for being witches and consorting with the Devil in 1693 at Salem Village, Massachusetts.* COPYRIGHT © THE NEW YORK PUBLIC LIBRARY / ART RESOURCE, NY.

Fig. 13. *Satan's tempting of Jesus helps Jesus, in all his humanity, better understand his divinity and the important public ministry that awaits him.* COPYRIGHT © RÉUNION DES MUSÉES NATIONAUX / ART RESOURCE, NY.

Fig. 14. *The legendary Battle of Clavijo, fought around 844 between the nearly defeated Spanish Christian King Ramiro I and the Moors, was reversed when St. James the Apostle (who supposedly brought the gospel to Spain) appeared as a knight and slew sixty thousand Moors, hence his name Santiago Matamoros (St. James, the Moor-slayer).*

oppression forced upon the wretched of the earth. To be saved calls for new relationships—not just with God, but also with each other. Satan becomes the opposite of God, an idea that is in tension with the Judeo-Christian doctrine of monotheism.

Nevertheless, to reject Christ as Savior is to reject his salvation and to condemn oneself to Hell along with Satan and all of his demons. The choice in the minds of the early Christians was clear: salvation with Christ or damnation with Satan. Choose ye the way, to Good or Evil. There was no in-between. The cross becomes the place where the devil is conquered, where the chains of bondage are broken. Suffering and martyrdom at the hands of the empire becomes redemptive; gore, à la Mel Gibson's *The Passion of Christ*, is glorified. Making Christ's death a necessity for salvation seems to justify unjust suffering, thus undermining any effort in dealing with the millions who are being crucified on the crosses of race, class, and gender oppression. Can indeed the evil of the cross save us from evil? Can the demonic act of crucifixion save today's crucified people? Or does injustice, the unjust crucifixion of Christ, beget more injustices? Does Jesus die as ransom or in solidarity with all today who are being forced to carry a cross so that the elite few can enjoy privileged and abundant lives?

For those who are being crucified by oppression and injustice today it is hard, if not impossible, to see anything redemptive about unjust suffering. A ransom paid to Satan relies on a Satan who actually has something owed to him. But for those who live on the underside of history, the crucifixion makes more sense when understood as an act of solidarity. Christ does not die to pay any ransom, or, as suggested by Anselm of Canterbury (c. 1033–1109), to pay the debt of human sin. Christ stood in solidarity with those who were dying at the hands of the political and religious leaders of his time. It was on this point that Christ and the Church Fathers turned the tide against the Hellenistic-Roman world's indifference to oppression and injustice, against the temple priests who refused to hear the cries of the poor, or against the senators and philosophers whose idea of civic *devotio* was preoccupied with idolizing the emperor and the Roman state. The disenfranchised are constantly called upon to offer up their lives so that the few can live. Jesus Christ, in the ultimate act of solidarity, makes a preferential option for the crucified and as such becomes a model for those who wish to stand in solidarity with the disenfranchised who wrestle with the demonic, death-bringing social structures.

## Wrestling with Tricksters or Demons? A Case Study

It would be difficult to trace accurately and count how many times Christian polemicists or apologists among the Church Fathers described or dismissed the deities of other nations and peoples as "demons" or "devils." And yet, in this way of talking about the religious beliefs and practices of others, we find the seeds of future acts of intolerance and violence that one cannot imagine Jesus Christ ever condoning, even as he chided the disciples, when stating: "I am the way, the truth, and the life; no one comes to the Father but by me" (John 14:6). Nonetheless, liberation from the pagan elemental spirits and zodiacal demons and protection against all sorts of ethereal and malevolent demonic powers was the ultimate goal of ancient Egyptian, Chaldean, Greek, and Roman magic.

This idea and the practice of magic might best be compared with our modern faith in science as a means of gaining liberation from the suffering caused by disease or illness and from anxiety over our inability to control the forces of nature. From this perspective, ancient magic is more like modern science, since both approaches seek to gain mastery over nature and alleviate human suffering—characteristics with significant implications for anyone either gifted with healing wisdom or called to heal the sick as a minister. As observed by Helmut Koester, "If the fate of human beings was determined by the stars, and if good and evil demonic powers constantly interfered with human life, magic offered to make the demons subservient to human interests and to outwit the dictates of fate" (1987, 380). The popular *daimōn* who served as the lord of magic and transformation, and perhaps the favorite trickster-figure among the masses of ancient men and women who venerated him for thousands of years, was also known as the messenger of the gods among both the Greeks and the Romans, who respectively called him Hermes or Mercury.

In contrast, ancient Christians believed liberation from the principalities and powers of the demonic realm had been made possible to them by the incarnation of the Logos in Jesus Christ and then assured by his rising from the dead and ascending to heaven just as suggested in Galatians: "When we were children, we were slaves to the forces of elementary spirits. But when the time had fully come, God sent his son, born of woman and born under the law so as to redeem those under the law, so that we might be adopted as sons and daughters" (4:3-5). Paul then goes on to rebuke the Galatians quite sternly:

"Formerly when you did not know God, you were slaves to beings that by nature were not gods. But now that you have come to know God, or rather are known by God, how is it that you can turn back again to the weak and beggarly elementary spirits? Do you want to be once more their slaves?" (4:8-11).

Many among the ranks of ancient men and women who converted to the worship of Jesus Christ from the various pagan cults, mystery religions, or philosophical schools would have been familiar with the theme of healing maladies of the soul as well as maladies of the body and mind. They also would have been aware of the different "gifts" bestowed upon mortals by the gods and of the miraculous forms of communication and interpretation that sometimes happened when mortals and gods came close to touching each other's realms of existence. For ancient magicians and sorcerers, conjuring angels or gods through the practice of magic was a means of gaining power over the realm of spirit to bring about positive effects in the physical realm of existence. The generally positive lore and pastoral legends about the Greek god Hermes posed quite a problem for the Church Fathers because Hermes, who was known as "the Good Shepherd" among the ancients, possessed a few symbolic attributes that were very similar to some of the virtues of Jesus Christ.

Paradoxically, Hermes was also the alleged demonic figure at the center of the ancient magical and alchemical arts whose influence persisted throughout the Ancient, Medieval, and Modern periods as a "trickster" playing hide and seek with humanity in the natural world as well as in the realm of literary interpretation. Indeed, our modern English word signifying the interpretation of texts, "*herme*-neutic," attests to this ancient god's persistent influence through the ages; a most confounding and perplexing set of circumstances when one realizes that such fine Christian scholars and saints as Albertus Magnus (c. 1193–1280) and his pupil Thomas Aquinas (1225–1274), were believed to have known plenty about the alchemical and magical arts attributed to this alleged pagan devil called Hermes. We are forced to ask the question: Were pagans and Christians who practiced magic worshipping devils and demons, or were they just playing the so-called "golden game" of Hermetic magic with this quick-witted and elusive trickster-spirit who was also known to the ancients as "the Good Shepherd"?

The history of this mysterious *theologia magica Christiana* (Christian magical theology), practiced openly by Medieval and Renaissance Christian laity and clergy, begins in the Hellenistic-Roman world of the ancient

Mediterranean. From its earliest beginnings, this tradition emphasized the fusion of Egyptian and Greek principles concerning astronomy, mathematics, medicine, and literary interpretation. Zosimos of Panopolis, who taught in ancient Alexandria around 300 CE, was the first sage to discuss the processes of transmutation and describe the goals of the alchemical work. The esoteric tradition later known as *alchemy* derived its emphasis on the transmutation of matter and spirit from the scientific context of Hellenistic Alexandria. Practices and techniques from ancient goldsmiths and metallurgy became intertwined with astrological and cosmological beliefs about human potential and the awesome powers concealed in nature. It was about this same time in Hellenistic Egypt (c. 200 BCE–c. 200 CE) that the *Corpus Hermeticum*, or "Books of Hermes," were compiled, perhaps under the supervision of Zosimos of Panopolis.

However, as we pointed out earlier in this chapter, among the ancients the older a civilization was the more prestige it possessed on matters dealing with spiritual wisdom. Other sages maintained that all genuine truths should harmonize or correspond to each other like the universal application of sacred astronomy and sacred geometry, which the Egyptians claimed to have received from their Ibis-headed god, Thoth. Egyptians believed that the four areas of study cited above were given to humanity as "gifts" by which to improve human life and learn the secrets of nature and how to read the signs in the heavens for communicating with the gods who dwelt in the unseen realms beyond the stars and the planets. Among the Greeks, these traditions became equated with Hermes, whom we are told was the son of Zeus and the mountain nymph Maia; a family pedigree that, according to the Church Fathers, only a devil or a demon would boast about.

Hermes also served as the "messenger" of the Olympian gods. He was known among the Greeks as the protector of travelers, as the trustworthy guide of souls in their sleeping hours as well as in their journey after death from the world of the living to the realm of the afterlife. Clues to the etymology of Hermes' name may be derived from the words *hermaion* and *hermen*, which respectively signified a "pile of stones," erected to guide travelers on ancient Greek roads, and the "stone-pillars" erected in front of ancient Greek homes as dwelling places for the protective spirit of Hermes and sometimes also as fertility symbols (Lurker 1987, 150–51). The Greeks also referred to Hermes as *kriophoros*, meaning "ram-bearer," an epithet designating his role and manifestation as "the Good Shepherd." The prevalence of this epithet led many early Christians to equate Hermes with Jesus Christ as "the Good Shepherd." Thus, a bewildering association of paradoxical beliefs about Hermes came to be espoused among such Christian apologists as Justin Martyr and among such Christian theologians as Augustine.

Among the ancient Romans, the figure of Thoth-Hermes was equated with the Roman deity Mercurius, the god of tradesmen and merchants, as well as the patron lord of thieves. But in his loftier role as divine mediator and messenger of the gods, Mercury would be equated among Christians with the inspiring and comforting presence of the Holy Spirit. This was due in part to one of Hermes' Latin epithets, *medius currens*, which literally signified "running in the middle" or "mediator" between the human and divine realms. In the medieval Christian calendar, as in Roman times, Wednesday (*dies Mercurri*) was the day of the week set aside for honoring Mercury. Hence Hermes, as the Roman god Mercurius, continued to exert a profound influence upon the Western imagination as an intermediary figure capable of bridging the gap between human existence and the Word of God and between matter and spirit.

The syncretistic blending of traits shared by Hermes and Christ, however, went even further. While the apologists and Church Fathers were busy appropriating and demonizing pagan religions, Hermes' association with sacred stones and biblical references to Jesus as the "cornerstone, chosen and precious," yet rejected by the builders of the temple (1 Pet 2:4-10), attracted much attention among early Christians. The *Corpus Hermeticum*, or "Books of Hermes," for example, describes the Hermes-Thoth procession as that of a supernatural being incarnated three times in the history of the world. Thus, Thoth begat the first Hermes known as *Agathodaimon* or the "Good Spirit" (*agathon* = "good"); who then begat the famous Hermes Trismegistus, who was the father of the third Hermes known as Tat, the son (Faivre 1995, 17). Thus, Hermes' appellation among Hellenistic-Roman sages as "Trismegistus" derived from the epithet "Thrice-Greatest" and would later influence various esoteric Christian currents, such as Renaissance magic and alchemy. Hence, the idea among the Church Fathers was that Hermes was both a pagan herald of the one, true God and the founder of trinitarian theology among the pagan religions and philosophers.

Another significant conception about Hermes-Thoth circulating among ancient and medieval Christians was the legend echoed in Saint Augustine's *The City of God* that this deity had been the Egyptian sage who, by the grace of God, taught Moses how to command the forces of nature. This is a legend that was still alive and well in the High Middle Ages judging by the fact that the Cathedral of Siena features a large fresco below the main entrance featuring Moses receiving the "Books of Hermes" (*Corpus Hermeticum*) from Hermes Trismegistus. In J. K. Rowling's best-selling Harry Potter book series, the character of Professor Albus Dumbledore most closely resembles medieval and early modern depictions of Hermes-Trismegistus. Furthermore, Dumbledore's prized bird, the phoenix, functioned for centuries in European literary and artistic contexts as a Christ-symbol because its fiery death and rebirth signified both the process of transformation and the miracle of Christ rising from the dead and ascending to heaven.

Although many of the early Church Fathers dismissed the Egyptian deity Thoth as nothing more than a pagan demon, the rich legends and pastoral epithets about the Greek deity Hermes and the Roman deity Mercury helped preserve their status among the emerging Christian cosmology and beliefs of early Christians. Hence, their stories and significance were preserved as beneficent pagan myths that signified anonymous aspects of Christ revealed in their fullness only after the incarnation of the Word and the ascension of Christ to heaven. The leading theologian and most prolific writer among the Church Fathers of the later empire, Augustine of Hippo, summarized the perplexity he and his fellow Christians felt over the so-called gold and silver of pagan wisdom in these words: "We should not think that we ought not to learn literature because Mercury is said to be its inventor, nor that because the pagans dedicated temples to Justice and Virtue and adored in stones what should be performed in the heart, we should therefore avoid justice and virtue. Rather, every good and true Christian should understand that wherever he may find truth, it is his Lord's" (1958, 54). Thus, the universal truth claims of the one God of Judaism and Christianity came to drive out the many gods and goddesses of the ancient pantheons reflected in the starry heavens and among the elemental forces of nature.

## Satan Matures in Early Christian Discourse

Jesus preached about and prayed to a loving and merciful God he referred to as *abba*; relational theology is founded on the premise that there exists a primordial link between God and humanity as exemplified in Gen 1:26-27, where it is written that Adam was created in the image and likeness of the Creator. Adam's fall from grace for disobeying God and falling prey to

Satan's sinister trickery and temptation alienated the descendants of Adam and Eve from the privilege of this relationship and its originating concept known as the *imago Dei*. Many among the ranks of the Church Fathers believed fervently that in Jesus of Nazareth God as Logos had become incarnate so that human beings might ascend to heaven and reclaim their angelic or divine natures.

Athanasius of Alexandria (c. 298–373 CE) was one among the many early Christian leaders who shared this belief in the meaning and promise of the Incarnation, the cosmological reality of which also had profound implications for the entire tone and trajectory of human history since God's act of love and self-sacrifice by giving his only child was understood by Christians as both a cosmic and historical event. If this view were true, then the Incarnation offered the potential liberation of humanity not only from sin but perhaps also from the principalities and powers unleashed in the practice of magic and sorcery, from the devils of wood and stream, and from the demons of the skies and the seas, as well as from the elemental spirits of the zodiac and those who dwelt on Mount Olympus.

Faced with the prospect of explaining the reality and power of evil to a civilization whose philosophers, religious visionaries, and political leaders believed that evil was no more than human ignorance of the "Highest Good" (*Summum Bonum*), the Apostles and the Church Fathers who succeeded them redefined the entire cosmological history of civilization as one big schematic vision of Judeo-Christian time known to most scholars as *salvation history*. However, the Fathers of the early Christian movement were also divided about how best to explain their beliefs to the Gentile elites of the Hellenistic-Roman world. Among today's scholars of New Testament studies and the history of Christianity, the Church Fathers' reinterpretation of past, present, and future was rooted in the Hebraic tradition of God's covenantal relationship with humanity since the creation of the cosmos.

This first period of salvation history culminated in the episodes discussed in the previous chapter about Adam's fall from grace when tempted by Satan to eat of the tree of knowledge and the subsequent expulsion of Adam and Eve from the Garden of Eden. A second period of salvation history was believed to have lasted from after the flood to the eras of Moses and the later Hebrew prophets. The Incarnation of Jesus Christ inaugurated the next period of salvation history, and the prophesied return of Christ will open the doors to the millennium-long reign of Christ's kingdom of peace and justice on earth.

The key point in this trajectory of salvation across time and place is that the universal truth of the Logos radiated in a line of apostolic succession after the resurrection and ascension of Christ. Following the lead of Justin Martyr, the Church Fathers became intensely suspicious and critical of any truth claims that lay outside these Judeo-Christian trajectories of salvation history. Indeed, truths outside of this epistemological pyramid were equated with Satan and the desire of his legions of demons and devils to possess, deceive, tempt, and lead astray as many human souls as possible. This relentless level of discourse among the Church Fathers had the effect of providing Christianity with power over the pagan past and power over whatever truth claims were to be found among Hellenistic-Roman religions, philosophical systems, and civic culture. It was a discourse aimed at equating the opponents and rivals of the Christian movement with a totally vile and despicable otherness personified in the realm of absolute Evil by figures such as Satan and a host of devils and demons. The imperial courts and provincial governors responded with their own hateful discourse by branding Christians as antisocial and ignorant believers in an unseen deity, as well as issuing the much more serious charge of being enemies and traitors of the Roman state. Hence the Church Father's rhetoric of portraying much of the empire's culture and truth claims as issuing forth from Satan cannot be separated from the persecutions and eventual martyrdom that befell many of them in the second and third century.

For example, the story of Polycarp's ministry as one of the earliest Church Fathers and of his remarkable yet tragic martyrdom inspired many Christians to resist the oppression of Rome and its cult of emperor worship. Polycarp (c. 70–c. 155 CE) studied with the apostle John and distinguished himself by exhorting the Christians at Philippi to endure in their faith, refuting heresies and guarding the early church against corruption. He ardently wrote to the Philippians: "For everyone who does not confess that Jesus Christ has come in the flesh is an anti-Christ; and whosoever does not confess the testimony of the Cross is of the devil; and whosoever perverts the oracles of the Lord for his own lusts, and says that there is neither resurrection nor judgment—this man is the first-born of Satan" (1977, 293). While serving as Bishop of Smyrna, Polycarp was arrested on charges of being a Christian and at his trial was asked by the Roman magistrate to proclaim "Caesar is Lord" and offer incense before a statue of the emperor to honor the *genius* in his veins and soul. Polycarp refused and according to the traditions of the apostolic Church Fathers told the judge: "Eighty-six years I have served Christ, and

He never did me any wrong. How can I blaspheme my King who saved me?" He was then burned at the stake alive. The legend of his martyrdom recounts how by the grace of God the flames did not consume his skin right away so that Roman soldiers had to stab him with a sword only to witness how blood gushing from the wounds helped extinguish the flames. Polycarp was executed for refusing to honor the Roman cult of emperor worship, which was inextricably tied to second-century notions of citizenship, civic loyalty, and respect for imperial authority.

Not only are there forces hostile to Christianity, like the demon-inspired Roman Empire, but there are also, according to Irenaeus, those whose theology is demon-inspired within the church. Such "heretics" may claim to be Christians, but in reality they use Jesus' name to teach demonically inspired doctrines and are following the lusts of their flesh.[4] Tertullian will go on to claim that those who interpret scripture differently are inspired by the Devil, "to whom belong the wiles that distort the truth."[5] The "Other" is not just the world outside the church but those within the church that disagree with the Church Fathers. Another of the Church Fathers, Hippolytus, who served as a rival Bishop of Rome (c. 200 CE), wrote his *Refutation of All Heresies* aimed at uncovering the lies and falsehoods of astrologers, Gnostic sects, sorcerers, and magicians while steadfastly upholding the doctrine of Christ as the Logos against the dreaded influence of Satan and the demons. Heresiarchs, also known as "heretic hunters," became a common development among the early Christian leadership of the third century. These men, most of whom also served as high-ranking Bishops of major cities, also wrote heresiologies, in which they compiled lists and descriptions of the various heresies of the times and set about explaining how such false teachings were an entrapment and a snare inspired by Satan and the demons.

However, perhaps the most effective and eloquent summary on the supremacy of Christian truth claims over the demonic origins of pagan spiritual wisdom was expressed in the early fifth century by Saint Augustine in his *De doctrina Christiana:*

> All the teachings of the pagans contain not only simulated and superstitious imaginings and grave burdens of unnecessary labor, which each one of us leaving the society of pagans under the leadership of Christ ought to abominate and avoid, but also liberal disciplines more suited to the uses of truth, and some most useful precepts concerning morals.

Even some truths concerning the worship of one God are discovered among them. These are, as it were, their gold and silver, which they did not institute themselves but dug up from certain mines of divine Providence, which is everywhere infused, and perversely and injuriously abused in the worship of demons. When the Christian separates himself in spirit from their miserable society, he should take this treasure with him for the just use of teaching the gospel. And their clothing, which is made up of those human institutions which are accommodated to human society and necessary to the conduct of life, should be seized and held to be converted to Christian uses. (1958, 75)

## Saint Augustine and the Problem of Evil

The period of the late Roman Empire, also known among professional historians as Late Antiquity, was an age of uncertainty and anxiety about the future of the empire. The military might of Rome had steadily declined and the division of the empire into an eastern half, with its capital at Constantinople, and a western half, with its capital at Rome, had weakened the overall political unity and economic prosperity of the once vast and glorious "Pax Romana." Instead, the Western Roman Empire was now economically inferior to the wealthy provinces and territories of the Eastern Roman Empire that included Egypt, Palestine, Greece, and Asia Minor. The West was also under constant threat of invasion or attack from the so-called barbarian tribes, who did not hate the Roman Empire but who were in awe of its wealth and sophistication.

Most of these tribes, which included the Alemanni and the Visigoths, wanted only to be allowed to settle down and farm on Roman land, or work in the towns and cities for a decent wage and better standard of living. Others, like the Huns, were highly skilled warriors capable of attacking and fighting with great speed on horseback in strategically effective ways the Roman military had trouble defeating. Nevertheless, the Romans repeatedly pushed them all back and kept them from enjoying the benefits of Roman citizenship. Sometimes these encounters were quite violent. Rome spent about two hundred years building walls along many of the empire's border regions. In this anxious context of apocalyptic fear and expectation, Augustine formulated his doctrine of Disordered Love as an explanation for the evil and sinfulness of a world perched on the threshold of its own tragic destruction and collapse. Indeed, the Western Roman Empire fell in 476 CE, a mere forty-six years after the death of Bishop Augustine of Hippo, whose career as a Christian writer and leader placed his life and theological treatises in a prominent position.

In his youth, Augustine had been a highly curious intellectual and student of rhetoric who was deeply troubled by his carnal passions and desire to ponder the philosophical problems of certainty and evil. As he struggled with his deep moral and spiritual questions, Augustine experimented with various sects and movements, including the Skeptics and the Manicheans. He eventually converted to his mother Monica's Christian faith and soon became a celebrity among the rising tide of Christian clergy around the same time that Emperor Theodosius the Great declared Christianity as the empire's official state religion in 395 CE. In addition to concerns over the origins of evil, the Christian church of the late fourth century was also deeply troubled over the problem of doctrinal heresy and what to do with bishops deemed heretical by the Theodosian dynasty. It was an era of extreme anxiety and fear all over the empire, which was only made worse by Christian leaders' denial of religious diversity and harsh treatment of religious dissent, as evidenced by the numerous pages set aside to deal with heretics in the Theodosian Code of laws compiled and released in 380.

Apocalyptic expectations about the future, which most readers associate with Christian beliefs about the end-times, witnessed a dramatic resurgence of interest during Augustine's lifetime as a Roman citizen and minister of Christ. The infamous Battle of Adrianople was fought against the Goths in August 378 CE and many came to regard this colossal military failure as a sign of the decline of the Roman Empire. Then in August of 410, the Visigoths sacked Rome over a three-day period and dealt a serious blow to the security and imperial prestige of the city. It was about this time that, according to French researchers Jean Hubaux and Jérôme Carcopino, an old Roman myth attributed to the city's founder, Romulus, resurfaced in response to public and civic fears of Rome's impending demise.

The myth was about twelve eagles that Romulus had seen at the time of Rome's founding. Over the centuries, interpretations of this myth had changed to the point of equating each eagle with a century in the history of Rome. As often happens in the space between apocalyptic interpretation and apocalyptic expectation, nearly twelve centuries had passed from the founding of Rome around 753 BCE by Romulus to the sacking of Rome by the Visigoths in 410 CE.[6] Still others maintained that the disasters befalling Rome and her empire were already written and announced by ominous portents, signs, comets, and wonders in the astral realm of the heavens.

Pagans eventually blamed the calamities that were occurring on the Christians for encouraging society to abandon the worship of the old gods and goddesses in favor of the new faith of the imperial family. On the other hand, Christians blamed the downturn in the Roman economy and the threat of more barbarian invasions on the wrath of divine retribution from the one, true God of the Hebraic tradition for the previous three centuries of state-sanctioned martyrdom and persecution against innocent Christians. Augustine countered all of these apocalyptic fears and expectations with his conviction expressed in *The City of God* that the omnipotence of Christ, the Father, and the Holy Spirit transcends the influence of those principalities and powers of the astral realm that the once mighty empire and its people worshipped in their pagan ignorance.

Eventually, factions in each camp of pagans and Christians (that is, the Manicheans) reasoned that perhaps God was the source of evil in the world. This nihilistic notion of God's nature was popular among Christians in the late Roman Empire who were scared of the possible fall and destruction of their civilization. The Church Fathers had never fully discredited the dualistic arguments of Gnosticism that a truly loving God would never condemn his creatures to living in a transitory body at the mercy of illness, disease, and physical suffering amid the looming specter of death. Perhaps the physical world was the creation of a sinister god, known as the Demiurge, who was not the highest god or the highest divinity in the cosmos. These and other dualistic notions about the nature of God threatened the foundations of Christian monotheism and exacerbated the question of evil in ways that disrupted notions of God's love, mercy, and grace for all of creation. If, as the Christian community was pondering in those days, God had indeed created the universe and the world out of nothing (*creatio ex nihilo*), and God is the omnipotent source of all love and grace, then where did evil come from? Some Christians were beginning to speculate in a quasi-gnostic way that God was the source of evil. After all, did not God create the angels and was not Satan also one of God's fallen archangels?

Augustine reasoned that an all-loving, all-powerful God who sent his only begotten Son to die for the salvation of the human race could not be the source of absolute Evil in the universe. He was intrigued by how our attractions and attachments often lead to poor moral choices, sinfulness, and, as he believed, sometimes even to obsession or madness. His training in neo-Platonism also taught him that Eros was the mysterious and cohesive force that held all things in harmony throughout the universe, while his Christian convictions and knowledge of the Holy Scriptures taught him that the redemptive power of Christ's miraculous birth and resurrection centered on the mystery of God's love and grace for humanity. Augustine's own syncretistic identity and moral convictions testify to the undeniable relationship between the human person and God, which human beings could "turn away from" or "fall away from" by exercising free will, just as Satan had chosen to disobey God's will and commandments. For Augustine, this turning away or falling away from the source of all love and life in the cosmos was the beginning of diabolical (*diabolos*) patterns of thought and behavior.

Augustine explains that each person has the capacity to enjoy four main loves in his or her life that needed to be experienced and honored in order of priority according to Christ's two Great Commandments (Matt 22:35-40). The highest and most important of these is the love of God, for as Jesus said about the greatest commandment in the Law when addressing the Pharisees and Sadducees, "You will love the Lord your God with all your heart, all your soul, and all your mind" (Matt 22:36). Next, Augustine addresses the love of others and the love of self, followed by the fourth and final attachment as the love of objects. As he reasoned, excessive love of self leads to selfishness or self-centered attachments. Excessive love of others can lead to possessiveness, misguided or carnal passions, and, in extreme cases, to crimes of passion based on obsessive attraction or attachment to other persons.

Finally, excessive love of objects leads to materialism, greed, raw ambition, gluttony, and so forth. When a person's attachments and attractions are unbalanced by not being ordered according to Christ's great commandment, our souls become disordered. Augustine's main point comes down to a simple theological principle and is perhaps valid across time and place as an existential and psychological perspective on misguided human pursuits, obsessive attachments, and overly passionate attractions: disordered souls commit sins and crimes as a result of disordered love and the exercise of one's free will. Hence, evil is not lodged in the heart and mind of God as creator but in the moral disobedience and sinful attachments of human beings misusing their free will against the will and commandments of God. In effect, evil becomes a privation of goodness (*privatio boni*), a turning away from God's goodness—from God's love and grace.

Over the centuries, some Christian theologians have criticized Augustine's moral philosophy for denying or diminishing the power of absolute Evil in the universe. For Augustine, Satan was not just a fallen angel but one of the foremost examples of sin and anger leading to a falling away from the divine. It is important to point out that Augustine believed in the reality of evil and Satan, but his emphasis on free will and divine grace undercuts the power of Satan and his devils in an almost Platonic way. However, is it possible that his notion of evil as disordered love was an example of the early Christian recognition of how the "trickster" feature of Satan, and his league of demons, actually helps the Lord lead men and women to their higher natures by tempting and provoking them, just like Christ's encounter with Satan in the desert had a formative and decisive role in fulfilling his redemptive mission? Even though Satan may will evil, God is able to use Satan to accomplish his divine plan.

Preaching in Carthage, Augustine seems aware of the give and take that was going on all around him between the pre-Christian pagan past of his civilization and the alleged triumphant Christianity of his times:

> There are those who say: "God is good, He is great, supreme, eternal and inviolable." It is He who will give us eternal life and that incorruption He promised as the resurrection. But these things of the physical world and of our present time belong to the *daemones* and to the invisible Powers. They leave aside God, as if these things did not belong to Him; and by sacrifices, by all kinds of healing devices, and by the expert counsel of their fellows . . . they seek out ways to cope with what concerns this present life.[7]

In a universe structured by disordered love and sin, Augustine argued that for those who have God's grace, these worldly structures and practices are benign because one can still be led to conversion and redemption while the believer focuses on the things of God and heaven, perhaps with Satan being used by God as a means for correcting the shortcomings of humans.[8] Augustine's Christian forbears and contemporaries had seen the Emperor Constantine end the persecution of the church by signing the Edict of Milan in 313 CE, calling the Council of Nicaea in 325 CE, and then witnessed the Roman Empire, under the rule of Constantine's descendants and successors, swaying back and forth between heresy and orthodoxy for nearly fifty years until the rise of the Theodosian dynasty and its new law codes in 379 CE. We will return to the theme of absolute Evil versus absolute Good, and to Satan's role as a "trickster" figure capable of leading humans to a higher moral potential, in the last chapter.

## Conclusion

Early Christianity emerged as a synthesis of first-century Greco-Roman and Jewish beliefs about the fundamental worth and dignity of the individual in relation to the perceived power and supremacy of the highest divinity signified by the Logos, or the Word of God, and in response to ancient society's need for justice and healing and care for the poor. The transformation of Satan's role into that of God's adversarial archangel and the reinterpretation of the problem of evil, which occurred from the first through the fifth century of the Christian era, cannot be separated from the early Christian drive toward converting its rivals and establishing mastery over the pagan past. However, this approach to dealing with religious diversity and cultural differences rendered the gods and goddesses of all non-Christian peoples as the offspring of Satan, as the principalities and powers of the Prince of Darkness, and as malevolent and evil demons seeking intercourse with humans while turning them away from the Holy Trinity of the Father, the Son, and the Holy Spirit. Historian Robert Muchembled reminds us that by the time of the Council of Toledo in 447 CE, Satan is physically described as being "a tall, black creature, horned and clawed, with asses' ears, glittering eyes and gnashing teeth, endowed with a large penis and giving off a sulphurous smell" (2003, 17). The incarnation of Satan as Christ's enemy on earth, that is, giving flesh to the spiritual, made Satan a more frightful creature in the religious imaginations of the faithful than ever before; a terror to common folk and the educated alike during the coming thousand-year Medieval period.

The quest for the historical Satan leads us to reconsider how the early Christian discourse against pagan demonology versus the power of Christ's Holy Spirit to vanquish these unholy ghosts and devils exacerbated the problem of evil while laying the foundation for Christianity's intolerance of other religious traditions and our civilization's predisposition toward the dichotomy of absolute Good versus absolute Evil. These moral and cultural features over time became intimate features of how Christianized Western societies and nation-states dealt with its various "others" and with those deemed heretics or deviants—characteristics that led to persistent episodes of violence and persecution as Christian heretic hunters and exorcists battled Satan and his army of demons during the Medieval and Reformation eras as manifestations of the prophesied and dreaded Anti-Christ. We will now examine those highly superstitious periods in the elusive life and times of Satan. ✳

# Chapter 4

# SATAN COMES OF AGE

I n 305 CE, the Emperor Diocletian abdicated and partitioned the Roman Empire among four contentious corulers. The Empire was divided among Licinius, Maximinus Daia, Constantine, and Maxentinus, the latter being an unpopular ruler among the people and considered a usurper by the other three coemperors. Sensing an opportunity shortly following the death of Diocletian, Constantine gathered his troops in Gaul, crossed the Alps with a fairly small army, and marched toward Maxentius's capital—Rome. Rome was a well-fortified city and could probably have outlasted any siege that Constantine might engineer; but Maxentius consulted the Sibylline books, where he discovered a prophecy stating that the enemy of Rome would perish that day. Interpreting the oracle to be a reference to Constantine, Maxentius rode off to meet the invader on the field of battle, gathering his forces at the Milvian Bridge in late October of 312 CE.

Meanwhile, Constantine was anxious about the upcoming encounter. Outmanned and outgunned, he prayed to whichever god would come to assist his demoralized legions. According to several Christian chroniclers who knew Constantine, it appears that the God of the persecuted Christians responded. Constantine's mother, Helena, had also been a devout and loyal Christian for many years. The historian Eusebius states that Constantine saw a vision of the cross in the sky above the sun accompanied with the words *in hoc signo vinces*, "by this sign, conquer."[1] Another historian, Lactantius, says that it was during a dream the night before the battle that Constantine was commanded to place a Christian symbol on his soldier's shields.[2]

However we wish to imagine how God appeared to Constantine, one thing is certain—Constantine ordered his troops to paint upon their shields the superimposed Greek letters "chi" and "rho," a recognizable Christian symbol. What began as a battle for power—who would eventually rule the empire—became the very first Christian religious war between the forces of the true God and the false idols of the enemy. For the first time, the symbols of the Prince of Peace became the means by which conquest and warfare was justified, and human blood was spilled on the battlefield as an offering to the crucified God. Christ the pacifist became Christ the warrior, accompanying the Roman soldiers who were fighting against the forces of darkness.

The battle went well for Constantine. Maxentius fell off the bridge (or jumped attempting to retreat) and drowned in the Tiber River, pulled down by the heavy armor he wore. His bloated body would be found the following day. Constantine won the western half of the Roman Empire and became sole ruler. The eastern half was partitioned between Licinius (his brother-in-law) and Maximinus Daia, the latter eventually losing his share to the former. Even though Constantine continued to worship the god of the soldiers, the Unconquered Sun, he expressed his gratitude to the Christians through the Edict of Milan in 313 CE, a decree that supposedly ended Christian persecution throughout the empire. With time, Constantine would move against the more powerful Licinius on the charge that he was persecuting Christians; which he was, seeing them as a fifth column aligned with the "Christian" Constantine within his own regime. As we know, Constantine the Great proved victorious, and with his victory both the Empire and Christianity—for good or bad—were radically changed forevermore.

Until now, it was the Christians, according to Roman rumors, who were the Other, believed to engage in incestuous orgies (how the "holy kiss" was misunderstood) and infant cannibalism with the drinking of a woman's menstrual blood (how Communion was misunderstood).[3] Such rumors justified the previous two centuries of persecutions as Roman civic and imperial morality moved to decimate the perceived evil of Christianity. But with Constantine's battle-field "conversion" at the Milvian Bridge, Christianity ceased being the misunderstood faith of the persecuted and marginalized, becoming instead the faith of the powerful, including the emperor and all those who wanted to be close to power. Those seeking the emperor's favor started attending the emperor's church and preferring his new-found faith tradition as the superior religious cult of the time. The triumph of Christianity provided the age of Constantine with the power to create the discourse, misrepresenting—as they were once misrepresented—the beliefs of the non-Christians in order to make them appear evil. Those once accused of meeting secretly to engage in cannibalistic infanticide and incest would come to accuse their own Others of meeting secretly to engage in cannibalistic infanticide and incest. Of course, such views of pagans did not start when Christianity obtained political power at the beginning of the fourth century CE; for much earlier, Christian thinkers such as Tertullian dreamed of such a day when he wrote, "Who would lose by a Christian world except pimps and procuresses and all who make profit from vice? Paid assassins, poisoners, magicians, soothsayer, fortune-tellers, and astrologers."[4] With time, those with power viewed themselves as representatives of God's grace and mercies on earth, and those who were Other to them, as Satan made flesh.

In the previous chapter we explored the historical development of Satan alongside Christianity's contentious relationships with other religious and spiritual traditions. In this chapter, we will focus on the incarnation of Satan in the clash of civilizations and cultures from the fall of the ancient world to the colonial period, for out of those lost centuries, Satan took on flesh and began to dwell among us. This chapter will explore who you say—or better still, who *we* say—the devil is. More precisely, it looks at who we say is in league with the devil. Once Christians determined among which group or individuals Satan is enfleshed, then moral justification was often provided to conquer and vanquish the enemies of God—usually at a tidy profit for the crusading or colonizing Christians.

Specifically, this chapter examines the cultural representations of Satan alongside Christianity's persistent preoccupation with the problem of evil from the medieval period to the colonial era of the early modern period. It might be objected that combining cultural, theological, and literary examples from such a vast stretch of time spanning over a dozen centuries presents a historiographical problem. However, our quest for the historical Satan thus far has led us to the realization that much of what Christians believe about the Prince of Darkness was forged in the Middle Ages and then amplified over the centuries as medieval civilization waned and Western European Christianity became involved in the colonial enterprise.

For example, the church's long struggle with the medieval and early modern State influenced the idea that national identity went together with a loyal and orthodox Christian identity. The formation of modern Western

European nation-states from the violence and scattered debris of the colonial empires of the early modern period witnessed the denigration and exclusion of indigenous peoples from all over the world by accusing them of worshipping devils and demons or of being heretics, since many of them refused to abandon their old religious ways and native cultural styles. Breaking down the long span of time from the Roman Empire to the late colonial era of the 1700s into smaller segments might offer a clearer picture of local examples. Still, the advantage of taking a much wider view of Satan's life and times is precisely in facilitating a sharper focus on those trans-local ideas, themes, symbols, and patterns of representation that make up the collective and historical conceptions of evil that are the main focus of this book's quest. Therefore, our aim in this much broader chapter is neither to be too exhaustive nor to offer up too vast an overview of these diverse times and places. We emphatically maintain that certain themes and patterns assumed as belonging to the medieval period seem to have been transferred into the consciousness and unexamined assumptions of more recent periods in the life and times of Satan and that the Western world's collective discourses on both "Otherness" and on the problem of evil are inextricably bound to these early Christian and medieval legacies of dealing with heretics and dissenters, demonology and witches, and other religions such as Islam and Judaism.

## Greco-Roman Cults and Magicians

Two persistent characteristics emerged from our discussion of the Church Fathers in the previous chapter: the tendency to equate all forms of heresy with the perversion of sacred doctrine and of religious truth by Satan and his legions of demons, and the tendency to deploy medical or psychiatric terminology to dismiss heretics as suffering from illness, madness, or lunacy. As these ways of excluding religious dissenters and of dismissing their philosophical and theological arguments gained momentum during the transit of the early Christian church toward the triumphant imperial dynasties of Constantine the Great (c. 305–337 CE) and Theodosius I (379–395 CE), a new form of persecution and state-sponsored violence replaced the earlier practice of dialogue and debate among the early Church Fathers and heretic hunters. This time around, it was not the pagans who were persecuting and ordering the arrest of enemies of the State; rather, it was now Christian leaders and laity who were behind the emergence of these new forms of religious persecution and incarceration.

Two centuries before Constantine conquered through the cross, we recall that Justin Martyr advanced the concept that Jesus Christ, through this same cross, destroyed the power of the serpent that instigated Adam's transgression in the Garden of Eden.[5] As we saw in the previous chapter, Justin argued that the gods of pagans were in reality the fallen angels who were cast out of heaven after they rebelled against God's authority, choosing to follow Lucifer.[6] It was these fallen angels who worked their magic through the Pharaoh's magicians (Exod 7:8-13)[7] or conjured up the dead for King Saul through the witch of Endor (1 Sam 28:3-14).[8] Any supernatural power or manifestation that does not come from God was automatically attributed to the demonic. The issue is not that false gods are impotent but rather that any power or influence they do possess comes from Satan. Nevertheless, it is through the cross that humans are liberated from the bondage of demons masked by human ignorance as the gods of other religions and faith traditions.

Prior to Constantine's victory at the Milvian Bridge, magic had been an integral part of the Greco-Roman world. This was the case not just among the so-called civilized empires of Greece and Rome but also among the lands of the "barbarian" peoples, specifically the Germanic, Celtic, and Slavonic tribes. These cultures used magic to control the weather, create prosperity, win battles, and cure illness; hence, this form of ceremonial and sympathetic magic was a necessity within society. But if magic could be used for good, could it not also be used for evil? How else can misfortune be understood? So, while good magic was sponsored by the state, participating in bad magic, the type that brings harm, was considered illegal (Baroja 1961, 18–19). Through such magic, for example, humans could be changed into animals, as illustrated by Circe who transformed Ulysses' fellow sailors into pigs—pigs that were still able to keep their human mental capacities.[9] Changing humans, usually men, into animals harkens to the fertility cult of the Roman goddess Diana (depicted in medieval Germany as Perchta or Holda), who could also turn would-be suitors into animals. Although the early Christian church rejected such metamorphoses, it nevertheless held that believing oneself to be an animal was a mental derangement caused by the Devil.

As mentioned, the deities of the former ancestral faith of the people, as per Justin Martyr, became the demons of the new Christian religion. The resemblance of the Devil to the Greek and Roman god Pan, who possessed cloven-feet, horns, and goatee, or to the fertility goddess Diana, complete with female breasts, has left scholars to support the thesis that Satan replaced the pagan deities that once presided over and participated in ancient magical rites. Thus, those labeled witches were in reality practicing ancient fertility religions (Levack 1987, 28). The indigenous traditions of the people who relied on magic were now dismissed by Christian authorities as really being the work of Satan. The Evil One became more than simply the tempter, someone who leads humans astray; Satan was the impetus or muse of those who the church said were not followers of Christ.

Not surprisingly, by the fourth century laws deriving from the newly empowered Christian church started to appear within the Roman legal code, specifically laws forbidding the practice of any kind of magic and laws that condemned any form of idolatrous worship. By 364 CE, under Emperors Valentinian and Valens, laws were enacted that made the honoring or invocation of devils a capital offence.[10] A civic battle erupted outlawing the public practice of any spirituality other than Christianity. Identified as necromancy, as "the arts of the Devil," or as Black Magic, in European societies the maintenance of the pre-Christian spiritual and magical traditions was now forbidden, punishable by death (although arbitrarily enforced). Although leaders and followers of religious cults and those who participated in magic were outlawed, their habitués in the form of witches and sorcerers continued in the imagination of the public centuries after the collapse of the Roman Empire as an alternative to, and/or form of resistance to, the rise of a dominant socio-political Christianity.

## The Collapse of an Empire

Throughout the long period of the Middle Ages, European Christendom was both haunted and perplexed by the fall of the Roman Empire. The word "haunted" is appropriate here because it was a tragic event the likes of which our contemporary civilization might possibly experience only through the devastation of a global nuclear war, or perhaps through the doomsday impact of a comet or large meteorite striking the planet and plunging us all into an apocalyptic ice age. But medieval intellectuals and leaders were also perplexed that Europe's most powerful and advanced civilization, the Hellenistic-Roman Empire, completely perished despite its military and financial power and the vastness of its territories and provinces. By 550 CE many of the empire's cities and towns were abandoned and its people scattered in different directions. Of course, the Eastern Roman Empire with its capital at Constantinople endured for another thousand years as the Byzantine Empire until its overthrow by the Ottoman Turks in 1453. Yet for the western half of the old Roman Empire, as the centuries passed the ruins of that once mighty and now lost world surrounded the peoples and cultures that later became Medieval Western Europe.

The hierarchical and sophisticated governance system of the Christian church served Europe well during the Dark Ages that followed the collapse of imperial rule in the west. Studies of the decline and fall of the Roman Empire abound and have captivated the European and Christian imagination for centuries. Edward Gibbons' seven-volume masterpiece of historical prose *The History of the Decline and Fall of the Roman Empire* (1776–1788) was a best seller from the time of its first publication in the eighteenth century to the late twentieth century. Gibbon was also highly critical of the role Christianity played in the demise of Antiquity and the rise of medieval societies, which he and his generation of early modern intellectuals tended to see as an inferior and narrow-minded civilization too preoccupied with church-sanctioned persecution and censorship. As discussed in the previous chapter, Saint Augustine of Hippo (354–430 CE) pondered the meaning of this decline even before the Roman Empire's fall in the late fifth century and concluded that the once mighty and glorious empire had been allowed to exist by God's will as a vehicle for the spread and triumph of the Christian religion throughout the Ancient world. Hence, as the breakdown of law and order accompanied the erosion of civic government and social services in Italy, Spain, France, the British Isles, and so forth across the continent, many turned to the medieval Christian church as the preserver of Christian learning, provider of social services, and diplomatic peacemaker among the feudal warlords and barons of the Germanic and Scandinavian peoples.

Among the ranks of Christian clergy, there were those who perceived the presence of Satan and his demonic legions in the events surrounding the fall of the Roman Empire and the subsequent collapse of a politically centralized and economically vibrant ancient Mediterranean world. This contributed from early on to the medieval fascination with prophecy and apocalyptic theorizing about the future of humanity and the world as the universe came to be perceived by some Christian thinkers and visionaries as a battlefield between Christ and a mighty host of blessed saints versus Satan and his sinister bands of demons and devils. From these notions of absolute Good versus absolute Evil and a longing to understand the mysterious meanings of the book of Revelation arose the medieval enthrallment with deciphering the identity of the Anti-Christ.

Such fear and foreboding should come as no surprise, since, after all, the empire had been converted and officially sanctioned as a Christian civilization since Emperor Theodosius I declared it to be so in 395 CE, ordering the closure of all the remaining pagan temples across the empire. How could such a powerful society have collapsed? Was it their decadent and corrupt lust for more worldly power that led to the fall of Rome, or was it some circumstance of God's judgment over humanity that brought weakness and calamity upon the Romans? Perhaps the glories of that lost world, and the understanding by later generations of the so-called triumph of Christianity over paganism, left indelible marks on how the Christianized offspring and descendants of that forgotten world would treat all those future generations of pagans looming on the horizons and frontiers of Europe as Western-Latin Christendom was forged out of the chaos, forgetfulness, and illiteracy that characterized the Dark Ages, that is, from the late sixth to the tenth century CE.

## Fear and Evil in the Early Medieval Imagination

The medieval conception of Satan and the problem of evil derived much of its influence from the intersections of biblical literature and the theological legacies of the Church Fathers with notions of both beneficent and malevolent spirits taken from the popular myths, legends, and stories of the diverse pagan peoples who migrated into Europe during the centuries following the collapse of the Western Roman Empire. Among these biblical precedents we find the Fall of Adam and Eve in the Garden of Eden, humanity's capacity for sin and disobedience of God's commandments, Lucifer's temptation of Christ in the desert, and Christ's various acts of casting out demons and performing miraculous healings throughout the New Testament.

We find that the devotion of the pre-Christian, pagan tribes to fertility rites and nature-worship was particularly vexing to early medieval evangelists and missionaries seeking to convert them to Christianity. Indeed, their collective and individual devotion to the Divine Feminine, associated with the cycles of the moon and with the return of spring each year, was personified in deities such as the Earth Mother, the Lady of the Lake, the Goddess of the Moon, or the Celtic triple-goddess associated with sacred wells known as Coventina. These beloved maternal images and the loyal following each inspired presented a significant challenge to those striving to convert the Celts, Welsh, Saxons, and innumerable other ethnic groups. Bodies of water such as lakes and ponds, rivers and streams, and peat bogs were revered by these pagans as doorways to the spirit world. Winter and summer solstices were also marked and commemorated as a means of honoring the masculine aspects of divinity and the natural world. Trees, especially the oak and the hawthorn, were regarded as sacred beings that could be cut down only under the most extreme circumstances. The cosmological- and nature-based paganism of these diverse tribes and their shamanic bards must be understood as a major point of contention with the Christian missionaries who sought to evangelize them in favor of a strictly masculine-centered monotheism and the moral message of the New Testament.

Hence, in order fully to understand the idea of Satan and the role of evil among the imaginations of the peasantry, or of the rising public servant and merchant middle class, as well as among the nobility and high-ranking clergy of medieval society, we must examine the origins of medieval religious and cultural history. It is important to point out that during the millennium known as the Middle Ages, much of what came to be known as Satan or as issuing forth from the demonic realm—we are thinking here of those aspects that were not specifically tied to biblical passages or antecedents—had its earliest beginnings in the conceptions of heresy and evil that ancient Christianity bequeathed to medieval Christianity. Secondly, we need to examine the ways in which early medieval Christian missionaries sought to evangelize and convert the resistant pagan tribes and ethnic groups who later became the various peoples and nations of Europe.

For example, during the migration and conversion phases of early medieval history, tribes such as the Celts and Danes, or the Franks and Normans, or the Goths, Angles, and Saxons were often on the move, be that for climatic reasons or as a result of competition for natural resources and food supplies. These phases lasted for several centuries, a timespan that coincides with what modern historians since the 1600s usually referred to as the "Dark Ages" (c. 476 CE/c. 525 CE to about 800 CE). During these years chieftains from each of these tribal ethnic groups, and others too numerous to cite, interacted with Christian missionaries dedicated to coaxing them and their subjects away from an earth-centered paganism toward the Judeo-Christian monotheism and religious beliefs of the Bible. This conversion and acculturation process led Christian clergy into a new phase of eradicating the gods and goddesses, spiritual beliefs and practices, and sacred places and cosmology of a different set of pagan peoples whose major differences from the Greeks and Romans, Egyptians and Phoenicians was that they lacked an urbanized citizenry and in a few instances also lacked the written languages and literatures of these former ancient rivals.

Whenever an event of major historical importance happens, it almost always leaves a trace in the ways that chroniclers, bards, and storytellers choose to mark or commemorate such events. One of the clearest examples of this tendency is found in the lore and majesty associated with the coronation of the king of the Franks, Charlemagne, as "Emperor of the Romans" (*Imperator Romanorum*) in the year 800 CE. For nearly two centuries his family had distinguished themselves as loyal Christians and defenders of the Bishop of Rome, as well as skilled warriors and military strategists with territorial possessions across a vast region that would later be known as modern France, Germany, Austria, and Northern Italy. According to tradition, Charlemagne was crowned in Rome on Christmas Day by Pope Leo III with the solemn title "Holy Roman Emperor." Ironically, this was a symbolic phrase and title that looked back to the lost and forgotten world of the Roman Empire, as well as forward to the dream of rebuilding a *Respublica Christiana* in the ninth century from the ruins of the past.

This new arrangement brokered by Pope Leo III rested upon Charlemagne and his descendants honoring the Roman Church and the Bishop of Rome as the trustworthy arbiters of civilization against the superstitious paganism of the Franks and the other clans and tribes that surrounded Latin Christianity at that time. The pope's diplomatic strategy was not new. The church had been following a policy of converting Germanic pagan leaders and their families for about two hundred years before Charlemagne in the hope that such conversions might produce a trickle-down effect of Christianization.

If these events happened as depicted later by German and French medieval triumphalism and modern romanticism, then the absurdity of the Pope's ploy is clearly a political tactic at a time when the real and surviving Roman imperial throne at Constantinople was vacant. In one of his military campaigns against the Saxons, Charlemagne had referred to his opponents as "devil-worshippers," and after the war he granted the surviving Saxon warriors and lords clemency as long as each accepted Christian baptism and pledged loyalty to the Frankish Crown at Aachen and to the Bishop of Rome. Charlemagne's ruthless approach of containing the spread of Saxon power in Western Europe during the late eighth and early ninth century through forced conversions has been described by Mark Ellingsen as a "military-evangelistic policy," one by which "All heathens would either be baptized or slaughtered." Ellingsen further observes how this policy of forced conversions had a long-term effect on the Saxons and across Germany during the ensuing five centuries: "In the late Middle Ages, Germans, and the Saxons in particular, were highly regarded throughout the Church for their piety. Consequently, filled with zeal (and ruthlessness), the Saxons began practicing this means of mass conversion among their neighbors" (Ellingsen 1999, 191).

On the other hand, the Byzantine Emperor was the symbolic and cultural descendant of Constantine the Great, who regarded southern Italy as one of the empires' most cherished provinces and the Pope as one of his most cherished subjects. However, Constantinople and the lands of the Byzantine Empire were so far away and struggling with numerous governance issues of their own that by the time of Charlemagne's death in January 814, it had taken little notice of the growing relationship between the Papacy and the fledgling Germanic empire based at the Frankish capital of Aachen. Although a generation after Charlemagne's passing his descendants declined into a long period of feudal warfare for control of his lands and resources, the Germanic heirs of Charlemagne became the rulers of the infamous Holy Roman Empire.

Throughout the Middle Ages, the Holy Roman Empire often tried to control the Pope and the city of Rome, resisting the dynastic claims of the French Monarchy and the territorial and ecclesiastical claims of the Byzantine Empire in southern Italy. This intermittent and violent struggle for control of a religious institution, the Papacy, led to the most disastrous and dysfunctional of all medieval conflicts that pitted the State against the church. Capturing or kidnapping the Pope while he traveled around Europe, and appointing a replacement pope (*anti-pope*), whose loyalty to a particular royal faction could be guaranteed, became a frequent occurrence throughout the High Middle Ages. If the Pope died while in captivity, then the better the outcome for the usurping faction's political and feudalistic ambitions. For some medieval religious and apocalyptic visionaries this manipulative sinfulness and sad degree of disrespect for the Holy See was sometimes perceived as an earthly conflict in which Satan's presence as the dreaded Anti-Christ fought steadfastly against the heavenly forces of God and Jesus Christ.

The conversion processes that led to the miraculous accomplishment of Charlemagne's Carolingian-Frankish collaboration with the Pope and the Church of Rome had been in the making for over a century before the coronation of Charlemagne. As early medieval church leaders and their secluded monasteries and majestic abbeys found themselves increasingly outnumbered by the diversity of these tribal warlords and chieftains whose domains were not always easily accessible from the main centers of church activity and influence in towns and cities, Christian leaders and missionaries decided on a policy of converting the tribal leaders and their immediate family in the hope that such conversions from the top would trickle-down to the warriors and laity among these pagan flocks. This approach, of course, failed to accelerate the conversion of the vast majority of men, women, and children who numbered in the tens of thousands among these ethnic clans across continental Europe, Ireland, and the British Isles and who identified far more with the gods and goddesses of their ancestors than with the Holy Trinity and good news of the Gospels.

For the rank and file of these various tribes and clans, avoiding conversion and the pressure to attend church each Sunday was as easy as moving to the highlands, or relocating deeper into the lush forests that existed in those times (that is, before the monastic labors and feudal practices of clearing ancestral lands to expand villages into towns and cities, which reached fever-pitch in later medieval deforestation cycles). While they did sometimes refuse to stop celebrating pagan feast days such as the onset of spring around the first of May each year, or the cosmic cycles of solar renewal around the annual summer and winter solstice, in other instances they created elaborate syncretistic blendings of pre-Christian pagan festivals with Christian feast days, such as the merging of Celtic May Day and June springtime celebrations with the annual Feast of Pentecost. Before resuming our journey through the medieval conception of Satan and the problem of evil, we will take a brief detour to examine how pre-Christian myths and pagan symbols were blended with political and military themes to create one of the most enduring chivalric adventure stories of the Christian imagination.

## Evil Characters in Medieval Arthurian Literature

Numerous examples of syncretistic responses to early medieval conversion practices survived in the popular literature of the times, especially among the Arthurian and Grail-quest romances, whose popularity and entertainment value has continued up to our own times. While an exhaustive treatment of the theme of evil in such an extensive and diverse literary tradition is beyond the scope of this present study, an overview of popular and literary understandings of certain characters from the pages of Arthurian literature will illustrate these points. Stories about King Arthur and the Knights of the Round Table, the sorcerer Merlin, and the quest for the Holy Grail began to appear all over Europe in the 1100s but were most likely based on a blending of pre-Christian legends with chivalric adventure chronicles dating to the period of the Dark Ages. Nearly every school-age child and adult familiar with Euro-American culture knows something about the Druid sorcerer Merlin and how he helped the young and reluctant future king of England, Arthur Pendragon, cope with the challenge of learning to govern, gaining spiritual insight from the forest and its animals, and become aware of where evil lurked in his kingdom.

Most of us can recall at least one instance of a movie, cartoon, or children's story book in which King Arthur pulled his magical sword, Excalibur, from the impregnable and immovable stone in the forest. But many of us do not realize that in most of the medieval stories and ballads about the once and future boy-king, Arthur pulls Excalibur from the stone on Pentecost Sunday, which was also code-language for the pre-Christian Druidic celebrations that took place in "the Merrie Month of May" (which was also the title of a much beloved fourteenth-century English ballad). This festival celebrated the revivification of nature in the spring and honored the Goddess in her sacred time of the year. The figure of Merlin, although a favorite among modern readers and devotees of Arthurian romance, has also been reviled intermittently over the centuries by orthodox and conservative Christians as an example of the pagan devil-worshippers who regarded trees, stones, rivers, and streams as nature spirits or benevolent beings instead of as demonic and evil harbingers of Satan's kingdom of sinful lies and spiritual falsehood.

In Thomas Malory's fifteenth-century version of the Arthurian saga, *Le Morte d'Arthur*, we find the mythical figure of the Lady of the Lake, most likely based on the ancient Celtic legends and ritual practices of figures like

Coventina or the Earth Mother. As the various stories of the boy-king attest, Arthur's mentor, Merlin, already had a relationship with the Lady of the Lake. In some versions of the story, Merlin and the Lady of the Lake, known as Nimue, share a love interest, while in other versions of the legend she is an enchantress who tries to detain Merlin from his destined work across Britain and in Camelot. In Malory's epic tale, the sword that King Arthur drew from the stone on Pentecost Sunday was later broken in battle. Merlin then goes to the Lady of the Lake on behalf of King Arthur, and for the sake of peace and harmony among all of the peoples of Britain, he prays that she might grant Arthur the privilege of wielding Excalibur once more for the greater good of all who dwell in his kingdom and across Britain. Hence the famous images portrayed in so many story-book illustrations, romantic paintings, and modern movies of a woman's arms and hands bearing Excalibur, eerily protruding from a body of water, while King Arthur wades through the shallows and reaches out nervously for the sword of power.

The British archaeologist Barry Cunliffe states that "since water came from the earth, it was appropriate for the deity of the source to be female reflecting one of the powers of the earth mother" (Cunliffe 1979, 89). The close association of Celtic conceptions of the goddess with lakes and ponds, rivers and streams is well attested in the works of archaeologist Miranda Green, who points out that "the Celtic mother-goddesses may also have influenced early Christian cults, such as those of the Virgin Mary and certain female saints" (Green 1996, 116). Ancient swords, along with many other ritual offerings, have been found in bodies of water throughout Europe, especially in sacred wells and springs dedicated to the Celtic water-goddess Coventina, who is often accompanied by three water nymphs linked with healing and maternal nurture and possibly signifying the three stages of human life: birth, adulthood, and death.

The most famous of the sacred wells associated with Coventina is located near the village of Carrawburgh along Hadrian's Wall in England. Since its discovery in the 1800s, the site has been extensively excavated and studied by several generations of archaeologists and historians (Allason-Jones 1996, 107–19). This Celtic triple-goddess image offers an interesting contrast with the masculine designation of the three persons of the Holy Trinity, but herein also lies the key to why these beliefs and the revered practices associated with them were suppressed as Christianity spread across medieval Europe. Nonetheless, the role of the Lady of the Lake in Malory's overall narrative is fascinating and echoes the persistence of pre-Christian myths and pagan legends in the popular literature of the Middle Ages.

King Arthur's half-sister, Morgana, who is also known throughout this literary corpus as Morgan le Fay, has been much maligned as well for her association with the cult of the Goddess and for interpretations of her character as a witch or sorceress. Generations of poets who rewrote the saga for their own times, and generations of pious Christian readers who simply despised her character, helped create a strong disdain for Morgan le Fay—perhaps an inevitable prejudice that seems to have been set forth already in many of the primary-source versions of the story as she undermines King Arthur and works to destroy Camelot. Her character is strong-willed, versatile, and form-changing. Her character also appears to be the target of gender-bias and demonizing because of her identity as a woman healer with mysterious spiritual powers and significant temporal influence at court as the king's sister. It seems that she too is associated with the spiritual and life-giving properties of "water," or perhaps even with a water-nymph or fairy, since in Welsh "Morgan" means "sea-dweller."

In certain modern adaptations of the Arthurian sagas, such as Marion Zimmer Bradley's *The Mists of Avalon* (1987), Morgana arrives in Camelot dressed in the black-garb and cloak of a priestess from the mystical Isle of Avalon, which was sacred to the Druids long before the arrival of Roman legions or Christian evangelists in the Celtic lands and the British Isles. Her style of dress leads some at Arthur's court to mistake her for a Christian nun, which opens many doors, hearts, and minds to her cunning and diplomatic savvy. In most versions of the narrative, she is soon thereafter wrongfully accused of alleged demonic and evil influences at Camelot as she plots Arthur's downfall by both natural and supernatural means.

In more recent nineteenth- and twentieth-century versions of the story, however, Morgana is infamously scorned for her incestuous and adulterous affair with King Arthur that results in the birth of his only heir, Mordred. Sir Mordred, who is both the king's son and nephew, was born on the pagan festival of May Day (May 1st) and becomes the archenemy of everything good that King Arthur and Camelot signify. His name can mean either "brave" or "evil." Given the frightful connotations of his son's name, and the final and decisive battle between father and son portrayed in Malory's version of the Arthurian legend, some readers and commentators over the years perceived parallels between Mordred and Satan. But Malory is not responsible for the incestuous and adulterous twist on Morgan le Fay and King Arthur because for Malory Mordred is the offspring of Arthur with his other half-sister, Morgause—which may explain the troubling conflation of the two characters, Morgan and Morgause, in post-Malory versions of the Arthurian story. It is, however, also possible to contrast King Arthur's significance as a Christ-symbol with Mordred's possible meaning as the prophesied Anti-Christ who sets in motion the wheels of chaos and turmoil to bring about the ruin of the Round Table fraternity and the downfall of Camelot and a unified Britain, which in turn functions also as a symbol for the victory of a Christianized European political order of kings and knights over a prehistoric matriarchal paganism and tribal factionalism.

Our society's simultaneous fascination and fear over the reputation of strong-willed women, or women who wield spiritual and temporal power, such as Morgan le Fay, is perhaps best summed up in Mark Twain's 1889 novel *A Connecticut Yankee in King Arthur's Court*:

> I knew Mrs. Le Fay by reputation, and was not expecting anything pleasant. She was held in awe by the whole realm, for she had made everybody believe she was a great sorceress. All her ways were wicked, all her instincts devilish. She was loaded to the eyelids with cold malice. All her history was black with crime; and among her crimes murder was common. I was most curious to see her; as curious as I could have been to see Satan. To my surprise she was beautiful; black thoughts had failed to make her expression repulsive, age had failed to wrinkle her satin skin or mar its bloomy freshness. (1979, 188)

No one knows for sure how ancient are the oral tales and poetic traditions from which the Arthurian and Holy Grail sagas emerged. The varied stories are certainly pre-Roman as well as pre-Christian, and most of the legends seem firmly rooted in the prehistoric lore of the Celts. Many contemporary scholars and archaeologists would argue that an actual historic person known as King Arthur lived and ruled in Dark Age Britain around the middle of the sixth century and perhaps may even have been a former Roman knight and cavalry commander who defended the region against migrating bands of Saxons, Angles, and Danes. Ironically, however, as Thomas Malory's epic narrative closes, readers catch a glimpse of King Arthur's body resting majestically on a boat with three queens aboard, one of whom is his sister Morgan le Fay. The ship is bound supposedly for the sacred Island of Avalon where the women will heal his mortal wounds and restore him to life under the auspices of the Divine Feminine. Thus, long before the migration and conversion phases of the early medieval period, a close association among water, healing, and women existed among the Celts and Britons that was later transmitted to the oral and literary sagas of the Arthurian tradition. The medieval Christian church never officially condemned this literature, nor did it pay the sort of attention that set this corpus apart with an "official seal" of church approval. Nonetheless, the negative associations and alleged wicked intentions assigned to Arthurian characters such as Merlin, Morgana, the Lady of the Lake, and Mordred attest to yet another formative episode in the life and times of Satan and ethical discourses on the problem of evil, during the early Middle Ages and beyond.

## Satan's Role in Destruction and the Coming of the Anti-Christ

As the centuries passed and European Christendom grew, other conceptions of potent evil forces led by Satan's alleged aims of undermining the church's mission to establish the kingdom of God on earth emerged and developed their characteristic medieval inflections. Among the claims of unrestrained evil forces in the cosmos and Satan's destructive role in natural disasters and social calamities, we find two examples of collective and individual fears that haunted the medieval religious and social imagination. The first is the profound fear and suffering associated with the persistent reality of plague outbreaks and the unseen effects of disease and infection that often decimated the population of medieval towns and cities. The second is the theological idea of the Anti-Christ and the coming apocalyptic transformation of the world in a final battle between Good and Evil.

Each of these medieval terrors was usually accompanied by either the demonization of Jews and Muslims as sinister agents of the Devil for not accepting the divinity of Jesus Christ or by accusations that Jews had somehow conspired to assist in the spread of the plague. Given the fear mongering, apocalyptic speculation about future disasters, and public hate speech against Muslims during the first decade of the twenty-first century, we must admit that a few aspects of this disturbing *medievalism* are alive and well in our modern times. Perhaps, as some evangelical Christians claim, Satan and the demons have been very busy stirring discord and anger around the world since the tragic events of September 11, 2001.

Outbreaks of plague and disease were common throughout the Middle Ages. The populations of town and cities were often decimated by the spread of these epidemics. But considering the pre-modern understanding of science, and given the poor state of general health knowledge and hygiene practices, such outbreaks were often seen as manifestations of evil under the auspices of Satan and the demonic legions of Hell. In a desperate and hateful search for answers, sometimes members of the Jewish community, and single or widowed women alleged to be evil witches, were accused of poisoning water wells, crops and livestock, or food supplies to set off these waves of illness and death. The most infamous and distressing medieval spate of plague arrived at the ports of northern Italy in November 1348 on ships from the east and went on to devastate the population of Europe over the next three years. Modern researchers believe the real culprit was not a malicious band of demons and devils but a powerful strain of bubonic plague that spread from Asia across the overland and sea-borne trade routes until it spread all over Europe.

By the time the epidemic began subsiding in 1351, it is estimated that 25 to 50 percent of the population of most villages, towns, and cities had been decimated. In some areas with higher than average population densities the mortality rate may have been as high as 75 percent of the adult population. It took Europe over a century to recover from the social, political, and economic effects of this horrible epidemic that forever altered the local and trans-local cultures of the continent. The Black Death, however, had an equally devastating effect on notions of religious belief and personal morality, as many asked themselves: "Where was God in the midst of the pestilence, suffering, and death?"

Some chose to enjoy themselves and indulge in all manner of desires and vices since it seemed at one point as if all men, women, and children were going to die regardless of gender, age, rank, or social class. Many assumed the Day of Judgment was upon them and that the plague was Satan's way of inflicting maximum suffering and disillusionment upon the people of God and Christ's earthly church. Fourteenth-century chroniclers reported that people were dropping dead everywhere within two to seven days of the onset of symptoms and that never before had so many welcomed death with such joy, the pain and cruel suffering of the disease being particularly nasty. Perhaps Giovanni Bocaccio's personal account of the plague's effects in Florence in *The Decameron* (1353) best conveys the tragic horrors of the Black Death:

One citizen avoided another, hardly any neighbour troubled about others, relatives never or hardly ever visited each other. Moreover, such terror was struck into the hearts of men and women by this calamity, that brother abandoned brother, and the uncle his nephew, and the sister her brother, and very often the wife her husband. What is even worse and nearly incredible is that fathers and mothers refused to see and tend their children, as if they had not been theirs. (1353, 3)

However, this was only the beginning of intense eruptions of plague and pestilence that would ravage Europe and much of the world until the introduction of modern medicine, public hygiene, and water and sewage treatment systems in the 1800s. The city of Naples, once the flower and pride of a revitalized medieval economy and ambitious building program, was ravaged by plague five more times after 1351, with an estimated death toll of about fifty thousand more citizens by the early 1400s. Hence, one of humanity's most primordial fears about the association of evil with the effects of natural disasters and epidemics was unleashed in the wake of the pandemic plague of 1348–1351.

Despite the eschatological and end-times implications of medieval and early modern Europe's persistent spate of deadly epidemics, the biblical idea of a cosmic struggle between Satan and Christ as suggested in the book of Revelation offers us yet another episode in the life and times of Satan's sojourn through the Middle Ages. For example, Christ's promise that he would someday return to vanquish Satan and establish the kingdom of God on earth took on increasingly apocalyptic dimensions as European Christendom approached the turn of the millennium around the year 1000. The spread of Islamic caliphates and kingdoms with powerful military forces and robust economic success across the Near East, the Iberian Peninsula, and the Mediterranean basin since the fall of the Roman Empire was interpreted as a sign of the approaching age of the Anti-Christ. The persistence of such themes over the centuries should not surprise us, since in our own recent historical memory the approach of the year 2000 triggered multiple waves of apocalyptic expectation (for example, fears over the Y2K computer bug), and gave rise to a fervent Millennialism that still influences the imaginations and beliefs of millions of people around the globe—concerns that remain quite strong at the time of the present volume's publication.

As the year 1000 passed and no major conflagrations occurred, rather than subsiding, instead Christian speculation about the struggle between

Christ and Anti-Christ increased. The Prince of Peace and the King of Kings was set to do battle against the Prince of Darkness, the battlefields being the human heart as well as the earthly realms of the church and State. Thus, in addition to notions of individual temptation by Satan, and of demons luring otherwise good men and women astray, fantastic interpretations of Satan using bishops and popes, kings and emperors to destroy the church and undermine the State emerged as key strategies in Satan's imminent sending forth of the Anti-Christ. Some would-be seers were content to study the Holy Scriptures for signs and clues as to the future of humanity; while others founded movements of the Holy Spirit predicated on the notion that a transformation had indeed occurred at the turn of the first millennium. But the dysfunctional terrestrial struggle between the church and the State, and Christendom's inability to convert the Jews and the Muslims, was impeding the full manifestation of God's new spiritual kingdom across the earth.

However, the magic of believing is a very powerful potion for the human imagination, and in time, all manner and types of political or social events were perceived as signs or portents of the coming apocalypse and final judgment of humanity. The book of Revelation took on an increased significance among medieval biblical scholars and theologians, as did the other books of the Bible with apocalyptic connotations or passages. Biblical prophecy became a major focus of theologians and visionaries such as the Calabrian Abbot Joachim of Fiore (c. 1135–1202), who was authorized to write about his prophecies and visions by three different popes. His predictions about the future expendability of the institutional and hierarchical Latin Church of Rome in favor of a more egalitarian and decentralized "Church of the Holy Spirit" were declared heretical after his death by Pope Innocent III.

It seemed as if the lust for world power and riches had corrupted the church and undermined the liberating message of the Gospels and Christ's call to serve the poor and the marginalized. The liberty and integrity of the *poverty of Christ* became one of the great monastic themes of the High Middle Ages as the followers of Saint Francis of Assisi sought to rebuild and reform the mission of the church. Claiming to be the true followers of St. Francis' rule of poverty and service to the poor, the Spiritual Franciscans (*Fraticelli*) attempted to break away in dissent from the Friars Minor until Pope John XXII (Pontiff: 1316–1334) authorized their arrest and violent suppression from his Papal Palace at Avignon in a misguided effort to silence their apocalyptic visions, stop their refusal to handle money, and quell their radical idealization of mendicant poverty against the regular priesthood.

The Spirituals, on the other hand, believed they were living out Christ's references in the Gospel of Matthew (22:34-40) about the two greatest commandments while preparing the way for Christ's second coming and a new outpouring of the Holy Spirit. This entire episode stands to this day as one of the saddest examples of clergy forgetting the meaning of Christ's Great Commandment resulting in the tragic loss of life and church-sponsored oppression. In keeping with an increasingly persistent theme in our quest for the historical Satan, well-meaning clergy on each side of this controversy believed the other was deluded by the Devil into being obstinately radical and demonically recalcitrant by refusing to compromise!

In the late Middle Ages, the Papacy was moved from Rome to Avignon by the French Monarchy as a direct result of France's concerns about the Holy Roman Empire's meddling in the affairs of the church. This was known as the Babylonian Captivity of the Papacy that lasted from 1309 to 1378 and culminated in the Great Schism of the Latin Church, an event that saw multiple French, German, and Italian bishops claiming the throne of Saint Peter from 1378 until about 1418. News of these events, and the prolonged duration of this crisis of the *antipopes,* led the disillusioned hearts and minds of many devout Christians across Europe to conclude that the designs of the dreaded Anti-Christ were revealed in the French Crown's plans to control the holy office of the Pope and that Christendom was in dire peril as Satan's chaotic hold on the Latin Church lasted for nearly a century.

During this period, the Hundred Years War between France and England wrecked the economies and agricultural fields of Western Europe, the struggle between the Friars Minor and the Franciscan Spirituals erupted and was suppressed by Pope John XXII, and the Black Death exploded across all of Europe, killing millions and disillusioning the faith of thousands among the survivors whose lust for the pleasures of the world ran wild under the ever-present specter of death by bubonic plague. This was the century immortalized by Barbara Tuchman in her best-selling novel, *A Distant Mirror: The Calamitous Fourteenth Century* (1978), for its numerous natural disasters, political and social calamities, and general loss of faith in the power of Good to vanquish the power of Evil.

By the time the Council of Constance resolved the papal dispute between Rome and Avignon in 1417 and elected Martin V as the new and legitimate Pope, much damage had been done to the prestige of the Western Church and to the Papacy as an institution capable of wielding spiritual and temporal authority across Europe. The conflict was seen by many writers and theologians as a sign of the apocalyptic times in which they lived and increased the power and prestige of such rising nation-states as France, Spain, and England, which became the major European powers over the next two hundred years. In the collective imaginations of the late medieval populace, and amid a rising tide of apocalyptic speculation from all quarters of Christendom, Satan was alive and well and thriving on a steady diet of ecclesiastical chaos and political violence as these and plenty of other tragic events unfolded. We now turn our attention to the fantastic section about Hell and Satan depicted in the medieval world's greatest literary masterpiece, *The Divine Comedy*, which is still widely read among modern high school and college students.

## Satan in Dante's *Inferno*

Dante Alighieri (1265–1321) was born into a noble and influential family in Florence, Italy. Today he is considered Italy's greatest poet and one of the medieval world's most outstanding humanist scholars and religious visionaries. Dante's family background and Guelph party allegiances were tied to the conflict between the Papacy and the Holy Roman Empire discussed above. In Italy this intermittent strife manifested itself for centuries and saw the pro-papal party, known as the Guelphs, putting itself against the pro-imperial party, known as the Ghibellines. In 1302, after two separate Guelph factions (the Whites and the Blacks) fought bitterly for control of Florence, Dante's faction ended up on the losing side, and he was subsequently exiled from his native city for the rest of his life.

He then traveled around Italy and France without ever settling down for too long (although he eventually married and had children). The exiled Florentine politician, scholar, and talented poet turned his labors to writing *The Divine Comedy*, which he tells us in the opening verses was about the time when he "reached the midway point in life" (that is, reaching "middle-age" at about thirty-five to forty years of age). He boldly chose to compose the epic poem in the Italian vernacular of the commoners instead of in the polished Latin of the schoolmen and nobility. Although Dante's allegorical poem is regarded as one the great artistic monuments of the medieval literary imagination, it also offers us a highly intriguing fourteenth-century window for examining images of Satan, the role of demons and devils, and the problem of evil in the medieval religious imagination.

It is a major incongruity that, given the contemporary denial of evil forces and Satan's existence, modern society pays scant attention to the other more edifying sections of Dante's *The Divine Comedy*, sections describing the poet's journey through Purgatory and Paradise. Remarkably, Dante's journey through the depths and sufferings of Hell are required reading in English classes and humanities programs across North America, especially among high school students and college undergraduates. For the general reading public, however, the popularity of Dante's *The Divine Comedy* subsided several decades ago. The poem is essentially a journey of transformation through the different realms of an earth-centered view of the universe and through the different levels of spiritual existence beyond the terrestrial plane as each of these views was understood in Dante's era. Thus, we proceed from a dark wood where Dante is met by the ancient Roman poet Vergil, who guides him through Hell and Purgatory, following which we proceed from one of the penultimate sections of Purgatory through the astral levels of Paradise. Here Dante is guided by the late Beatrice Portinari, since Vergil was a pagan and therefore forbidden from entering the heavenly kingdom of God and Christ.

Dante met Beatrice at age nine on an evening when his father took him to a May Day party at the Portinari household. She was eight years old and Dante fell in love with her instantly—a "beatific" love, as her name surely signified to the passionate and idealistic boy. Although Beatrice later married another man, Dante revered and loved her from afar for the rest of his life, and then even after her untimely death around the age of twenty-four. Her role in *The Divine Comedy* is largely allegorical as her name suggests and reminds us of the role of courtly love and Platonic philosophy in the medieval imagination. Despite all of the transcendent beauties and sublime moments that Dante experiences on his journey toward paradise, it is the first part of his masterpiece, the descent into the bowels of Hell, that concerns our quest for the historical Satan.

The legendary torments and punishments of Hell depicted by Dante in *The Inferno* offer a good example of medieval conceptions of sin and evil. It is worth noting that while Dante populates the different levels of hell with historical persons and biblical figures that were already infamous among his contemporary audience for various misdeeds, a fair amount of his imagery is not simply derived from his fanciful poetic imagination. For devout medieval Christians, eternal damnation for acts of sin and evil while alive on earth and the fear of being consigned to Hell by God's judgment were very real preoccupations. Take, for example, the series of diabolical relief sculptures, attributed to the French Romanesque artist Gislebertus (c. 1120–1135), that decorate the Last Judgment doorway of the Cathedral of Saint Lazare at Autun, France. Here we see a visual representation of the reality of demonology and the chastisements that await the wicked and the sinful on Judgment Day. We see one demon tipping the scales as an angel attempts to weigh the souls of the deceased; a pair of demonic claws lowers another human soul to the depths of hell while serpents gnaw and tear at the breasts of another figure already judged and descending into hell [see Figure 5]. Although sculpted nearly two centuries before Dante composed *The Inferno*, these visual images of suffering and punishment from Autun Cathedral bear a remarkable resemblance to the literary images of misery and anguish described by Dante.

The inferno that Dante presents us with is located beneath the city of Jerusalem in the form of a massive triangular-shaped pit with a series of circles, or leveled terraces, into which are cast those who were judged for certain sins and crimes. Before he and Vergil enter, they see a terrifying sign that reads: "Abandon hope, all ye who enter here." The geography of Hell that Dante offers us is as intriguing as it is complex and provides specific torments for specific sins. For example, those who spread violence that costs others their lives and the needless deaths of innocent victims are condemned to drown forevermore in a river of blood. Dante's primary sins are incontinence and malice. The first deals with uncontrolled passions or appetites that one cannot subdue by the usually benevolent force of reason, and the latter deals with acts of violence and fraud aimed at the amassing of power over others through deception, lies, and cheating.

Throughout the various circles of Hell laid out by his poetic structure, we note that there are realms set aside for the gluttonous, the lustful, fortunetellers and makers of discord, evil counselors, and so forth. The lowest region of Hell, however, is set aside for traitors, who are considered to have engaged in the worst form of fraudulent sins. Among these we find those who have betrayed kinfolk, their country, their guests or masters (that is, Judas Iscariot for betraying Jesus Christ as well as Brutus and Cassius for betraying Julius Caesar) [see Figure 6]. Their place in Hell is literally at the lowest level, which Dante identifies as Cocytus, the mysterious "river of wailing" from ancient Greek mythology. Dante wanted to show us the state of the unrepentant soul after death and why it was important to lead a life of virtue and balance in the here and now. Indeed, the ultimate anguish of the unrepentant sinner's soul is akin to being devoured by Satan, whose mouth is the lowest level of Hell, and then passing through the Prince of Darkness' bowels before being defecated into the refuse and stench of this demon-infested and depraved realm.

While much of Dante's imagery and cosmology is typically medieval, he also embellished quite a bit with his own moral ideas and political concerns. For example, given his status as a life-long Florentine political exile after about 1300, he spares no kindness in his portrayal of politicians and leaders from his native city. On the other hand, the struggle between the Papacy and the Holy Roman Empire, which in the imaginations of many late medieval writers and visionaries was analogous to the cosmic battle between Christ and the Anti-Christ, found ample expression in the pages of Dante's *The Divine Comedy*. In Alain Boureau's landmark study on the birth of medieval demonology, *Satan the Heretic* (2006), we learn that it was during the years from 1280 to 1330 that European Christendom became obsessed with demonology, the presence of witches, and the idea of certain persons signing a "blood-pact" with the Devil in order to gain unlimited spiritual power over others (2006, 8–40). Ironically, this period coincided with much of Dante's lifetime, and the presence of demons tormenting the damned and serving Satan's every command is well attested throughout the circles and regions of *The Inferno*.

## Medieval Witches

During the reign of Pope Nicolas (assuming it was Pope Nicolas V who reigned from 1447 to 1455) some unnamed bishop from Germany was visiting Rome on business. While there, "he fell in love with a girl, and sent her to his diocese" along with other acquired possessions, specifically some rich jewels. On her way to the bishop's diocese, this girl "with the usual greed of women" grew covetous of the jewels, so she placed a curse on the bishop. Were the bishop to die, she concluded, she could then take possession of the jewels. The next night, the bishop became gravely ill. On the third day, when all hope was gone, an old woman came to him and stated that she could heal him. She told the bishop: "Your illness has been caused by a spell of witchcraft, and you can only be healed by another spell, which will transfer the illness from you to the witch who caused it, so that she will die." After consulting with the Pope, the bishop agreed. The narrator explains what happened next:

> It is to be understood that at the very same hour and moment the illness left the Bishop and afflicted the girl witch, through the agency of the old witch; and so the evil spirit, by ceasing to plague the Bishop, appeared to restore him to health by chance, whereas it was not he but God Who permitted him to afflict him, and it was God Who properly speaking restored him; and the devil, by reason of his compact with the second witch, who envied the fortune of the girl, had to afflict the Bishop's mistress. And it must be thought that those two evil spells were not worked by one devil serving two persons, but by two devils serving two separate witches. For the devils do not work against themselves, but work as much as possible in agreement for the perdition of souls.

The bishop eventually visits the dying girl, offering forgiveness; in response, however, she turns away her face, saying, "I have no hope of pardon, but commend my soul to all the devils in hell." After uttering these words, she died miserably (Kramer and Sprenger 1486, 158–59).

This fifteenth-century tale provides a glimpse into a worldview wherein Satan totally occupied the imagination of European humanity. It is a world were bishops take on young girls as mistresses without concern for improprieties, where the misogyny is a given, where illnesses are assumed to be caused by the Devil, and where nobody flinches when the Pope agrees to allow a witch, who made a pact with the Devil, to heal his bishop. For modern readers, this is a strange world where the boundary separating evil spirits from humans is porous. It is also a world whose religious views and masculine extremism would eventually bring great misery and death to countless women created in the image of God.

By the late Middle Ages, demons were everywhere. It was believed that one-third of the angels of Heaven were cast out with Satan. That means, according to the thirteenth-century bishop-cardinal of Tusculum, Peter of Spain (who in 1273 became Pope John XXI), of the estimated 399,920,004 angels that existed, 133,306,668 became demons. Of course, not all medieval doctors of the church agreed on this number. The estimates ranged from a low of 7,405,926 to a high of 2,665,866,746,664 (Medway 2001, 56). Regardless of which number is ultimately used, let alone how one arrived at such numbers, in the mind of the general Christian population of that era, they lived in a world infested with demons. They were everywhere creating mischief, hoping to lead humans away from God [see Figure 7]. In the earlier medieval period, non-Christians were seen mainly as ignorant or misguided idolaters, led astray by the master deceiver and tempter, Satan. Yet with the church's consolidation of power in the High Middle Ages, these idolaters began to be seen as willful followers of Satan, if not demonically possessed. For those in power, specifically the official church, the institutionalization of Satan and the increasing social and religious discourse on the problem of evil created a means by which the populace could be controlled (Boureau 2006, 93–118).

As the Christian church expanded its power over Europe, fear of evil—then as now—proved to be a powerful tool used by those demigods wishing to exercise and maintain control. Not only was the church interested in control, but it also sought the eradication of any residue of indigenous pre-Christian European spirituality. In this battle for the fidelity of the populace, the church's opponents were not only portrayed as evil but as nonhuman—a shift in thinking that would have dire consequences upon humanity. The witch came to be linked with Satan, a move no doubt caused by the social conditions and attitudes that arose during the Middle Ages. But just as important are the historical origins of the witch. Although difficult and complex to delineate, witches can partly be understood as the reinterpretation of the pre-Christian cults (that is, the cult of Diana, which flourished in the fifth and sixth centuries, or the cult of the Earth Mother, which flourished among the Celtic peoples of the early Middle Ages). These pre-Christian priestesses usually prayed, made sacrifices, or participated in magical traditions that often included conjurations (Baroja 1961, 17, 21, 65).

Toward the end of the Middle Ages, specifically the thirteenth century and the rise of Scholasticism à la Thomas Aquinas, the Devil's powers became less ambiguous as they started to be identified with entire groups of people. During the Middle Ages women, specifically the traditional village wise woman, were considered the vessel of ancient knowledge, as manifested in herbal and nature-based healings. In many cases, she can be understood as the town healer or midwife. Yet if she could use magic to do good, could she not also use magic to do evil? Regardless, to engage in certain forms of magic, whether to do harm or good, was characterized as witchcraft. Ironically, there was a much older tradition known as "white magic" or Christian magical theology (*theologia magica Christiana*) that was reserved for male practitioners who generally were not condemned for their dangerous alchemical games and experiments. Thomas Aquinas and his teacher Albertus Magnus were among the renowned Scholastic theologians whose names were often associated with this type of beneficent or alchemical magic aimed at understanding the natural world and amplifying Christian knowledge. All other magical practices not approved of by the church were deemed as malevolent or "black magic" and regarded as under the auspices of Satan, the conjuring of demons being part of the so-called "Devil's pact."

It was during the late Middle Ages that thinkers and theologians began to ask through what power witches performed their magic. To answer this concern, a demonology was attached to witchcraft, a move that created a simple dichotomy: those who used magical power (for example, witches) did so through the power of Satan; furthermore, anyone who was not a Christian was a follower of Satan. Not to follow Christ according to the dictates of the church was to be in league with the Devil. This of course was not a new position, since the Church Fathers had developed a similar discourse centuries earlier to discredit rival religions and philosophical schools in the ancient world. The persecution and punishment of witches became the established European Christian church's means of eliminating these practitioners of ancient traditions, who usually were women, of suppressing any competing spirituality or cultural tradition. It was to female practitioners of magic, to witches, that the various misfortunes that befell an individual, a community, a ruler, or a state were attributed.

The witch became the accomplice, lover, and covert human presence of Satan. She ceased using magic to achieve some desire or mere personal goal; rather, she was now used by Satan to achieve his goals on a grand scale. Because Satan lacks generosity, medieval scholars concluded that a reciprocal relationship had to exist. Acquiring magical powers implied that a pact with the Devil had to have been made, with the witch's soul being traded for supernatural knowledge. For the audacity of interpreting reality or healing the sick through folk-medicine and natural magic apart from the church, the penalty was severe, even though many of those who perished during the witch hunts were innocent victims that probably were not engaged in any specific indigenous non-Christian European religious or magical tradition. Still, in the zeal to strengthen the hold of the official church on the political and religious milieu, those seen as opponents were sacrificed on the altar of Christ in accordance with the biblical mandate: "You shall not allow a witch to live" (Exod 22:18).

As the threat of witches to Christian society spread, specifically in parts of Northern Germany, Pope Innocent VIII released the bull exhorting magistrates to hunt down these witches. He decreed that "all heretical depravity should be driven far from the frontiers and bournes of the Faithful."[11] In response to the Pope's wishes, two Dominicans, Heinrich Kramer (Henricus Institoris) and Jakob Sprenger produced the *Malleus Maleficarum* (Hammer of She-witches) around the year 1486, the first major treatise providing guidance on how to hunt down witches. In the age of the printing press, their manuscript was widely circulated, quickly becoming the normative understanding of witches and their unholy alliance with the Devil. These witch hunts led to tens of thousands, mostly women, being executed, usually by being burned at the stake. The number of those persecuted is difficult to determine. Estimates range from the thousands to the millions. From the start of the sixteenth to the late seventeenth century it is estimated that one hundred thousand women perished, half of these in Germany. Records have been lost, and the numbers have been inflated by officials wishing to show their fidelity in eliminating demonic influences from their jurisdictions and by more recent scholars in order to magnify the gravity of the persecution (Levack 1987, 19–22).

According to an earlier anonymous treatise (*Errores Gazariorum*) from 1430, the Devil would usually appear to these witches in the form of a cat while they met in synagogues. During these Sabbaths, the witches would invert the moral and religious norms by doing homage to Satan. Although not much is written in the *Malleus Maleficarum* as to what occurred during these secret nocturnal Sabbaths, popular rumors at the time included orgies, naked dancing to atonal music, aerial transportation by riding tridents or pitchforks (a symbol associated with the Devil) as well as brooms, kissing a cat's anus, ritual intercourse with Satan, engaging in a parody of the Catholic Mass where the Nicene Creed is recited backward, and eating the corpse of exhumed deceased children [see Figure 8]. Also contributing to the understanding of the demonic were the moralistic paintings of the period, for example, the works of the Early Netherlandish painter Hieronymus Bosch

(1450–1516). The medieval surrealistic Hell panels of the triptychs he produced, among his most famous being *The Garden of Earthly Delights*, created
a reality based on nightmares where the moral symbols employed elicited
fear, a fear that focused on the Devil and on the nature of woman as temptress. Bosch's painting illustrates a disturbing perception of Hell where those
who succumbed in life to the Devil's temptation find themselves reaping the
rotted fruits of eternal damnation—a damnation defined by cruel and brutal
scenes of torture and torment [see Figures 9, 10, and 11].

It is interesting to note that during the late Middle Ages evil most commonly took the *female* human form—a phenomenon that should not be
surprising when we consider the prevailing assumption that women were
the temptress of holy men. Women, according to the *Malleus Maleficarum*,
"know no moderation in goodness or vice. . . . When they are governed by
a good spirit, they are most excellent in virtue; but when they are governed
by an evil spirit, they indulge the worst possible vices" (Kramer 1486, 42).
Women were believed to be more superstitious than men and more carnal
than men; they were perceived as intellectually childlike (1486, 43–44).[12]
Hence, they were quicker than men to waver in their faith, making them
more susceptible to the influences of the Evil One. Or as Tertullian, the
third-century apologist succinctly stated: "You [woman] are the one who
opens the door to the devil . . . you are the one who persuaded [Adam] whom
the devil was not strong enough to attack. All too easily you destroyed the
image of God, man. Because of your desert, that is, death, even the Son of
God had to die."[13] A simple dichotomy is created due to women's weaker
nature. They are either virtuous—the Madonna—or wicked—the whore,
quick to engage in orgies attended by Satan.

One wonders if the constant portrayal of witches as sexual deviants constantly copulating in all sorts of orgies, coupled with how they were normatively interrogated,[14] encompasses the attempt of those judges to exorcise
their own suppressed sexual desires now projected upon female bodies. If so,
this might explain the cruel torture the female body endured—an offering
lifted up by which the male bodies of judges found salvation from their own
sexual sins. A simplistic binary relationship is created where the male bodies of holy men are defined through the negation of the demonic bodies of
women as witches. They—witches—are controlled by their flesh; we—holy
men—are controlled by the Holy Spirit. They are evil; we are righteous. They
belong to Satan; we belong to God. Once the Other is defined in these terms,

whether they be women accused as witches or colonized people accused as heathens and pagans, it becomes easy to include one more pair of binary oppositions. They are nonhuman; we are human. Their nonhuman construct allows those who self-define as human to visit all forms of inhumane cruelty upon them in an effort to dehumanize them. Their slaughter becomes justified because we—righteous Christians belonging to God—are acting in God's name against God's enemies.

In the mind of church leaders, these women were evil, if not inhuman, because they were engaged in something more sinister than simply providing the sick with herbal medicine. The power of healing they demonstrated could be gained only by making a pact with the Devil, whose prerequisite was the renouncement of Christ and Christianity. How else could these uneducated women hope to match the erudition and sophistication of male doctors who had studied the healing arts at church-approved universities and colleges? These women dealt in petty potions and petty evils while pretending to heal the sick and counsel the afflicted. Such a pact is important because without the assistance of witches, devils could not "bring about evil . . . either substantial or accidental, and . . . they can[not] inflict damage without the assistance of some agent [that is, witch], but with such an agent diseases, and any other human passions or ailment, can be brought about" (Kramer 1486, 11). In other words, while demons who are permitted by God can visit havoc upon humans, they prefer the assistance of witches (1486, 238). Any misfortune or sickness that befalls an individual, town, or country occurred because some witch channeled the power of devils. Employing herbal medicine was not some quaint innocent practice based on some benign ancient tradition—it was part of a pact that made the witch more malevolent and dangerous than Satan. The witch's ultimate goal was the same as Satan's, namely, the overthrow of the religious and political structures of the time. Not much has changed when we notice that even to this day, those who challenge or attempt to change the economic and political status quo are also characterized as demonic.

Anyone who renounced the true faith so as to participate in such diabolical practices deserved no mercy. The crimes of witches exceed the sins of all others, even exceeding the sins and fall of the angels who followed Satan in rebelling against God (1486, 77, 82). They have chosen to become enemies of God, and, as such, have no one to blame but themselves for the suffering awaiting them. Likewise, to argue that witches making pacts with the Devil really do not exist only proves that those holding this position "are to be regarded as notorious heretics" (1486, 8). For those who administer public justice against witches or prosecute them in any public official capacity (that is, Inquisitors) cannot be injured, afflicted, or influenced by their witchcraft (1486, 89–91). And if these administrators and public officials are negligent in their pursuit and persecution of witches, then it is God who is injured by their neglect and thus will permit witches to bring great affliction upon those lacking the zeal to prosecute and persecute these evil doers (1486, 118).

Evil ceased being a sole matter of human nature or an inclination of the human heart. During this the time of the burnings it became more enfleshed, more concrete—even able to produce a child that, while not being of the Devil, is born with a propensity for evil. But how? After all, how can demons—as spirits—impregnate a woman? According to Thomas Aquinas, a demon would shape-shift into a woman (succubus) and either seduce a man or visit him while he was asleep for the purpose of extracting his semen (hence explaining why men at times have nocturnal emissions, known as "wet dreams"). Then the demon would shape-shift into a man (incubus) and plant the stolen sperm into a woman.[15] This idea that demons can collect male semen and deposit it within women can be further traced back to Augustine.[16] The *Malleus Maleficarum* shows how witches could be found in fields or forests, lying on their back with the bottom half of their bodies exposed. Based on "the agitation of their legs" and the "disposition of their sexual organs" it was seemingly obvious that they were "copulating with incubus demons that are invisible to the onlookers" (1486, 114).

Not only can demons take the form of humans to conceive satanic children, but they can take the form of well-known Christians in order to destroy their reputation. This was the case with archbishop Silvanus of Nazareth. The demon, transformed in the archbishop's likeness, entered the private quarters of a respectable lady and attempted to rape her. Crying out for help, several came to her aid, finding the demon—in the form of the archbishop—hiding under her bed. The innocent archbishop's reputation was thus defamed; only to be restored when the demon in question was forced to confess at St. Jerome's tomb (1486, 134).

Witch hunts were not limited to Roman Catholics. In fact, the high point of the late-medieval witch-craze was a phenomenon of the Protestant Reformation period. Throughout the sixteenth and seventeenth centuries both Catholic and Protestant officials tried and executed tens of thousands of women on the charge of witchcraft. Leaders of the Protestant Reformation, including Martin Luther and John Calvin, may have done much to debunk Catholicism along with its theology and rituals, but their Protestant views of Satan and witches did not deviate much from their medieval Catholic counterparts. Protestants were quick to point out that the papacy was occupied, indeed possessed, by the Anti-Christ, while Catholics concluded that it must have been Satan who inspired the Protestant Reformation. Although Protestants and Catholics each charged the other with being satanic, agreement existed concerning the reality of Satan. Luther, whose own physical seizures were attributed to Satan, concludes during his lectures on Galatians that "it cannot be denied but that the Devil liveth, yea, and reigneth throughout the whole earth." Humans "are all subject to the devil" who is "the prince and god" of this world and responsible for "sorcery and witchcraft" (1531, 126). John Calvin would agree. He writes, "For the devil is said to have undisputed possession of this world. . . . In like manner, he is said to blind all who do not believe the Gospel, and to do his own work in the children of disobedience."[17] In short, whatever did not come from God, according to Reformation leaders, was evil. A simple dichotomy was created and maintained. Either you believe in the Protestant interpretation of the gospel or you are among the "wicked [who] are vessels of wrath."[18] For Martin Luther, Catholics who remained faithful to the church, Jews who refused to recognize the Messiahship of Jesus, peasants who rebelled against aristocratic landholders, and Protestants who were not followers of Luther were dismissed as being "agents of Satan" (Pagels 1995, 180).

Leaders of the Protestant Reformation exaggerated Satan's power, making his influence even more pervasive than their fellow Roman Catholics. In so doing, they increased the fear of him. Reformation leaders saw their earthly existence as a battle against the Evil One that could be won through the extirpation of witches. Martin Luther calls for the eradication of witches in 1526 when he delivers his *Sermon on Exodus*. "Women are more susceptible to those superstitions of Satan. . . . They are commonly called 'wise women'. *Let them be killed*. . . . The law that sorceresses should be killed is most just, since they do many cursed things while they remain undiscovered. . . . Therefore, let them be killed."[19] It is important to note that the first century of the Reformation coincides with the most intense period of the witch hunts, which began during the 1560s. Ironically, while Protestants and Catholics saw each other as demonically influenced, Protestants still joined their Catholic opponents in ferreting out witches and cleansing society of female-induced evils.

Like Martin Luther (1531, 126), John Calvin captured the common theological understanding that Satan could do nothing without the consent of God. "With regard to the strife and war which Satan is said to wage with God, it must be understood with this qualification, that Satan cannot possibly do anything against the will and consent of God."[20] We are left wondering why, if God is so powerful, God allows Satan and his horde of demons such power among humans. It is because God, according to the *Malleus Maleficarum*, is so heavily offended by human sin that God grants the devil greater power in tormenting humanity (1486, 116). John Calvin would agree:

> God thus turning the unclean spirits hither and thither at his pleasure, employs them in exercising believers by warring against them, assailing them with wiles, urging them with solicitations, pressing close upon them, disturbing, alarming, and occasionally wounding, but never conquering or oppressing them; whereas they hold the wicked in thralldom, exercise dominion over their minds and bodies, and employ them as bond-slaves in all kinds of iniquity.[21]

Probably the best-known example of a Protestant-led witch hunt unfolded in colonial Massachusetts from February through May of 1693. Salem Village (later renamed Danvers), where the witch hysteria began, was rife with disputes over grazing rights and property lines. The ministers to the village found themselves thrown into internal disputes over land, with several leaving the parish as a result of the non-payment of their wages. Eventually, the decision was taken to call Reverend Samuel Parris, though significant levels of division remained within the church given that the vote to send for Parris had only a slim majority in favor. Ironically, the witch hysteria began in the home of Reverend Parris when his daughter Betty Parris (age 9) and his niece Abigail Williams (age 11) began to throw uncontrollable fits, barked like dogs, and fell into trances. It was believed that these ailments began with a game these girls played with the household's indigenous Caribbean slave, Tituba. Egg whites were poured into water (creating a type of crystal ball known as the Venus Glass) so as to ascertain, based on the shape taken, the occupation of future husbands.

Soon these two girls were joined by others in bizarre fits. When examined by the village doctor, William Griggs, he concluded that there was no physical ailment responsible for their condition; thus, they must be bewitched. The question then became: By whom? The girls subsequently began to accuse neighbors of being witches responsible for causing their afflictions. They began by first accusing outsiders: Sarah Good, a homeless beggar; Sarah Osborne, who did not attend church; and the ethnic Other, Tituba the slave. Over the course of the hysteria, more than 150 individuals were imprisoned for being witches and consorting with the Devil [see Figure 12]. Of those accused, fourteen women and five men were executed on the capital felony of witchcraft. The "spectral evidence" that was admitted in the trials at Salem consisted of the testimonies of the "victims," who stated that they were attacked by phantoms having the form of the various accused. Though these phantoms were invisible to others, such evidence was considered acceptable in the court of law run by chief justice William Stoughton. One man, Giles Corey, was crushed to death under heavy stones (*peine forte et dure*) for refusing to enter a plea on the accusation of being a witch. About five other individuals died while incarcerated. The hysteria came to an end when Royal Governor William Phips dissolved the court conducting the investigations because accusations had begun to be leveled against the colonial elite.

Although it is difficult to understand such hysteria and outbursts as occurred in Salem, such events did serve a purpose for the villagers. A powerful Satan helps answer the theodicy question. In an era pregnant with war and pestilence, an era of short and brutal life spans, an era of illiteracy and ignorance, having a Satan responsible for human suffering with God's blessings because of human disobedience to God's representative on earth, the church, starts to make solid theological sense. In a perverted form of logic, humans deserve demonic torment and the church-inflicted torture. Whenever misfortune befell good townsfolk, relief from the anxiety of the times could be had by denouncing the witch and projecting upon her all of the guilt and insecurity felt. In a sense, the witch played an important role as scapegoat, carrying upon herself all the sins of society. Through her stripes her neighbors were healed.

According to the influential French philosopher René Girard, scapegoating serves an important task during times of crises, especially crises that remind humans of their mortality, such as political disturbances, famines, or plagues common during the late Middle Ages. Such monumental upheavals as the Black Death of the fourteenth century or the religious wars of the sixteenth century caused the collapse of the "social order evidenced by the disappearance of rules and 'differences' that define cultural divisions" (1986, 12). During times of crises, Girard argues, human society unites through what he terms a "victimage mechanism" (1987, 23–30). Those suffering the misfortunes of the time "convince themselves that a small number of people, or even a single individual, despite relative weakness, is extremely harmful to the whole of society" (Girard 1986, 15). The shedding of blood is required to cover the sins of the many, bringing unity and reconciliation among the perpetrators of violence. Ignorant of the true causes of the crises, those calling for a witch hunt find strength and reassurance in the collective persecution of victims in order to eliminate the perceived cause of the crises (1986, 12–15). By offering up scapegoats, those in power, namely the church, eliminate potential "troublemakers" and "rebels." Those labeled "witches," who are perceived as openly and aggressively challenging the social and political supremacy of Christianity, quickly find themselves in precarious situations. Normalizing witch hunts becomes a powerful instrument in maintaining the status quo, effectively silencing potential opponents.[22]

Natural cataclysms, wars, and epidemics may have led to the sacrifice of scapegoats accused of bringing about disaster, but there was no need to wait until these calamities occurred. It became profitable for individuals to testify that their political enemies were in league with the Devil in order to remove those who would oppose their drive for power and/or privilege. In some cases, an accusation would lead to the accuser obtaining the land and possessions of the accused. In other words, there existed profitable incentives to "out" those who were in cahoots with Satan or who practiced black magic and sorcery. This form of scapegoating for profit began in the early fourteenth century, when the king of France, hoping to overturn the papal decisions of the deceased Pope Boniface VII (whom ironically Dante placed in the inner circle of Hell where simony is punished), posthumously accused him of obtaining his position as Pope with the help of demons (Medway 2001, 73). As recently as 2006, Governor Timothy M. Kaine officially pardoned Grace Sherwood of Pungo, Virginia, who was accused of witchcraft on July 10, 1710, and served seven years in prison after being dunked in the Lynnhaven River. The fact that she had floated back up to the surface of the water was taken as proof of her diabolical status as a witch. Notably, Pungo is located in the central part of Virginia near Norfolk and Virginia Beach, and Grace Sherwood was a widow with good grazing lands and desirable property that local rivals likely hoped to confiscate following her trial and conviction. After she was released from prison, she lived to be about eighty years old. The case of Grace Sherwood passed into the lore and legends of colonial America as the infamous "Witch of Pungo," a home-grown historical incident that reminds us of how very recent and factual the witch-craze nightmare really was.

## The Colonized Other

While Europe was ablaze with the consequences of the hunt for witches, a lost sailor named Cristóbal Colón (Cristóbal means "bringer of Christ" and Colón means "repopulate") was discovered in 1492 when he came ashore by the Taínos, the indigenous people of the Caribbean. The Taínos's discovery would soon lead to their decimation, for Colón's adventure occurred at a time when the holy fight against the forces of the devil was fused and confused with the imposition of a Christianity that lacked tolerance for any deviation of doctrinal diversity. Queen Isabel of Castile,[23] in spite of her work in reforming the faith and advancing scholarship, secured from the Pope authority to implement the Inquisition as a tool of protecting the faith from heretics, specifically Jews and "Judaizing" Christians (Jews who converted under threat of duress). Indeed, Spanish intellectuals and religious visionaries believed the remarkable events of 1492 hailed that their young nation-state would serve all of Christendom as the agent of Christ's Second Coming and vanquish Satan by converting the Jews and Muslims to the Christian faith.

By 1492, the year the lost Colón was discovered, all Jews were expelled from Spain. This was also the year that the last Moorish stronghold, the Caliphate of Granada, fell to the Christians, ending seven hundred years of Muslim rule [see Figure 14]. Jews and Muslims faced a choice: convert, die, or leave Spain forever. In trying to understand faith traditions different from Christianity, it was simply assumed that such faiths were inspired by Satan. Jews were believed to be magicians complicit in witchcraft, practicing both sorcery and human sacrifice. As the "killers of God," they were accused of kidnapping Christian children in order either to feast upon them during Passover or crucify them in a reenactment of their supposed role in crucifying Christ. It did not help that the New Testament refers to their sacred assemblies as "synagogues of Satan" (Rev 2:9; 3:9).

The reconquest of the Iberian Peninsula created a Spain that was once again "Christian." The seven hundred years taken to reclaim the land was due to a religious obligation to fight all the enemies of the faith. By reading the narrative of Joshua 6 literally, a religious understanding of holy war developed that merged fidelity to Christ with the conquering of infidels. We recall that the Joshua narrative provided God's people with divine sanction to destroy the city of Jericho and slaughter all of its inhabitants (including women and children) because they were heathens. Spaniards, as the original chosen people of God, believed they too held a mandate from God to purify the land of all abominations and bear witness to the Christian faith among all the nations and peoples of Christendom.

As the last crusade ended in Spain, a newer crusade began in the Western Hemisphere. This spirit of conquering God's enemies was not finished with the expulsion of Jews and Moors from Spain's domains in 1492 but journeyed with Colón to the so-called New World, thus fulfilling in the minds of conquering Spaniards the biblical prophecy of Isaiah 60:9: "The coasts shall await for me, vessels of Tarshish [understood as Spain] in front, to bring your sons from far away, and their silver and gold with them, to the name of Yahweh your God, and to the Holy One of Israel for he has made you glorious." Conquistadores were on an apocalyptic mission, believing they were fulfilling the great commission: "In your goings, then, disciple all the nations, baptizing them in the name of the Father and of the Son and of the Holy Spirit" (Matt 28:19). In so doing, the conquistadores were ushering in the Second Coming of Christ, conquering by means of sword and across the land of the heathens so as to establish Christ's messianic kingdom on earth.

Still, how can those who call themselves "Christians" rape, kill, and plunder people from other lands? Colonizers must convince themselves that the unchristian violence they unleash is not only justified but is in accordance with the will of God. The humanity of those about to be conquered is dismissed, relegated to a lower stage on the evolutionary scale in need of Christian tutelage. The white man's burden becomes the Christianization and civilization of primitive and barbaric people. In exchange for the "good" work of freeing indigenous people from the grip of Satan, those perceived as inferior (in other words, non-whites) can repay the colonizer's generosity by contributing their cheap labor and natural resources, enriching the Christian colonizer in the process. Refusing to do so signified a denial of the authority of the church and rebellion against God's perfect will. Not serving the colonizer was akin to waging war against God.

The builders of Christian empires justified what otherwise would have been a cruel and blatant imposition of oppressive structures that resulted in the accumulation of personal wealth and power by convincing themselves that their actions were against those who were worshipping demons. Justifying conquest by the glorification of God meant that the spirituality of the indigenous people ceased to exist as an error due to their ignorance concerning the good news of Jesus Christ: the indigenous worshippers, like the European witches, had to be in league with Satan. It was not sufficient simply to define the conquered as inferior and thus responsible for their menial existence—they had also to blame them for the misfortune that befell them as punishment by or disfavor before God. The same themes previously used to demonize witches were now being used to demonize those non-Christians whose lands and resources were desired. They, like the witches, were the mirror opposite of faithful Christians, doing publicly what Christians do privately, participating in acts that Christians find disgusting, defiling what Christians hold sacred. Specifically, both witches and Native people were accused of sexual irregularities (non-heterosexual matrimonial relationships), cannibalism (specifically the eating of children), and the reversal of "proper" gender roles (where women were socially and physically on top). The typical non-Christian indigenous person was seen as a homosexual and an onanist who also practiced cannibalism and bestiality.

For example, Gonzalo Fernández de Oviedo, chronicler of the colonization venture, refers in 1535 to Native people as sodomites in *Historia General y Natural de las Indias* (in English: *General and Natural History of the Indies*). Even though no hard evidence concerning the homosexual practices among the aborigines existed, de Oviedo still makes the claim that anal intercourse by men with members of both sexes was considered normal (Mason 1990, 56–57). The first bishop of Santa Marta, a Dominican friar named Tomás Ortiz, wrote:

> The men from the mainland in the Indies eat human flesh and are more given to sodomy than all generations ever . . . they are sorcerers, soothsayers, and necromancers . . . they turn into brute animals; in all, I say that God never created people so set in vice and bestialities. (López de Gómez 1946, 155)

The human sacrifices Indians in Mexico and Peru were accused of committing were offerings that the conquistadores believed were being made to

Satan. Toward the close of the sixteenth century, a Jesuit named José de Acosta argued that "the human bloodshed in various ways in honor of Satan was infinite" (Rivera 1992, 159).

Juan Suárez de Peralta, a late-sixteenth-century resident of Mexico, describes the inverted patriarchal patterns of Native society when he writes:

> The custom [of Native Americans is] that the women do business and deal with trade and other public offices while the men remain at home and weave and embroider. They [the women] urinate standing while the men do so seated; and they have no reluctance to perform their natural deeds in public. (Pagden 1982, 175)

The sins against nature in which indigenous people participated threatened the institution of the patriarchal family and by extension the very fabric of civilized society. Conquering Spaniards, along with other Europeans, had in their minds a moral obligation to enter the land and restore a proper, phallocentric social order. The Conquest in which Spaniards partook became a just war to punish the Indians who have willfully sinned against God and nature, as well as a holy war so as to remain faithful to God's first commandment of having no false gods before the Lord.

The sins of Native people became more than just rebellion against the true God, it was an indication that they were subhuman. According to Ginés de Sepúlveda (who debated with Bartolomé de Las Casas over the humanity of Indians), Native people lacked *humanitas*. Relying on Aristotelian differentiation between the nature of free humans and natural slaves, he concluded that Indians as *humunculos* (barely human) deserve to become slaves, lose their lands, and be forcefully converted to Christianity (1951, 35, 63, 119–22). Understanding Indians as beasts that walk on two legs justifies the stripping of their lands and enforced servitude to the benefit of believers in Christ.

While the Natives were assigned a subhuman status, the indigenous local gods and/or spirits of the soon-to-be-colonized were incorporated into the pantheon of demons standing against the more powerful Jesus Christ and his army of Saints. The enemies of the Indians equated Native spirituality with Satan and his demons. Gerónimo de Mendieta, a Franciscan missionary who arrived to Native territory in 1524, wrote:

> They are in error and deceived by the devils, enemies of the human race, concurring in abominable vices and sins, which will bring them

to damnation and to suffer the sorrows and eternal fire of hell. (1596, 3.13:214)

And yet, consider the words of Bartolomé de Las Casas, long hailed as the so-called defender of the Indians. Even those who are supposed to be allies in protecting the Indians from the genocidal advancement of Christians still relegate their spirituality to the demonic. Las Casas writes:

> [The Taínos] did not have idols, only rarely, and then not for worship, but only to be used imaginatively by certain priests used by the devil. . . . They did not have external or visible ceremonies, but only a few, and these were conducted by those priests whom the devil appointed as his ministers. (1967, 1.3.120:632)

No qualms existed among Spaniards, even supposed defenders, in toppling the idols or razing the temples of Native people and building upon their sacred sites Christian churches. As Nicolás de Witte, an Augustinian friar, reminds us in 1554, such sacred sites for Indians were in fact like a "temple of devils" (Cuevas 1914, 222). Dethroning Native beliefs was in effect dethroning Satan. The destruction of Native spiritual symbols was perceived as a cosmic battle in which God proved victorious over Satan and his horde of demons, who had been masquerading as Indian spiritual elders.

In 1553 Pedro de Cieza de León, reflecting on the Native people of the region that was to become Peru, concludes that the Devil, from whom the Spaniards were redeemed through the "cruel death on the cross" of Jesus Christ, is the same Devil "who possessed these [Indian] people, with the permission from God, [and] kept them oppressed and captive. Their only hope for redemption and salvation was conversion to "the holy mother church" (1553, 27–28). Conversion and baptism into the Christian faith became a rejection of one's identity, culture, traditions, and society equated to and symbolized by the renouncement of Satan. As Elaine Pagels remind us,

> To this day, Christian baptism requires a person to solemnly "renounce the devil and all his works" and to accept exorcism. The pagan convert was baptized only after confessing that all spirit beings previously reverted—and dreaded—as divine were actually only "demons—hostile spirits contending against the One God of goodness and justice, and against his armies of angels. (1996, 214)

Obviously, the Spaniards were not the only ones who saw Native people as demon worshippers in need of eradication—the Northern Europeans who mostly settled the Northern Hemisphere held similar views. They created and promulgated the Black Legend to deflect the depths of English inhumanity toward the Indians. The Black Legend was a propaganda campaign perpetuated by the English against the Spaniards to highlight and caricature the unmitigated cruelty of the conquistadores by translating their writings into English. It was an attempt to contrast the Spaniard quest for gold with the English so-called quest for God. In reality, the English quest was as much for land as the Spanish search was for gold. And like the Spaniards, the English to the north unleashed their own genocidal atrocities, justified by equating those who occupied the land as nonhuman worshippers of demons and devils.

For the Puritans, natural order was the result of the creative force of God. Yet the Indians they encountered were seen as representing the wilderness, a disruption of God's natural order (Pearce 1953, 3–24). Hence, they were the agents of the Devil, challenging God's will to consecrate the Puritan mission with the bountiful blessings of Indian land. One of the most troubling examples of demonizing the Other occurred in colonial Connecticut on May 26, 1637, when a group of Puritan settlers from the Massachusetts Bay Colony, along with allies from several local native tribes, attacked the Pequot village at Missituck (modern-day Mystic, Connecticut). This is the infamous chapter of colonial American history known as the Pequot War. Economic and territorial competition between European settlers and Native American tribes aside, one of the cruelest ironies of this entire colonial episode is the rhetoric of justification used by Puritan clergy and military leaders who blamed the alleged demonic and satanic beliefs of the Native savages for the atrocities that were unleashed upon them in May 1637. As recorded in Captain John Underhill's journal,

> It may be demanded, Why should you be so furious (as some have said)? Should not Christians have more mercy and compassion? . . . Sometimes the Scripture declareth women and children must perish with their parents. Sometimes the case alters, but we will not dispute it now. We had sufficient light from the Word of God for our proceedings. (1638, 40)

Many reading this kind of material today may find it hard to believe that so-called God-centered people as devout and pious as the English Puritans could ever use the Word of God, a well-known New Testament reference to Christ reminiscent of the Logos from the Gospel of John, as the justification for starting this war and authorizing the massacre of four hundred to seven hundred men, women, and children whom the English feared, despised, and dismissed as worshippers of demons. Such fatal characteristics invalidated both Pequot claims on the land the settlers called "the New Jerusalem" and their right to live in the world order the Puritans brought to North America.

Probably one of the earliest North American religious leaders to make a seamless transition from witches being worshippers of Satan to Indians doing likewise was Cotton Mather (1663–1728), a Puritan minister who played a supporting role in the Salem Witch Trials. For Mather, to be "Indianized" meant to serve the Devil. This is what he thought occurred to a young girl named Mercy Short. Short, who was earlier kidnapped by Indians, now suffered from tormented fits of memory from her captivity. According to Mather, Short had seen the Devil. In describing what Short saw, Mather wrote: "Hee [Satan] was not of a Negro, but of a Tawney, or an Indian colour . . . he wore a high-crowned Hat, with straight Hair; and had on Cloven-foot" (Takaki 1993, 41). Satan, in other words, was Indian. Defining the Other as demonic allowed Mather to see the English colonial venture through a God-versus-Satan, good-versus-evil, us-versus-them lens. He wrote, "The wilderness through which we are passing to the Promised Land is all over fill'd with fiery flying serpents" (Ibid). The Indians, Mather observed, are "so Devil driven as to begin an unjust and bloody war upon the English, which issued in their speedy and utter extirpation from the face of God's earth. . . . The Devil decoyed those miserable savages in hopes that the Gospel of our Lord Jesus Christ would never come here to destroy or disturb His absolute empire over them" (Ibid., 43).

The common assumption held by Cotton Mather, as well as other early colonial religious leaders—including Jonathan Edwards (1703–1758), a Western Massachusetts preacher, theologian, and missionary to the Indians best known for helping to shape the First Great Awakening—was that the Indians encountered were the remnant of the Ten Lost Tribes of Israel, a remnant that had lost all knowledge of God's teachings. The Lost Ten Tribes of Israel refers to the ten tribes that settled in the northern lands of Canaan forming the Kingdom of Israel. Around 720 BCE they were invaded by the ancient Assyrians. With the destruction of their homeland, they disappeared from history and the biblical account. Based on Deut 28:64—"Yahweh shall scatter you among all nations, from one end of the earth to the other, there you shall serve other gods of wood and stone, which neither you nor your fathers have known"—early North American religious leaders believed that Satan led these former Israelite tribes eastward through Asia and across the land bridge or ice flows to North America.

These lost ten tribes settled in the new lands of the Western Hemisphere, becoming the devotees of Satan (Edwards 1989, 155, 433–34). For Jonathan Edwards, all who "worship the sun and moon and worship the devil don't worship the true God that made the [world]," and thus are destined to Hell (McDermott 2000, 127).[24] In effect, Indians were the "devil's captives," living in the "kingdom of Satan" (Ibid., 194–95).[25] Referring to the Natives, Edwards insists that "the devil sucks their blood" (Ibid., 1995).[26] According to Edwards,

> [T]he occasion of the first peopling of America was this, that the devil, being alarmed and surprised by the wonderful success of the Gospel which there was the first three hundred years after Christ . . . and seeing the Gospel spread so fast, and fearing that his heathenish kingdom would be wholly overthrown through the world, led away a people from the other continent into America, that they might be quite out of the reach of the Gospel, that here he might quietly posses them, and reign over them as their god. . . . [But] God has sent the Gospel into these parts of the world, and now the Christian church is set up here in New England, and in parts of America, where before had nothing but the grossest heathenish darkness. . . . Satan's kingdom shall be overthrown. (1851, 468–69)

Views of Indians as Satan's minions were not limited to the Puritans in the north. Further south in Virginia, the same views held true. Take for example the official reply to a March 22, 1622, Indian rebellion against English encroachment upon their land. Native leader Opechancanough of the Powhatan Confederacy led a coordinated series of surprise attacks on more than thirty of the surrounding settlements outside of the Virginia Company base at Jamestown, killing 350 to 1240 people. Writing a report on what occurred for the Virginia Company, Edward Waterhouse, a Calvinist lawyer, believed that the cause of the massacre was due to the settler's naïve belief that the Indians, hopelessly possessed by the Devil, can be converted from their savage ways to Christianity and civilization. Waterhouse wrote:

[T]he true cause of this surprise was most by the instigation of the Devil (enemy of their salvation) and the daily fear that possessed them, that in time we by our growing continually upon them, would dispossess them of this country, as they have been formerly of the West Indies by the Spaniards. (Williams 1990, 217)

The consequences of portraying North American Natives as savage Devil worshippers were not limited to the early American colonial period. Its consequences are evident to this day. We are reminded by Native Americans Kidwell, Noley, and Tinker that the association of North American Indians with the demonic was not relegated to some colonial past.

Throughout the United States, Native place names for sacred and ceremonial places were become designated as Devil's Lake, Devil's Highway, Devil's Canyon. Christians who gave places these names assumed that those associations with Indian beliefs gave them demonic qualities. (2001, 146)

Conquest, enslavement, and genocide was not restricted to Native Americans. Characterizing the Other as demonic did not stop with the conquest of the Western Hemisphere. The branding of practitioners of Native forms of religion as worshippers of demons disguised as idols has been used in Africa and Asia also—in short, throughout the Global South—to justify the colonial venture. We cannot help but wonder if Satan's greatest gift to humanity was the merging of Empire with Christianity and then convincing Christians that any threat to the sovereign's law and order, including witches, or any obstacle to fulfilling its manifest destiny, including Indians, must be tools of the Devil. Whoever they are, the enemies of Empire become by definition the enemies of God. This prevailing viewpoint continues to this present day. During the Cold War, Communism was more than just an opposing economic and political system—it was Godless Communism, or as former President Ronald Reagan dubbed the Soviet Union, "the evil empire." We, capitalists, believed in God; they, the Communists, did not. To underscore the point, in 1954 the U.S. added the phrase "one nation under God" to the Pledge of Allegiance to highlight the difference between "us" and "them." Of course today, Communism is no longer the threat it once was.

Since September 11, 2001, we have constructed and identified a new satanic enemy, radical Islam. Rather than concentrate on those who perpetuated the horrors of 9/11, a broad brush was employed to demonize all who stood in the way of Empire. Not surprisingly, former president George W. Bush gave us, during his 2002 State of the Union address, the term "axis of evil," which included the countries of Iraq, Iran, and North Korea. It would take only a few months before the list was expanded. Warning that the U.S. stood ready to take action, then Under Secretary of State and future U.S. representative to the United Nations, John Bolton, added three more countries to the "axis of evil" list in his May 2002 speech, "Beyond the Axis of Evil." The countries added were Cuba, Libya, and Syria.

Yet enemies of Empire and God need not be the only ones defined as evil. Anyone who questions U.S. exceptionalism or supremacy finds themselves labeled as Satan's mouthpiece. Academics, liberals, and politicians (including presidents) have all been portrayed in demonic terms for going against the prevailing mindset that equates America with that "shining city upon the hill." Unfortunately, such characterizations only stifle constructive discourse. As we move toward the final chapter of this book, we are left wondering whether humanity would have been better served if there had been no such figure as Satan, the personification of absolute Evil. How many so-called witches might not have been burned? How many holy crusades to rid the world of evil would have been averted? What if, instead, Satan was to be understood differently? What if Satan, or absolute Evil, played a different role in determining moral agency? ✳

# Chapter 5

# The Devil Made Me Do It

O ntologically, there is no Satan—but that does not mean Satan does not exist. Natural disasters such as hurricanes, tornadoes, tsunamis, or earthquakes illustrate the randomness by which nature can strike out and bring death and misery to believers and unbelievers alike. But if natural disasters were not enough to cause us to pause, we have a human history that has made inhumanity and violence the moral norm. Mass murder, genocide, inquisitions, torture, terrorism, crusades, concentration camps, colonialism, child abuse, and wars may convince us that radical evil personified as Satan is alive and well on planet Earth but may make us wonder about God and God's goodness. When we consider the many centuries that have seen humans using violent means on one another and how these abuses have been normalized and legitimized, we are left questioning the metaphysical.

This would certainly not be the first time that someone has looked around and wondered why evil triumphs. Psalm 73 notices that the "wicked" grow rich, having strong and healthy bodies (vv. 3-4), while the "pure" are plagued all day long, leading the psalmist to wonder "why should I keep my own heart pure?" (v. 13). Maybe Billy Joel had it right when he sang "Only the good die young." Even during the ministry of Jesus, his disciples asked for an explanation concerning both the randomness of natural disasters and the cruelty of humanity. They ask Jesus to explain moral evil as demonstrated by Governor Pontius Pilate who slaughtered Galilean worshippers, mixing their blood with that of their sacrifices, and natural evil as demonstrated by the fall of the tower of Siloam crushing eighteen people. Jesus responds that they were no guiltier than all the people living in Jerusalem, and unless his hearers repent, they too would perish in a similar fashion (Luke 13:1-5). If we are honest with ourselves, Jesus' answer is unsatisfying. We are left wanting. We are no closer to understanding why evil happens. We are left wondering if what is good and what is evil continues to be determined within the Christian world by those who have a stake in maintaining the present division of power and their station within those structures. If so, it should not be surprising that warnings of eternal damnation in Hell can be a more effective motivator than promises of salvation in Heaven.

Nevertheless, as effective as the Satan figure may have been, and in some circles continues to be, at scaring people into the Kingdom of Heaven, for all intents and purposes Satan (to paraphrase Nietzsche's famous idiom concerning God) is dead, and we (specifically the Enlightenment project) killed him. Satan may have reigned supreme in a world where he could be blamed for natural disasters, mental and physical illness, or the inhumanity of humans, but with the advent of scientific discoveries and the development of studies in medicine, psychology, and physics (to name but a few), Satan was defanged. Within our own culture, we went from the Salem Witch Trials where good religious townsfolk in terror of the Prince of Darkness hanged fourteen women and five men on the charges of consorting with the Devil, to Jon Lovitz dressed in red tights with horns and a pitchfork performing a comedic rendition of Mephistopheles for the popular, late-night television show *Saturday Night Live*. Satan went from being a creature to be feared to a creature to be mocked, from the real Lord of Evil to the figment of our childish imaginations. And just because Satan has been recognized as a construct to explain evil, a way of alluding to the worst of which humanity is capable, this does not mean that Satan does not exist. Although dead, he is not yet buried; and no doubt, he will rise again as long as we deny the reality and power of evil.

But Satan is not the only one the triumph of science dismisses. If the symbol of absolute Evil becomes passé, so too does the symbol for absolute Good. Must the death of Satan be resisted lest it also lead to the death of God? Although our focus is on Satan's death, it is important to note that lurking behind the conversation is a dismissal of the need of a God. Our failure to have an adequate understanding of Satan perverts how God is understood. Probably the best way of comprehending God's character is to begin with Satan, or more specifically, the problem of evil. We begin with the natural and moral evil, then ask: Who is God? What is God's response to evil? And based on God's response, what are we to conclude about God's character?

The answer to these questions may be disturbing. Take for example the story of Job. In all honestly, if we would have joined Eliphaz, Bildad, and Zophar, sat with Job on the ground weeping, examining the evil that had befallen Job from Satan's hand, and all with God's blessings, we might have ended up being more sympathetic to Job's wife, who advised her husband to "curse God and die" (2:9-13). Neither the rational nor the mystical suffices to answer the question of a grieving parent who asks, "Why my child? Where was God?" What makes the book of Job particularly disturbing is that when God finally gets around to explaining why God allowed such calamities to afflict God's faithful servant, God responds by basically saying, "Because I felt like it." And while, yes, God did replace the sons and daughters whom God allowed Satan to kill, any grieving parent knows that the loss of one beloved child can never be replaced by future offspring. What does God's response to Job say about God's character? Who is this God that on the whim of a dare from Satan brings tragedy into the life of a faithful follower? When one considers the centuries of violent anti-Semitism experienced by God's chosen people, we can better appreciate the humorous quip spoken among Jews: "God, would you mind choosing some other people once in a while?"

Not only are we left wondering if we can have a God without a Satan, but more importantly, we can ask what is the relationship between the two. If Satan is an illusion, is God also an illusion? Do we need a Satan to describe a God in the way right is understood when contrasted with left, or up when contrasted with down? Can good be understood in the absence of evil? But does an existence absent of a Satan or a God lead to a type of nihilism where finite mortal beings are tossed between the meaninglessness and futility of life. Can there be a universal ethical foundation informing moral reasoning that determines right from wrong if there is no transcendence? Or is all ethics relative? Does the absence of a universal set of values make our world more precarious? Could it be that the underlying reason for the spread of atheism is the failure of theologians and clerics to explain evil adequately? After all, there exists no official creed or doctrine that provides a proper explanation. And frankly, Jesus' explanation to his disciples, or God's response to Job, as discussed above, are not helpful.

What specific church doctrine or creed can explain the Holocaust, the killing fields of Cambodia, Jim and Jane Crow, or how global power is distributed to cause misery and death on the vast majority of the world's population? If there is no God or Satan, then they must be created to establish a source of moral authority, a standard by which evil can be named. We try to understand Satan and what he represents in order to find proper perceptions about the problem of evil. Still, the defanging of Satan may have left him lacking the diabolical gravitas once possessed to serve as the means by which evil is defined.

## Satan's Death

Most scholars would pinpoint the start of Satan's death pangs to 9:40 a.m. on November 1, 1755, during the Christian holiday of All Saints' Day. As the faithful began celebrating God's graces, an earthquake, estimated to have been a magnitude nine on the Richter scale, rocked the devout Catholic city of Lisbon, Portugal. Accounts at the time claimed the earthquake was felt as far away as Switzerland and North Africa. This natural evil was followed by fires that spread throughout the city and a tsunami that engulfed the downtown area. Thousands died in the initial seismic wave on that fateful morning, while thousands more died in the ensuing chaos of hunger, dehydration, tidal waves, and the fires sparked around the city by the large number of All Saints' Day candles burning in churches, houses, and apartments across the cosmopolitan city.

The vast majority of the city (some estimate 80 per cent) was utterly destroyed. Ironically, on this important Catholic feast day, almost every Catholic church of importance crumbled, causing great angst among the faithful. How can God allow devotees to perish on such a holy day? Is this really the work of the Devil? And if so, is God so impotent that God is unable to protect God's children as they are praising and worshipping the Almighty? Or maybe God was simply punishing the inhabitants of the city for the massacre of unarmed natives and missionaries in colonial Paraguay, ordered by their king and carried out by their armies during the previous year?

The discourse that preceded the Lisbon earthquake further developed the religious conversation about theodicy—literally, the attempt to justify God or God's goodness and/or power in the face of evil manifested as natural (that is, the earthquake) and moral (evil and harmful actions committed by humans). In short, theodicy attempts to justify God in an unstable and tragic world. If God is personal, transcendent, omnipotent, and benevolent, then either God wills the removal of evil but is unable, or God is able to remove evil but does not will it. Either way, God ceases to be personal, transcendent, omnipotent, or benevolent.

Numerous and random tragedies mean we live in a suffering and hurting world, making it difficult if not impossible to speak about visions of establishing a more just society. Surely if God can raise Jesus from the dead, God could have prevented the earthquake from striking Lisbon. At the very least, the God who could make the sun stand still at Joshua's command so that his invading army could commit genocide to rid the land of its inhabitants (Josh 10:13) surely can stall the car of a drunk driver before she or he plows into a family with small children. Think of all the millions upon millions who perished due to smallpox before Edward Jenner developed a vaccination in 1796. The fact that a cure was found indicates that this particular suffering could have been prevented if God had willed it sooner, and all those who died, especially those who died so young, died in vain. God chose to allow greater suffering to run rampant until a human being, through the exercise of rational science and experimentation, put a stop to the disease. And this is but one disease, one tragedy among the many that plague and torment humanity. The number of nameless victims becomes greater than the stars in the heavens when we start multiplying the sum of human tragedies. Some might argue that the dark side of life teaches us the purpose of the good and confirms the notion that evil ultimately serves a divine purpose. And maybe a little bit of evil might accomplish this goal. Nevertheless, the body count is too high and the stench of senseless death too putrid. The problem is that there is too much evil, so much that it almost swallows any remnants of good. Maybe God is simply choosing to allow human and natural freedom to work itself out, creating a world where it feels as if there is no God, or at the very least a God that is absent?

The horror and randomness of the Lisbon earthquake ignited a new debate among the European Enlightenment philosophers over the concept of evil. The very theological foundation of how the church understood theodicy and the role of Satan was shaken to its core and like the ornate churches of Lisbon came crumbling down. The dichotomy between absolutes simply failed to be reconciled with the emerging corpus of scientific rationalism and philosophical thought. Evil, inherently tied to Satan and centuries of religious discourse, was beginning to be understood as existing beyond the transcendent.

Religious leaders across Europe soon began explaining the cataclysmic earthquake as God's chastisement for the sins of the people of Lisbon or as a stern warning for genuine repentance and a turn to deep prayer for all of Christian Europe. Theological responses to this horrific event, which claimed about sixty thousand lives, became one of the rallying points for the philosophers, revolutionaries, and antireligious skeptics of the Enlightenment. David Hume, Benjamin Franklin, John Wesley, Voltaire, and Jean Jacques Rousseau, along with a host of other major figures of that era, were affected by the shadow of the Lisbon earthquake of 1755. Indeed, the vehement debate that erupted between the advocates of scientific rationalism, like Voltaire and Hume, versus the advocates of divine punishment and Satan's role in the catastrophe represented by clergy from many different denominations, came to be interpreted by later historians as a turning point in the intellectual and religious history of the modern world. Our quest for the historical Satan throughout this volume has brought us face-to-face with this decisive moment of the past several centuries regardless of the collective amnesia that led us all to forget the impact of that fateful earthquake on modernity's conception of Satan and the problem of evil.

Religious responses to the Lisbon earthquake among French and Spanish Jesuits provoked the famed contemporary philosopher Voltaire into coining the rallying cry of the Enlightenment's anticlericalism, *"Ecrasez l'infame!"* ("Crush the infamy!"), with "infamy" referring, among other things, to ignorance, superstition, and ecclesiastical oppression. He wrote an ode on this tragic earthquake, which he titled: "Poem on the Lisbon Disaster, or an Examination of the Axiom, 'All is Well.'" Voltaire's reflection on the fate of Lisbon's tragedy in 1755 offers an interesting contrast to Pat Robertson's interpretation of the more recent earthquake of 2010 in Haiti:

> To those expiring murmurs of distress,
> To that appalling spectacle of woe,
> Will ye reply: 'You do but illustrate
> The Iron laws that chain the will of God?'
> Say ye, o'er that yet quivering mass of flesh:
> 'God is avenged: the wage of sin is death?'
> What crime, what sin, had those young hearts conceived

That lie, bleeding and torn, on their mother's breast?
Did fallen Lisbon deeper drink of vice
Than London, Paris, or sunlit Madrid? (1756, 77)

Additionally, Voltaire used the Lisbon earthquake[1] as a setting from which the main character of his famous literary and satirical masterpiece, *Candide, ou l'Optimisme* (in English: *Candide: Or, the Optimist*), wrestled with the problem of evil. Published four years after the momentous event in Portugal, Voltaire attempted to counter the accepted theological norm of the seventeenth-century rationalist Gottfried Wilhelm Leibniz, who believed in a benevolent deity that guided all things to work for the best. *Tout est pour le mieux dans le meilleur des mondes possibles* ("All is for the best in the best of all possible worlds"). The novella's main character, Candide, who is raised and engulfed in Leibniz's optimistic theodicy, eventually becomes disillusioned by the trials and tribulations of his life, forsaking his original optimistic belief for the task of simple work to avoid boredom and vice while preventing want. He concludes that the only option left is to live in seclusion within a garden of his own making. He concludes his misadventures with the statement "we must cultivate our garden" (1991, 87). Although the book would eventually become part of the Western literary canon, it was originally banned by the authorities for Voltaire's ridiculing of normative religious theological assumptions and the clerics and theologians who perpetrate these assumptions.

Immanuel Kant was another contemporary of the earthquake whose thinking was impacted by the tragedy. Although a major proponent of the power of reason upon which to base moral reasoning, still, in his last major work and main theological writing, *Religion within the Limits of Reason Alone* (1793), he attempts to provide some freedom for humans from the rational, concluding that radical evil is "incomprehensible" (1960, 39). For Kant, the only way to describe or explain evil was to deny any explanation of an external demon or deity and instead introduce the term "radical evil." Humans are evil because they are "conscious of moral law but [have] nevertheless adopted into [their] maxim the (occasional) deviation there from" (1960, 27). Such evil is a "*radical* innate *evil* in human nature (1960, 28)—it is an evil that is radical,

> because it corrupts the ground of all maxims; it is, moreover, as a natural propensity inextirpable by human powers, since extirpation could occur only through good maxims, and cannot take place when the ultimate subjective ground of all maxims is postulated as corrupt; yet at

the same time must be possible to *overcome* it, since it is found in man, a being whose actions are free. (1960, 32)

Projecting evil on some mystical figure or waiting for protection from evil from some sacrificial scapegoat simply will not do for Kant. Dualities between absolute Evil and absolute Good are overcome. Kant roots evil within human nature, thus refusing to demonize it or those who do evil, for even the wicked person does not will evil for the sake of evil but brings it about by choosing to ignore and abandon moral law (1960, 30–32). There is no original sin, and no original goodness of humans, except what originates within human free will and radical autonomy. Evil becomes a choice made freely by humans who are "partly good, partly bad" (1960, 16), not the result of some seduction from Satan. As long as humans externalize evil in the form of a Satan, they fail to deal with its root causes in human choices and actions. For Kant, the battle is not with Satan; the battle is with evil human will. Thus he moves the discourse from theodicy to anthropodicy—evil not as a cosmic reality tied to religious concepts but as a human act of the will. Kant provides a more practical, less theoretical understanding of evil that emphasizes the responsibility of human actions. As long as humans keep their attention on Satan or any other metaphysical source, Kant would argue that they will fail to act morally.

Through free will humans choose evil, following their predisposed natural tendency to place the particular over the universal, specifically their self-serving desires and interests before the categorical imperative of universalizing moral law. This tension exists because humans are rational beings and are distinctively predisposed to animality (1960, 21). Still, radical evil subjected to reason preserves human dignity because the will to do the good exists (1960, 31). Kant attributes humanity's intrinsic propensity to do evil to "the good or evil heart" (1960, 24), not to some primordial spiritual or mystical Fall of humanity. Ironically, even though Kant admits that humans may ultimately need divine help but should consciously ignore such a possibility for assistance, he reverts to religious language and symbols. And while he may reject the Christian concept of Original Sin, his understanding of evil as a natural propensity of humans (1960, 32) sounds eerily familiar. He even contradicts his notion of absolute freedom (radical autonomy) by admitting to the possibility, if not the need, for grace to those guilty humans who can become worthy of receiving absolution and/or aid (1960, 62–70).

Should evil actions be understood as part of what it means to be a finite, imperfect, and sinful human being? While modernity centered evil on the human will as opposed to the character of Satan, scientific advances being made in our present age are looking at acts normatively defined as evil as manifestations of chemical imbalances in the brain, DNA wiring, or psychological damage caused by earlier traumatic events. If this is true, can evil be cured or in some cases accepted. Or could it be that the Enlightenment project that gave us modern science and the rational understanding of evil is doomed to fail? After all, as Theodor Adorno reminds us, "to write poetry after Auschwitz is barbaric" (1983, 34). Is the attempt to understand evil (as in the case of the Holocaust) obscene, betraying the horror experienced by its victims. Massive, unjust suffering lacks meaningful resolution. After all, did not Hitler impose a new categorical imperative upon a humanity lacking freedom? According to Adorno,

> What the mind once boasted of defining or constructing as it likes moves in the direction of what is unlike the mind, in the direction of that which eludes the rule of the mind and yet manifests that rule as absolute evil. (1973, 365)

Our modern age managed to relegate Satan and/or everything he signifies to the field of rationality. But did this maneuver irrefutably and utterly fail? Do the Auschwitzes of history, both on a massive scale as well as in its limitation to the individual, prove that evil, either as Satan or as some rational concept, could not be so easily dismissed? If we try to picture the face of evil we usually see an Adolf Hitler, a Charles Manson, or a Jeffrey Dahmer. Is there something transcendent that embodies such evil? As much as our rationality has tried to do away with Satan, he does not seem to want to die—or if he did, he is surely resurrected in uncanny ways for our times.

## The Modern Myth of Dr. Faustus

Ironically, just as Christendom was emerging from the superstitions and fears of the medieval world, a new myth about Satan's desire to tempt human beings away from the humility and compassion of the New Testament message began appearing in European literary circles. It would eventually go through many versions and editions, and by the time Johann Wolfgang von Goethe (1749–1832) published his early nineteenth-century masterpiece,

*Faust*, it came to be viewed as a typical story of the early modern temperament. Some readers and critics hailed it as the quintessential myth of the modern German disposition to accomplish great deeds of knowledge and science as well as to conquer all of Europe. In the opinion of some scholars and literary critics, the myth of Dr. Faustus has been interpreted as the most characteristic myth of modern humanity, which, under the influence of science and rationalism, firmly believes one can sign a dangerous blood-pact with Satan and outwit the Prince of Darkness and his emissaries while deciphering the secrets and powers of nature and gaining limitless wealth and knowledge.

Despite its nearly unbounded popularity in nineteenth-century German and broader European circles, the tragic myth of Dr. Faustus was not new when Goethe published the first part of his highly popular poetic version in 1808 and followed it up with the second part in 1832. Goethe had been working on part one of Faust since about the 1770s, and he continued working on part two until just a few days before his death in March of 1832. The Faust legend or myth is not easy to place within the canon of European literature. It is neither a typical story of the Enlightenment nor a typical story of the Romantic generation that followed the Age of Reason; and yet aspects of its character belong more among the "Storm and Stress" movement of the early Romantics than among the rationalism of the Enlightenment philosophers.

The theme of the "Devil's Pact" was not new either but had been part of medieval Christian demonology and the "witch-craze" since the 1200s (Boureau 2006, 68–92). Hence, the myth of Dr. Faustus dates back to the period of intense theological and moral transition during the Renaissance and Reformation periods when so much new knowledge was being discovered about the world, the solar system, the human body, and medicine. This "new knowledge" threatened some people with fear and foreboding because it seemed as if only God and Christ should be capable of commanding such experimental power over the natural world. Indeed, the actual myth may have originated from the life and career of the historical Dr. Johann Georg Faust (c. 1480–c. 1540), who may have been a real-life wandering magician, alchemist, and astrologer who claimed he could reproduce all the miracles of Christ by the ethereal powers he commanded. His story scared and captivated the imaginations of thousands of readers around Europe, but he was largely regarded as a sorcerer dealing in witchcraft and black magic. Some regard him as one of the earliest examples of the modern myth of the "mad scientist" who became intoxicated with his incessant quest for knowledge and power in the laboratory. He was eventually denounced by church officials as a fraud and accused of being in league with the Devil.

Most scholars of that early Modern era dabbled in magic, and it was from the esoteric traditions of Christian magical theology and alchemy that the ideals of experimental science emerged in the 1400s and 1500s. This work rested on the conjuring of spirits, angels, and/or demons in the practice of what some regarded as "White" or beneficent magic. The Pre-Modern mind of those times, however, was terrified by the work of alchemists and magicians who claimed to be able to heal various diseases and command the elements of nature by conjuring the beneficent presence of angels or demons in the laboratory to effect changes in the physical realm or to produce various medicinal tinctures and healing elixirs. To the uneducated, it was all just hocus-pocus black magic and malevolent trickery in league with Satan. This also set the stage for the expansion of the theme of the "mad scientist," or the well-meaning "sorcerer," who gets so carried away with his search for secret knowledge and personal fame and fortune while trying to alleviate human suffering and improve human life that he ends up deranged and insane. On a lighter note, this desire to make life's labors and needs easier was precisely how Mickey Mouse got himself into so much trouble as the sorcerer's apprentice who wanted to use magical spells to make a short-cut of his cleaning chores in Walt Disney's rendering of *Fantasia* (1940). Mickey Mouse had no idea how much he had yet to learn about sorcery and did not realize how often short-cuts usually create more work in the long run. Of course, in the realm of ethics and theodicy there are no short-cuts that might prevent us from facing the existential challenges of our fear of evil and human frailties.

One of the earliest versions of the Dr. Faustus story appeared in Germany in 1587 and spawned numerous other versions of the story across Germany in the late-1500s as well as throughout the 1600s and 1700s. Perhaps the most well-known of these was the English version by Christopher Marlowe, *The Tragicall History of the Life and Death of Doctor Faustus* (1604), published eleven years after Marlowe's mysterious death by stabbing at just twenty-nine years of age following his arrest on charges of blasphemy against religion in May 1593.

In its basic outlines the story of Dr. Faustus was nothing more than the theme of "the Devil's Pact" signed in blood by the main character and

Satan's representative in the form of the alleged demon, Mephistopheles, who negotiates the deal on behalf of his master, Lucifer. Faust is given twenty-four years on earth, during which time he is to gain untold knowledge of science, increased wealth, and all the pleasures he could ever desire, with Mephistopheles as his servant throughout the duration of the contract. At the end, however, his soul will belong to Lucifer and he will join him in Hell for all eternity. Dr. Faustus seems incapable of recognizing that his salvation is still possible if he would simply repent and ask for God's mercy, but his unbridled lust for knowledge and supernatural powers blinds him to the love of Christ and the redemptive power of divine grace. He wants to gain so much more knowledge than he already possessed that only by magical and demonological means can he accomplish the object of his lust. The battle between Good and Evil is central to this story, as is the struggle between Christ and Satan for the human soul. In some versions of the story Faust is carried off by devils, while in others his brains and eyes explode all over the walls and floor of his study as he dies and his soul is consigned to eternal damnation and the torments of Hell.

However, as we review the evolution of the myth of Dr. Faustus in its various versions and retellings from the 1500s to the 1900s, it becomes apparent that a fundamental change in modern human consciousness about the dichotomy between absolute Good and absolute Evil had taken root. Those scholars and literary critics who have tended to perceive in this myth something of the modern temperament of radical individual freedom to pursue unlimited human happiness, scientific knowledge, and technological progress may have come closest to helping us understand why this story captivated the imaginations of millions all over the world during the past five centuries. Indeed, the Promethean visions and Herculean dreams of modern consciousness have led us to assume that all things are possible for the individual wills of modern man and woman.

From an allegorical and symbolic perspective, it does seem as if in marshaling the human will to defy and outperform the will of God while deciphering the secrets of the natural world, we modern men and women have signed a pact with Satan. We have each gained personal powers and other powers assisted by amazing technological gadgets that were inconceivable to our ancestors just a few hundred years ago, yet the trickster demons and devils with which we negotiated this emancipation from the bondage of religious superstition may have abandoned us to our own hubris and moral shortcomings somewhere along the way. We are like wanderers perched between utopia and oblivion, claiming we can do all sorts of amazing and magical things yet lacking the means to recover the inner peace and harmony we lost when we began our Faustian quest for scientific knowledge and for power over the natural order of things. We have gone one step better than Dr. Faustus, for we have outwitted Satan and Mephistopheles and are now the invincible paragons of modern individualism and technology. The real tragedy of Dr. Faustus is perhaps the tragedy of modern progress and the exuberance of modern consciousness whose demonic ego-inflation unleashed a torrent of evil, destruction, and death in the twentieth century on a scale never before witnessed in human history. Is Satan really dead? Or does he merely slumber contentedly, knowing that he tricked modern Faustian-man and Faustian-woman into believing ourselves invincible and emancipated from superstition and demonic deception? Our self-conceit and exuberance perhaps masks Satan's continued reign as the Prince of Darkness.

## Satan's Resurrection

Regardless of whether Satan died due to the rise of modernity or was simply slumbering, one thing is for sure—he has been resurrected for our times. Take the example of a small Italian agricultural village called San Giovanni Rotondo, where at Our Lady of Grace Church a sickly young Capuchin friar named Padre Pio prostrated himself in thanksgiving on the morning of September 20, 1918. He had just concluded celebrating the Mass and retired to the church's choir stalls for prayers. It was then that the priest saw before him a mysterious person with blood dripping from his head, hands, feet, and side. Soon, Padre Pio experienced the visible stigmata. This was not the first time the priest manifested the five wounds of Jesus' crucifixion on his body, but unlike the previous incident, this one lasted fifty years, until his death in 1968. Although medical professionals never were able to explain what caused the wounds or why the wounds never became gangrenous or infected, controversies and complaints concerning his stigmata and personal life still arose. Eventually cleared by church authorities of any wrong doing, Padre Pio became a spiritual celebrity with hundreds of thousands making the pilgrimage to see the priest and search for a message of hope in a world wracked with war and suffering. On June 16, 2002, Pope John Paul II canonized Padre Pio, declaring him a saint.

Several biographers confirm that Padre Pio would at times spend an entire evening literally, not figuratively, wrestling with the Devil. These encounters could last days and turn quite violent. His first encounter with the Prince of Darkness occurred in 1906. The devil would appear in many apparitions and at times in its own horrible form. One such event is recorded to have taken place in July 1964 at 10 p.m. Friars heard a commotion coming from Padre Pio's cell. When they went to investigate, they found the priest on the floor with a cut across his forehead. Padre Pio is reported to have told his fellow friars that Satan was trying to scratch out his eyes.[2] For some, the metaphysical is real, and millions of believers worldwide would agree, regardless of how modern, incredulous, or rationalistic we may perceive ourselves to be.

Since the so-called Age of Enlightenment, modernity has attempted to replace the metaphysical with the power of reason and the insight of the sciences. But replacing the transcendent with science proved problematic. First, signs of the transcendent continue to invoke the very thing they signify. Satan as sign is but a pale representation of that which is beyond science, an incomplete commentary on the incomprehensible. And second, science did not prove to be humanity's new savior but in some cases proved it could be quite demonic. Both science and the rationalism that undergirds it can just as easily lead to evil as it can lead to good. Science produced the efficiency of the concentration camps, the philosophy of eugenics, and the capability to build nuclear weapons that can incinerate the entire earth and everything in it.

Satan's death has left an empty space that was once occupied with the means (as imperfect as they may have been) with which to describe evil—a space that neither Modern nor Postmodern thought has yet to fill properly. Regardless of our march toward an enlightened secularism and its rejection of Satan as the manifestation of evil or the opposite of God's divine order, we are still faced with moral and natural evil—the Holocaust, the Rwanda massacres, and Darfur's genocide—as well as the effects of Hurricane Katrina, the Christmas Day tsunami of 2004 that killed over 250,000 people along the Indian Ocean, and the 1985 Armero tragedy, which saw lava bury that Colombian town and kill an estimated 23,000 people. We are left with no other terms to describe these unfortunate events but "evil" and "satanic."

Satan may have to be resurrected in our postmodern age, assuming that the Enlightenment project succeeded in killing him. Nevertheless, this new Satan must be more sophisticated than how he came to be known in the so-called pre-modern world. Satan's metaphysical existence can never be separated from the politics of domination, specifically colonialism. It provides the dominant culture with the ability to depict those whom they conquer, oppress, and repress as the Other. The Satan symbol has always been complex and has been used effectively to explain evil and scare people into embracing Heaven. But presently that figure, while still being used to accomplish similar goals of the past, has also become an effective tool by which groups of people can be controlled by those who are able to manipulate the Satan signs and symbols.

Our interest in Satan has less to do with explaining his existence and more to do with understanding his function. What is the function of churches constructing the "truth" about Satan and imposing this truth upon the rest of society, usually with the help of politicians attempting to consolidate their own political power? Linking the construction of religious knowledge (that is, Satan) with power[3] to defend oneself from evil legitimizes a status quo that is repressive if not more evil than what we are defending ourselves from.

Foucault reminds us,

> We should admit . . . that power produces knowledge . . . that power and knowledge directly imply one another; that there is no power relation without the correlative constitution of a field of knowledge, nor any knowledge that does not presuppose and constitute at the same time power relations. (1995, 27)

Power produces reality—a reality that creates truth and domination based on said truth. Satan, and what Satan represents, is what the religious experts, and the politicians they support, say Satan is. The content of our sacred texts is then employed to justify, through proof-texting, what has already been defined.

The central point of power is located on the enunciation of good and evil. Definitions of Good and Evil, God and Satan, are placed into a binary system signifying what is acceptable and what is forbidden, what is legal and what is illegal. What "we" do is moral and right; they are the "evil Empire" or part of the "Axis of Evil." Or as President George W. Bush eloquently reminded us during his first public appearance after 9/11, "This will be a monumental struggle of good versus evil, but good will prevail" (Associated Press 2001). No need for Bush to reference Satan by name—the word "evil" suffices. The term Satan may appear too premodern for our modern, if not postmodern, sensibilities; nevertheless, believers in Satan's existence knew what the self-proclaimed born-again President was signifying by the undefined word-sign "evil." Satan is present without needing to utter his name.

As in the old television westerns, we wear the white hats and they wear the black ones. How those in power define Satan and his followers (that is, terrorists) facilitates a moral system where violence can be exerted, where said violence can be appropriated to benefit the few, and where injustices can be conducted under the cover of morality and national interests. Whosoever is our Other is defined as all that is bad, with an absence of any good, so that we in return can define ourselves through their negation. I am what they are not. They, like Satan, are evil: I therefore must be godly, representing the forces of the good. In effect, Satan is created in our own image, for we project upon Satan, and those who are our enemies whom we define as satanic, all the evil that exists in us.

But people are not typically satanic—systems, social structures, and ideologies are. Once the truth of Satan and what he signifies is defined in the Other by those who claim to have more knowledge than the rest, then all actions taken to combat this evil, regardless as to how dubious they may be (that is, using torture to extract information from those we define as terrorists or invading another country under the false pretense that they were hoarding weapons of mass destruction), becomes the acceptable norm because, after all, we who are virtuous act for the sake of the good. Maneuvering to create a body of beliefs to justify social and political power masks the goal of empowering the few. Still, to embody either absolute Evil or absolute Good in a person or a people dehumanizes them and the one creating the dichotomy.

But such power is not limited to the corporal. Defining Satan exerts power over the individual, relieving him or her from the responsibility of implementing justice and transferring said responsibility to religious experts and other professionals. Those who do not obey the church or the Christian political leaders the church supports have placed themselves (consciously or unconsciously) under Satan's reign. Such individuals, through their sin of disobedience, have attached themselves to the forces of evil. Salvation requires conversion—a turning away from evil toward good, a turning away from Satan toward God, a turning away from disobedience toward obedience. The fruit of salvation becomes obedience to church and our Christian political leaders through self-policing. As newly saved creatures, our response is no to the devil and yes to those who have set themselves up as God's spokespersons.

And yet, for those who are disenfranchised within society, what the dominant culture defines as virtue (submission and obedience) and sin (rebellion and disobedience) are precisely the causes for their marginalization. No wonder U.S. Christian ethics seems indistinguishable from middle-class bourgeois respectability. The opposite of how the dominant culture defines the common good may be exactly what those on their underside must pursue. These virtues advocated by the dominant culture accomplish the justification of dominion through religious piety. Maybe Foucault is correct in asserting that

> a "soul" inhabits [humans] and brings [them] to existence, which is itself a factor in the mastery that power exercises over the body. The soul is the effect and instrument of a political anatomy; the soul is the prison of the body. (1995, 30)

Whosoever controls the soul, religious and political leaders of whatever stripe, end up training the body to obey those who get to define Satan and all that he symbolizes. Control through religious fervor over Satan and the satanic is more effective than any despotic theodicy.

We have seen how Satan has been used historically to explain moral and natural evil. He can also be used to explain the structural evil that, through theological thought, moves to exercise control over individuals by guiding their actions to define for them what is good and what is evil. This understanding of power leads to the crux of what truly is satanic. Satan and the problem of evil is not a theological mystery upon which academics should ponder; rather, it is an ethical issue. Satan and all he signifies raises consciousness about the prevailing injustices leading anyone who dares to be a Christian to ponder what types of moral or social praxes need implementation in order to bring about a more just environment.

Ethics, defined as praxis, means that good or bad ethics is defined by the results of the praxis employed. That which is satanic becomes the misuse of power (assuming power's moral neutrality) to satisfy the appetites of the individual or those of the dominant culture benefiting by how society is structured. The CEO who through the power of creating financial models is compensated obscene and unjust salaries, the priest who through the power of his office abuses the altar boy, or the petty criminal who profits through the selling of women's bodies can be defined as satanic because they bring death (literally if not physically) to others. Just as satanic are the actions of central intelligence services that eliminate or torture individuals for the sake of maintaining their state's superpower predominance, the theology and/or ethics of a dominant culture that justifies oppressive social structures, or the repression of a people by either the political Right or Left so that an elite group can benefit. While those with power and privilege define rebellion and disobedience, law-breaking and disorder, as satanic, those seeking liberation and salvation from oppressive structures see this praxis as salvific and the dominant culture's definition of virtues as submission and obedience, law and order, when used to maintain repression, as satanic. What those in power define as satanic creates cycles of victimization for the disenfranchised. Ironically, the dominant culture's vices are the required virtues needed to survive, fight abuses, and seek justice.

In short, the ethical dilemma is how to use the Devil to unseat evil. The answer may lie in how we reimagine Satan. How those in power define Satan is unsatisfactory for the dispossessed. The error made by most liberals is quickly to dismiss the spiritual, the metaphysical, if not the transcendent, as the results of hyper-emotionalism. Conservatives, on the other hand, usually dismiss everything and everyone with whom they disagree as being in league with, or at least influenced by, the Devil. What we need as we conclude our historical quest for Satan is a fresh start at understanding the metaphysical underpinnings of our struggle to comprehend and conceive of evil. To that end, we conclude by asking what a liberative ethical understanding of Satan might look like.

## Satan Reimagined from a Liberative Perspective

Personifying evil has more to do with the vivid imaginations of our forebears than anything appearing within the Christian Scriptures. Take for example Frank E. Peretti's description of demons as found in his best-selling Christian novel *This Present Darkness*. Peretti writes:

> He was like a high-strung little gargoyle, his hide a slimy bottomless black, his body thin and spiderlike: half humanoid, half animal, totally demon. Two huge yellow cat-eyes bulged out of his face, darting to and fro, peering, searching. His breath came in short, sulfurous gasps, visible as glowing yellow vapor. (1986, 35)

Peretti, like so many today, bases his understanding of demons, devils, and Satan on a historical tradition whose worldview found the threat of Hell more effective in motivating the public to act a certain way than the promises of Heaven. To this end, Satan and his armies of demons continue to be the antithesis of God. Satan, as a means by which people are scared into embracing Heaven and controlled here on earth, had to be imagined as signifying absolute Evil.

In Satan, nothing that is good, humane, or redeemable can reside. Unless the wretched sinners cling to the mercies of God provided through Jesus Christ, the reprobate would spend all of eternity suffering in the never-ending fires of Hell where they would be tormented by hordes of hideous creatures as described by Peretti above. Even if we wanted to move beyond dualistic notions of absolute Good (God) and absolute Evil (Satan), the fact remains that the current religious imagination of Christians, fueled by centuries of reinforcement from popular culture, is locked in this binary worldview that dates back to the early church and its struggle against paganism. To hint that evil may come from God (as did some biblical passages), or that Satan can lead believers to good consequences, continues to be considered blasphemy among most Christians.

Christian popular culture continues to simplify Satan as pure evil, even though, as we have already seen, the biblical text presents a more historically complex and ambiguously evolving figure. The problem of understanding who and what Satan is goes further than just understanding what the figure represents, either literally or symbolically. Missing from the biblical text, as well as from Christian creeds and doctrines, is a definitive statement on what actually is evil. Missing is a doctrine or definition on the very nature of evil. For most of us, to rephrase Supreme Court Justice Stewart's attempt to define hard-core pornography, when it comes to evil, we know it when we see it.[4] We are left with a reality that exists in our world and in our lives for which God might provide redemption but no official explanation. Our attempt to "fill in the gaps" in the absence of a cohesive theological understanding of evil has led many Christians throughout the past two centuries to simplify the dilemma by simply understanding Satan as the manifestation of everything that God is not, and thus the reason and cause of all evil that humans face.

In 1970 the American actor and comedian Flip Wilson crossed-dressed as Geraldine and made the phrase "the devil made me do it" a popular expression for that era. At times comedy, more so than theological tomes, can get to the heart of ethical dilemmas faster and more succinctly. Blaming Satan can absolve oppressors quicker than God's grace. I really am not that bad—so the logic goes—it is Satan, since the Garden of Eden, who has been leading humanity astray. I am really a good person, but I do wrestle with my secret demons. When I participate in the pain of others (not just physical but also caused by society and economics) of others, it is the devil that made me do it. Thankfully, Jesus took our place on the cross so that we do not need to pay the price for our sins. The devil made me do it, and Jesus cleaned up my mess. As a new creature in Christ "I" can move on without really addressing the consequences of or restitution for those sins the devil made me do. Hence, Nazi concentration guards can torture all week long and still attended worship services on Sunday mornings. Politicians can lead armies to war under false pretenses without addressing the tens of thousands, if not hundreds of thousands, who are killed or maimed because, after all, our intentions were pure—it was the enemy who was really evil. Repentance from Wall Street greed that tanked the U.S. economy and swindled thousands out of their life savings in 2008 can occur without having to deal with issues of public accountability and restitution to individual investors.

The complexity of oppression lies in its interconnectedness. A desire to oversimplify the complexity of how structures of power operate and how these structures cause disenfranchisement for the vast majority of the earth's inhabitants creates an attraction for necessary illusions that serve as answers for many of the evils that are present—specifically those evils that safeguard the privilege of the few. The illusion of Satan as the father of all evil not only excuses and absolves God of any responsibility for evil but also excuses and absolves those with power and privilege who benefit from the status quo that causes suffering for many who reside on the margins of society. Satan is the cause of all the world's hunger, disease, and oppression—instead of those humans who are enriched by such misery. The link between the riches and power of the few and the misery caused by poverty and oppression of the many is obscured. Satan, as cause of all human misery, becomes a necessity not just for God but for the elite few.

### Satan as Trickster?

Because of the very nature and complexity of the trickster figure, he[5] is difficult to describe or define. In some cases he plays the role of a noble trickster, elsewhere he is a mean, vengeful trickster. Regardless of how he is portrayed, agreement exists that he is the consummate survivor, a joker who is usually depicted as childish or clownish, competent in outwitting those who fancy themselves the trickster's superiors. Trickster figures can be described as ruthless, lustful, nasty, and greedy; nevertheless, their tricks can prove to be insightful, helpful, sage, and liberating. He is found on the crossroads of life, in the intersection of ambiguities and fluid boundaries. Although truthful in revealing what most wish to keep hidden, the trickster operates in a realm beyond good and evil, beyond the framework of what society, culture, or religion defines as right or wrong. Tricksters seldom recognize rules or regulations of either society or of the gods.

Possessing amazing abilities for survival and shape-shifting, tricksters also can serve as models for humans who must endure oppressive situations. Or more than likely, they are surrogate figures upon whom the survival tactics of the marginalized are projected. Trickster folklore, at times humorous, resonates with survival strategies that appear to be innocent, childlike stories. Not surprisingly, most oppressed or marginalized groups have stories concerning a trickster figure. Usually portrayed as physically inferior to more powerful enemies, the trickster relies on cunning and deception to exploit the greed, weakness, or false sense of self-righteousness possessed by those who are more dominant. The importance of the trickster is so significant to marginalized communities that they are often found embedded within their religious traditions.

The function of the divine messenger as trickster is to place humans and gods alike in compromising positions. The purpose of his tricks is to test others to consider the spiritual consequences of their actions and to force those seeking solutions to their dilemmas to explore possible alternatives previously unexplored. For these reasons, many faiths that possess a trickster figure neither fear nor villainize him; rather, they usually express admiration. Why? Because it is the trickster figure who undoes the order established by those in power, outwitting and subverting the status quo that is so oppressive to marginalized communities.

The trickster figure found within most religious traditions is never confused with the creator. Nevertheless, his deeds have the ability to alter creation and the usual outcomes of most ethical dilemmas. And contrary to the attempts of most Christian missionaries, the trickster is also never confused with a Satan-type figure that signifies absolute Evil. Nevertheless, many Christian missionaries reinterpreted the religions of their prospective converts by relegating their cherished trickster figures to the realm of the demonic (if not their whole faith tradition). The trickster cannot be understood as being moral, even though he is ethical. True, the trickster deals in lies and deceit, but only to reveal a deeper truth obscured by moralists. Through his tricks, he creates situations that force humans to imagine new possibilities that realism, conventional wisdom, or rationalism have ruled out. He refuses to remain a passive participant in social or religious structures that relegate him to the margins (De La Torre 2010, 105–6).

In his work *Domination and the Arts of Resistance*, James C. Scott argues that trickster figures are part of a group politics of disguise and anonymity that occurs publically and yet is designed to have a double meaning that allows the powerless to speak to authority while shielding and protecting their identity. Nearly every oppressed group has some type of trickster legend that usually appears as an innocent, entertaining tale about animals or human figures. For those who are able to hear, they are tales that celebrate the cunning wit of the trickster who navigates a treacherous environment geared for his destruction. Regardless of the traps set out to destroy the trickster, in the end the trickster triumphs over those who are more powerful. Usually too weak or too small to overcome their oppressors, the trickster studies the habits of his oppressors. By taking advantage of their voracity or credulity, and by using deceptive methods, the trickster manages to be victorious over more potent enemies (Scott 1990, 162–66).

The marginalized have little choice but to develop tactics and strategies to cope and survive when in the clutches of their oppressors. The trickster figure can provide oppressed groups a survival mindset or paragon of human potential to emulate. For the oppressed to challenge directly the more powerful might lead to their demise. Through deceptive and cunning resistance, however, the chances for success are greatly enhanced.

Most would argue that Christianity lacks a trickster figure, but we propose that originally Satan played this role. Although Satan has come to represent the embodiment of evil, we suspect that what the figure of Satan originally signified has its roots in the ancient trickster figure. It is to these roots that we wish to return. If Satan was to be conceived as a trickster, then his existence not only accomplishes the purposes of God but also those of marginalized groups. But what would a Satan as trickster who embodies relative evil as opposed to absolute Evil look like? What if Christianity were to return to the original biblical understandings of Satan, that is, Satan as a faithful servant of God whose responsibility, whose duty, is to serve as an adversary to humanity? Some would argue that it was this possibility of trickery versus personal salvation and repentance that lay at the heart of the intriguing popularity of the modern myth of Dr. Faustus and his contractual dealings with Mephistopheles. What if we allow this understanding of Satan to be influenced by other early faith traditions that emphasized a trickster figure?

To begin seeing Satan as a trickster is to move away from the binary concept that relegates him to the manifestation of absolute Evil toward a concept of him being capable of doing both good and evil. Or better yet, it involves seeing him as an entity that can be used by God to provide humanity with alternatives to either do good or evil. By creating havoc and bringing trials and tribulation into people's lives, humans might be moved from complacency and complicity with oppressive structures toward new options—options that include doing and moving toward the good. To conceive of Satan as a trickster is not necessarily to tolerate him nor to make him more palatable and less dangerous. Satan as trickster exists for the sake of the greater good of accomplishing God's will. Satan as trickster creates spiritual disorder, thus becoming a means by which God provokes the complicit toward sound moral choices. Prior to exploring the Christian ethical ramifications of moving away from a Satan who is absolute Evil toward a Satan who is a trickster, it would be beneficial to explore how the trickster figure has been understood within other traditions.

### Greco-Roman

Throughout this book's earlier chapters, we discussed a few of the diverse myths and legends about the gods and goddesses of the cultures and nations of the ancient Mediterranean basin. These deities played a dynamic role in the lives of the men and women who were their devotees and loyal followers for several millennia before the coming of Christianity and the waning of the ancient pagan world of Antiquity. While the Greek father of the gods, Zeus, sitting on his throne atop Mount Olympus and the Roman lord of the heavens, Jupiter, were by no means trickster deities, they each logged their fair share of stories and legends about how they interacted with mortals. Sometimes these deities acted playfully and other times more manipulatively.

On the other hand, the Greek messenger of the gods, Hermes, and his Roman counterpart, Mercury, were famous for their benevolent manifestations as the Greco-Roman trickster deities who often led people to their higher moral purposes and personal destiny. Hermes came to be regarded as the patron Lord of artists, scholars, and scientists for his allegorical role in shaping the ancient educational tradition of the Seven Liberal Arts. Indeed, Hermes was also known as the "Good Shepherd," an epithet that led many ancient pagans and early Christians to equate him allegorically with Jesus Christ. The Roman goddess Diana, the huntress, was a sort of trickster figure as well, leading both male and female devotees to an appreciation for nature and animals, the forest, and archery. Some of these deities had a tendency to play hide and seek with their devotees in a magical game of self-discovery and introspection whose outcome was often the spiritual transformation of their individual followers.

For example, the Greek god Eros and his Roman counterpart Cupid, signified the power and mystery of desire, love, and attraction. Eros and Cupid were notorious for firing off their sacred arrows of divine inspiration, or darts of "love at first sight," which no amount of human rationality or self-inflicted moral restraint could resist. The attractions triggered by Eros baffled the human imagination! Falling in love was often seen by the ancients as a type of madness of the heart. When Cupid's arrow takes flight, human reason beware! Modern readers mistake these arrows of attraction as always dealing with carnal lust or excessive hedonism, but as ancient philosophers knew all too well, it is entirely possible to be stricken with unexplainable love at first sight for an idea, a great book, a noble cause, or an artistic vision such as those that led to the construction of the Seven Wonders of the Ancient World. Looked at from this angle, Eros and Cupid performed a trickster function by compelling ancient men and women to peek over the walls of reason and rationalism and discover something wild and spontaneous about themselves that held a key to actualizing their full humanity. Hence, it was not mere carnal pleasure or reckless lust for one's appetites and passions but a desire to be more than one's mundane complacency and usual daily routines might suggest that one is destined by the gods to be.

An element of mischief, playfulness, and the theme of possibly being led astray were common motifs in the ancient mythological roles of Greco-Roman trickster deities. Despite the ongoing popularity of Greco-Roman mythology in today's world, Eros and Cupid, Hermes and Mercury, as well as all the other ancient gods and goddesses who manifested as trickster figures were dismissed by early Christian writers and theologians as demons or dangerous spirits capable of possessing unsuspecting or weak souls and leading them astray. Christians believed the Incarnation of Jesus Christ liberated them from the power of all pagan demons and devils and that by the power of the Holy Spirit sent forth at Pentecost they too could tread on serpents, cast out demons, and vanquish God's great enemy, Satan.

### African

Throughout numerous African indigenous traditions there exists an animal or a quasi-deity who plays the role of the trickster. And while much can be written comparing and contrasting different African trickster figures, for our purposes we will concentrate on just one, Eshu of Yoruba (present-day Nigeria), also known as Legba in Benin. Eshu's influence is not only felt in Africa but also in the Western Hemisphere where he is known as Elegguá in the Afro-Cuban religion known as Santeriá, Exu in Brazilian Candomblé, Legba in Caribbean vodou, and Lucero in Palo Mayombe. Of all the gods (known as orishas), Eshu is the most cunning.

One of the most popular stories concerning Eshu is based on a trick he played on two neighbors whose farms were adjacent to each other. Eshu decided to walk down the road that divided the two farms wearing a hat. One side of the hat was red, the other side was black (the colors red and black are sacred to Eshu). After walking down the road the two neighbors entered into a quarrel as to the color of Eshu's hat. Each neighbor accused the other of lying. Their squabble got so out of control that the king was forced to settle the matter. Eshu was eventually summoned to testify, where he produced the hat. His trickery shows the neighbors that neither one of them was a liar but that both were fools. In this fashion, Eshu reveals the truth about both of them, so that by revealing their weaknesses they might learn from their mistakes and change for the better.

### African-American

The concept of trickster among Africans came to the Western Hemisphere along with slavery. Within the U.S., the best known trickster among African-Americans is Brer Rabbit (probably a predecessor of Bugs Bunny). Stories concerning Brer Rabbit abound, but a brief review of just one of the more popular ones will suffice for our purposes. One day Brer Fox, who hated Brer Rabbit, decided to lay a trap in order to capture and kill him. So Brer Fox fashioned a cute baby figure made of tar and placed it at a crossroads. When

Brer Rabbit spotted the Tar Baby, he approached it and started a conversation, but the Tar Baby, obviously, did not respond. Frustrated about not receiving a response, Brer Rabbit shook the Tar Baby only to get his paw caught in the tar. Unable to free his paw, Brer Rabbit used his other paw for leverage, only to get that one also stuck. Aggravated, he used his two hind legs to push himself away from the Tar Baby, only to get them also stuck.

At this point Brer Fox jumps out from behind the bushes where he was hiding. With Brer Rabbit immobilized, he was at the mercy of Brer Fox. As Brer Fox pondered how to kill Brer Rabbit, Brer Rabbit began to think fast. Brer Fox asked Brer Rabbit what should be done. Should he be roasted and eaten? Maybe hung? Or maybe drowned in the river? Brer Rabbit responded by saying that any of those methods were fine as long as Brer Fox did not throw him in the briar patch. "The briar patch," thought Brer Fox, "Brer Rabbit would be torn to pieces." And with that he lifted Brer Rabbit and threw him into the briar patch. Brer Fox waited to hear the agonizing screams of Brer Rabbit, but all he heard was silence. After some time he saw Brer Rabbit on top of a nearby hill combing the tar out of his fur. Brer Fox had forgotten that Brer Rabbit was born and bred in the briar patch. The trickster, through deceit, overcame his near fatal predicament, brought on by his rashness, at the hands of a superior foe. The lesson the trickster teaches in this instance is that the oppressed must learn to curb their rash acts or temper and instead channel their anger into cunning acts of deception that might lead to their survival within a hostile environment.

### Native American

Among the lore of the indigenous Native nations are several trickster figures, most notably: Spider, Raven, Old Man, Wisagatchak (portrayed as Canadian Jay Bird or as Fox), and Coyote. For the purposes of our abbreviated discussion, we will concentrate on just one of the Coyote tales from one of the indigenous nations to illustrate how the trickster operates. The Karuk people, of what is now northern California, tell the tale of the three Yellow Jackets (another name for the wasp insect) who had fire. The three sisters refused to share the fire with the other animal relatives, many of which froze during the cold winter nights. Coyote devised a plan to steal the fire. With the enlisted help of the other animals, Coyote approached the Yellow Jackets and stole their burning stick. As he was running away, chased by the three sisters, he quickly passes the stick to Eagle, who passes it on to Lion, who hands it off to other animals lying in wait. Finally, the burning stick is given to Frog, who hides it in his mouth on the river's bottom. Unable to find the stick, the Yellow Jackets abandon the chase. Eventually, the Frog spits it out where it is immediately swallowed by Willow Tree. Coyote then teaches all the animals how to extract the fire from the tree. He shows them that if they rub two sticks together over dry moss they can retrieve the fire. Hence, from that day forward all animals had fire. Seeing an unjust hording of a commodity needed for the benefit and survival of the community, the trickster steals, considered an evil act, so that a greater good could be realized.

## Christianity

A simple good-versus-evil, binary understanding of reality leads to an ethical perspective that might cause more evil than good. A world where everyone and everything is either with or against God leads to great atrocities by those "with God" in their defense against the perceived threat of those "against God" (whom those on God's side usually define as Satanic). Because such an ethical framework causes more evil than good, we are in need of a new way of understanding what is satanic, what is Satan.

Throughout this book's quest for the historical Satan, we explored the development of the concept we have come to know as Satan. As we saw, throughout the sacred texts of Christianity and church history, the concept of Satan has remained fluid, constantly changing throughout the ages. So far, this quest has shown how Satan matured within the biblical text from being part of God's council serving God, who at God's request would become the judicial adversary to humans, to being absolute and pure evil, independent of God. But what if we were to return to an earlier understanding of Satan, specifically Satan as part of God's council fulfilling the role of trickster? Such a Satan would serve as God's adversary while accomplishing God's purposes, taking on the divine responsibility of revealing paths previously hidden by upsetting the status quo.

Learning to interpret Satan as the ultimate trickster rather than the embodiment of absolute Evil can lead to ethical praxes that are more liberative because they deal with the causes of oppressive structures in the physical world rather than simply blaming the present reality on the metaphysical presence of evil or on the moral depravity of humanity. Tricksters create situations that force the one being tested to look for new ways to deal with the discord that has entered their life. What society normalizes can mask oppressive structures that make resistance seem futile as both those who benefit and those afflicted by those structures are lulled into complicity. Seeking new alternatives to the surrounding trials and tribulations can lead the one being tested to discover opportunities previously unrecognized. Likewise, it could raise the consciousness of the one benefitting from the status quo, leading them to repentance and to a more liberative course of action that can result in the former oppressors discovering their own salvation.

Unfortunately, an original understanding of Satan as trickster has been lost by Christians. History has conditioned Christians to read into the biblical text an understanding of Satan as the evil antithesis of God. But what would happen if Christians were to reread some of the biblical texts with new eyes, refusing to impose their theology upon the text? What if they were to read the Scriptures conscious of Satan's role as trickster? If they employ this strategy in reading the text, they might discover a Satan that can be understood as a trickster, used by God for the benefit of humans or a being used by God for their ruin. Satan's role becomes a bit more complex than being simply evil incarnate. The trickster's role can lead to good, as in the case of conscientization. But it can also lead to destruction. It all depends on the one being tested, such as the failure of Dr. Faustus to be moved to humility and repentance, even as Mephistopheles reminded him of God's benevolence, before it was too late to save his soul. Trials and tribulations can lead Christians to be of good cheer because they recognize that Christ who is with them has overcome the world. Or they can lead them to greater misery and destruction because they refuse grace. If they believe the deception of Satan's tricks, rather than rise above it, they can face devastation. It does not depend on Satan, an implement used by God. Rather, it depends on humans and the choices they make.

As we have seen, there is not one clear portrait of Satan from Genesis through Revelation. Satan evolves over the centuries and millennia, leading to contradictory descriptions as to who and what exactly is Satan. It is not our task to reconcile these different portraits of Satan. Our task is to make a preferential choice for an earlier biblical understanding of Satan over and against what has become the normative portrait that resonates with popular culture across time and place. We propose to return to the early biblical Satan because it leads, in our opinion, to a better ethical framework from which to operate in the bringing about of justice and redemption. For example,

Satan in the book of Job leads Job beyond simplistic theodicy solutions that assume unfortunate circumstances are the result of God's punishment for peccadilloes. The Satan who confronts Jesus in the desert helps Jesus, in all his humanity, to understand his own divinity and the important public ministry he undertakes after the sojourn in the desert. Like tricksters of other various indigenous traditions we examined, Satan's temptation leads Jesus to understand his mission and purpose.

In order to grasp the concept and implications of Satan as trickster better, let us turn our attention to six biblical passages in which Satan plays a major role: Abraham's temptation and God's attack against Moses; the moral difficulties of the book of Job; the temptation of Jesus in the desert; Peter's temptation; and Judas' temptation.

**Abraham and Moses.** The two most revered patriarchs, Abraham and Moses, have strange encounters with God that do not shine a favorable light upon Yahweh. In the Abraham story we are told, "God tested Abraham, and said to him, Abraham. . . . Take now your son, your one and only son whom you love, Isaac . . . and offer him as a burnt sacrifice" (Gen 22:1-2). We can only imagine the repercussions if, today, someone took one of their children and attempted to offer him or her as a sacrifice to please God, professing that God had told them to do it. No doubt such a person would be arrested and placed under psychiatric care, as they should be. But the Abraham story has become so familiar that we fail to read its disturbing dark side. God decides to test Abraham his servant. And it is not until the knife is at the child's throat that God stops Abraham. What psychological harm must that boy have suffered for the rest of his life, trying to reconcile the everlasting love of his Father in heaven with the image of his father on earth holding a knife to his throat? If we who fall short of God's perfection would never consider suggesting the evil of filicide as a demonstration of loyalty, how, then, can God?

As disturbing as the Abraham story is, an episode with Moses, which is usually ignored for good reason, is more troublesome. God encounters Moses on God's holy mountain and commissions Moses to return to the court of the Pharaoh and demand that his children, the Israelites, for whom God makes a preferential option, be set free. Moses obeys and heads toward Egypt. The text tells us, "And it happened on the way [to Egypt to confront the Pharaoh], at the night resting place, YHWH met [Moses] and sought to slay him" (Exod 4:24). God tells Moses to go to Egypt to save God's chosen. Moses obeys and sets out on the return trek. But on the way, God appears and tries to kill Moses!

Abraham encounters an insecure God who must have God's creation prove their loyalty through filicide. Moses encounters a schizophrenic God who tells him to go back to Egypt and then attempts to kill him for doing what God demanded. In both cases, God is not portrayed in a positive light. What makes the Abraham passage distressing is that there is no Satan to test Abraham. God is doing the testing. Likewise, what makes the Moses story so upsetting is that God, not Satan, sets out to kill Moses for accomplishing the task set out by God. Were the text to have said that Satan put Abraham to the test, or that Satan tried to kill Moses, then the theology would be more in sync with how Christianity has presented the person of Satan through the ages. But as we have already seen, when the Torah was being written the concept of Satan was not yet fully developed. God is seen as being solely responsible for these disquieting acts.

The early rabbinical commentators also had difficulty with a God that would lead God's servant to commit the heinous crime of butchering his child, or with a God who would attempt to kill God's very own obedient messenger. Subsequently, an attempt was made to correct the biblical text so that God could be shown in a better light. To save God from such a negative reading, someone else needed to be blamed. This was accomplished by introducing a demon figure named Mastema (the personification of the Hebrew word for hostility) in the Pseudepigraphal book of *Jubilees*.

The Abraham story, as retold in the book of *Jubilees*, states, "And the prince Mastema came before God and said, 'Behold, Abraham loves Isaac his son, and delights in him above everthing else; tell him to offer Isaac as a burnt-offering on the altar, and you will see if he will do as you command. You will discover if he is faithful in everything you ask of him'" (17:16). It is Mastema, not God, who comes up with the idea to sacrifice Abraham's son. As for Moses, it was Mastema who attempted to slay Moses and deliver the Egyptians out of his hands, but God intervened and saved Moses from the clutches of Mastema (48:2-4). It is interesting to note that in the Abraham story, Mastema is subsequently replaced with Satan by the time we get to the Talmud (Sanhedrin 89b). It is Satan who, like in the case of Job, makes the suggestion to God to tempt Abraham. If we seriously consider a trickster role in Judeo-Christian thought, we are left with the ambiguity as to who exactly is the trickster—God or Satan.

**Job.** Job also presents a disturbing portrait of God. As if on a dare, God pours upon his faithful servant Job all manner of calamity to see whether Satan is right that Job's loyalty to God could be broken. God allows Satan to test Job by wiping out all of his livestock, all of his children, and finally all his health, but Job refuses to curse God and die. When Job asks why such evil has befallen him, God responds sarcastically to Job's hubris of asking why. After all, was Job present when God set the foundations of the earth? (38:4). In other words, how dare Job ask God to explain God's self? Still, we are left wondering, if indeed Satan is a trickster, who exactly is he tricking? Job or God?

We do learn from the story that innocent suffering does exist. Human suffering is not necessarily God's retribution for evils committed by humans. The book of Job does raise the theodicy question as to why bad things happen to good people. Maybe the ultimate message of the book of Job is captured in the bumper-sticker truism that "sh*t happens." True, by the end of the book God does restore Job's health and wealth. But really? What about the children? Job's children, seven sons and three daughters, are killed by Satan on God's authority (1:2-9). In a manner of speaking, God also restores Job's children. He fathers seven new sons and two new daughters, replacing those whom Satan killed (42:13-17). Still, for anyone who ever lost a child, no number of additional children can ever assuage the grief or replace the sense of loss of the original dead child. There really is no happy ending for Job.

**The Temptation of Jesus.** Who is this being that is tempting Jesus? All three Synoptic Gospels recount the story of how Jesus was led by the Spirit into the wilderness to be tempted by the Devil (*diabolos*); but only Matthew and Mark refer to this Devil as Satan (Matt 4:10; Mark 1:13). Matthew also refers to "the devil" as the *peirazō*, which can be translated as "the one who tests." This is an important descriptive term, because in his first appearance in the Gospel story, Satan is not introduced as absolute Evil, but as one who tests, as one who, as trickster, is testing Jesus. Satan as "tester" does not necessarily connote bad intentions. The one doing the testing may have the best of intentions for the one being tested. Still, if one of Satan's roles as trickster is to create situations where testing occurs, why then test Jesus? What could Jesus possibly learn from such a test?

Matthew tells us that Jesus fasted for forty days and forty nights. He was hungry. Three times Satan tries to test (trick) Jesus. The first test concerns possessions, "command that these stones may become bread" (4:3); then privilege, "If you are the son of God, throw yourself down" (4:6); and finally power, "I will give all these [kingdoms] to you if you fall down and worship me" (4:9). As trickster, Satan tests Jesus with the temptations faced by all of humanity, unearned possessions, privilege, and power, but Jesus refuses; and in so doing, thanks to Satan, Jesus learns something about himself and his mission. Only after the testing can Jesus begin his public ministry with a clearer understanding of his goals [see Figure 13].

**Peter's Testing.** Luke 22 describes the testing of Peter. During their last Passover meal together, Jesus singles out the disciple he calls "the Rock." He says, "Simon, Simon, behold, Satan *has obtained permission for demands to test you*,[6] to sift you like wheat. But I have prayed for you that your faith may not fail. And once converted, strengthen your brothers" (Luke 22:31-32). Similar to the story of Job, Satan tests the Apostles, specifically Peter. But here is the crucial point: before Satan can wreak havoc through Peter's temptation, Satan must first ask for permission, just as he did with Job. Why would Jesus grant permission for Satan to "sift" Peter "like wheat"? The answer: because through Satan's testing the apostle emerged stronger, better prepared to face all future forms of trials and temptations. Thanks to Satan as trickster, the apostle's arrogance is checked as he learns instead to rely on God's grace. Once Peter recovers from failing the test, specifically denying Christ three times before the cock crowed, and is converted by what he learned, he would be able humbly to strengthen his brothers.

This is not Peter's first encounter with Satan's trickery. Prior to their last meal together, Jesus asks his disciples, "Who do you say that I am" (Matt 16:15). Peter responds by saying, "You are the Messiah, the Son of the living God" (16:16). Jesus gives a blessing to Peter, for God the Father revealed this truth to Peter. Peter is to be the Rock upon which the church will be built, and not even the gates of Hades will prevail against this foundation. Not surprisingly, providing the correct answer goes to Peter's head, for a few verses later, when Jesus states he will be put to death when they reach Jerusalem, Peter arrogantly protested, saying that such a thing would never happen.

Jesus rebukes Peter's bravado with the words, "Get behind me Satan. You are an offence to me for you do not think about the things of God, but the things of humans" (16:23).

In one verse Peter is expounding God's revelation, only to be possessed by Satan's mind a few verses later. Did Satan replace God, casting God out of Peter so that instead of God doing the revealing it is now Satan? Is Peter simply a puppet, a mouthpiece for whoever happens to be in possession of him? One second God, the next Satan? Or is Peter simply a schizophrenic, literally having "a split mind"—one mind from where God's goodness provides revelations and another mind controlled by Satan to spew evil?

Or maybe it is not so black and white. Maybe Peter, like the rest of us, demonstrates how even those who listen to God can still be tricked into ignoring the things of God. When Jesus calls Peter Satan, Peter is not to be condemned for all eternity as being in league with the forces of darkness. Rather, Peter is tricked into focusing upon human things and in so doing forgets that he, as the Rock, will be the base on which Christ's church is to be built. The trickster Satan is able to accomplish God's purpose. Jesus' sharp rebuttal shocks Peter into remembering that it is not him who will build this church but Christ. Peter may stumble for being beguiled by Satan, but in the end he is made stronger and more resilient in doing the work of Christ.

**Judas' Testing.** Peter illustrates how Satan as trickster can lead the one being tested toward a higher consciousness for the sake of the good. But the tested one can always choose the option of doing what is wrong, not necessarily pure evil. The biblical example of Judas' temptation illustrates this point. During Jesus and the Apostles' final Passover meal together, we are told that "Satan entered into Judas, the one being called Iscariot" (Luke 22:3). How can one not feel sorry for Judas? Here he is, possessed by absolute Evil, whom he supposedly—according to our present-day understanding of Satan—is unable to resist. And to make matters worse, he is damned for doing what was beyond his control. Or was it?

Judas' satanic possession is unlike the other demon possessions found throughout the Gospels, where the victim manifests physical or mental distress. In the case of Judas, Satan's possession indicates a complete moral failure on the part of Judas. Like Peter, Judas is tested. Like Peter, Judas fails the test. Both betray Jesus, Judas for thirty pieces of silver at Gethsemane and Peter three times before the cock crows. But unlike Peter, there is no repentance by

Judas. Satan as trickster strengthens Peter's resolve as he discovers his need for God's grace. Satan also as trickster leads Judas toward ruin and destruction, because in the end he rejects grace and instead chooses death.

If the trickster figure uses deception and guile to overcome the one who is more powerful, then Peter and Judas, or anyone else for that matter, can only be harmed by Satan if they allow their greed or pride to be manipulated. The biblical text consistently reminds us that Satan has no power except for what God gives him and what we allow him to exert. According to James, we are to "resist the devil and he will flee" (4:7). In the temptations of Peter and Judas, although possessed, the tested humans retain the ability to resist being outwitted by the "powerless" Satan or to let the trickster defeat them.

## The Ethics of a Christian Trickster

Radical monotheism means that there is only one omnipotent and omnipresent God, creator of all that is and ever will be. To suggest that there exists another being that rivals God, that is omnipresent like God, that is so omnipotent that it can challenge the might and love of God, makes Satan into another God. Christianity is thus reduced to a good God and an evil God, which was one of the profound problems set off by the medieval dichotomy of Christ versus the Anti-Christ. Such a conclusion is problematic, for it portrays Satan as a hostile, independent entity assailing God's people in the quest for supremacy. But if Christians claim that there is only one God through whom all things are maintained and sustained, then Satan has no knowledge and no power that is not derived from God. Satan, like any other spiritual emissary, exists to serve God's purposes. The biblical text, specifically in the six passages just reviewed, seem to confirm the proposition that Satan has no power or authority except that given to him by God, concluding that Satan, and the havoc he causes as trickster, is necessary for God's ultimate purposes to be realized.

The de-emphasizing of a binary system of either absolute Good or absolute Evil moves us away from the impossible task of maintaining an ethical framework where we either emulate God's pure goodness or become wretched creatures under Satan's control. The concept of Satan as pure evil contributes to the theological concept of total depravity among humans found within most Christian faith traditions. How many religious leaders, congregations, and movements attempted purity and self-righteousness only to ignore their darker side, and in so doing fall victim to what they proposed to battle by persecuting others who fall short of their lofty and righteous expectations? The Spanish Inquisition serves as an excellent example of how, by denying one's darker side, great evils can be committed in the name of faith.

So can anyone ever really be good? The Gospel of Luke has an interesting exchange between Jesus and the one whom we have come to know as the rich young ruler. According to the text, "A certain ruler asked [Jesus], 'Good Teacher, what have I to do to inherit eternal life?' But Jesus said to him, 'Why do you say that I am good? No one is good, except one, God'" (18:18-19). Yes, we all fall short of the glory of God—and that's fine. In fact, it is probably healthier to accept the limits of the human condition than maintain any pretense of being totally good. This is not to say that moral ideals are wrong or should be discarded. Rather, it is about coming to terms with the reality that we could never achieve such ideals. And perhaps one of the trickster's favorite ploys is to convince us that such ideals are reachable. Our failure to recognize the evil within leads us to commit greater atrocities against those who fall short of our expectations while sincerely believing in our own goodness.

Satan as trickster serves a crucial role. Can we as humans ever truly advance without moral conflict? Without tragedy? Without struggle? How do we practice righteousness unless there is temptation in our lives? Although Satan as a trickster-hero becomes a scapegoat upon which humans can project their unrealized aspirations, their fears, and their failures, his trials and tests force humans to flex their moral muscles and in the process raise their own consciousness and self-knowledge. Without the darker side of the spiritual, we might never strengthen our own resolve to do good. In the final analysis, Satan as trickster is an agent of change. And here is the ultimate paradox: Satan as trickster teaches humanity how to walk humbly in the paths of the Lord. While possibly taking pleasure in testing human weaknesses and strengths, Satan can create situations that can lead humans to make proper moral choices.

Take the example of Paul, whose flesh was torn by Satan so that he "may not be made prideful" (2 Cor 12:7). Who "gave" Satan to Paul? The text does not say. And why is this Satan doing good, specifically keeping Paul from the sin of pride? Paul understood that Satan could be used by God to lead humans toward God's hope for their salvation. This is demonstrated by his recommendation to the church at Corinth that the man guilty of incest be handed over "to Satan for the destruction of his flesh so that his spirit can be saved on the Day of the Lord" (1 Cor 5:5). Yes, Satan may destroy the flesh, but he does so for a reason, to save the soul. But Paul also knew that the faithful could fail the tests of "the one who tests (*peirazō*)," the same word used for Satan in Jesus' temptation in the desert. When he writes to the Thessalonians, Paul expresses concern that they "might be tested by the one who tests and thus [Paul's] work might have been in vain" (1 Thess 3:5). The biblical text indicates that Satan's trickery can lead humans to sin or can prevent people from sinning. The hope of God is that through the tests administered by Satan, believers would mature in their faith. Yet there always exists the possibility that the test, like all tests, could be failed.

Through Satan's tests and tricks, those afflicted by oppressive societal structures can become aware of how racism, sexism, and classism are embedded within social, political, and economic structures that contribute to their suffering and disenfranchisement. What has been presented as legitimate and normative is disrupted. Through this process, Satan is able to lead those who are oppressed, making them conscious of how these structures operate to privilege a small elite group at their expense and allowing them to discover their ability to transform these structures toward a more just arrangement. The role of the trickster is to create situations that raise the consciousness of those relegated as "objects" being used by those in power for the dominant culture's gain. Satan as trickster, as the one who disrupts the norm, can illuminate new paths for the oppressed, even to the point of assisting them to become "subjects" of their own destiny by breaking through the accepted reasons given for their marginalization by those whom society privileges.

Trials and tribulations humanize the disenfranchised, who, until now, were seen only as "objects." The difficulties of their personal experiences, brought about by tests and tricks, have the potential to expose and unmask the contradictions within the prevailing social structures and the justification used by those in power in maintaining those structures. God can use Satan, as God did in the case of Job, Jesus, and Peter, to assist those who are seen as "non-persons" to uncover their identity and the causes of their station in life. The situations in which the marginalized find themselves, due to these "satanic" forces, becomes the starting point for all critical analysis. Upon evaluating the information based on the social location of the oppressed, the formulation of actions serving to change their situation becomes possible.

The trickster thus moves the disenfranchised away from a position of complicity with structures designed to maintain their marginality.

God can also utilize Satan to cause those who benefit from the status quo to discover their own salvation. Oppressors and sinners are also trapped in structures that dehumanize them due to their complicity with repressive structures. The ethics constructed by those privileged by the status quo is part of a false consciousness that accepts oppressive social structures as normative, one that does little if nothing to dismantle those structures. The ethics of the privileged and powerful can blame all misery caused by oppression that benefits them on Satan, or natural selection, or karma, or just bad luck while recusing themselves from all responsibility and liability. By bringing chaos to the "law and order" that protects the dominant culture's place within society, they too can achieve a conscientization that recognizes that even though the prevailing social structures privilege them, through the demonstration of solidarity with the disenfranchised, working with them for a more just social order, they can reclaim their humanity and thus their salvation.

Viewing Satan as trickster is not without problems, specifically the ambiguity that exists between Satan and God—an ambiguity that can find its full expression in the trickster figure. Rather than being God's antithesis, God's opposite, a certain ambiguity if not complimentary position is held by Satan. If Satan has no power except that given by God, we are left wondering whether evil can come from God, a proposition that the early biblical writers and ancient Church Fathers like Augustine raised. We heard the prophet Amos asking "If there is evil in a city, has Yahweh not done it?" (Amos 3:6). More disturbing is the passage where God sends evil spirits to torment King Saul (1 Sam 18:10). Such a proposition has the potential of dismissing any notion regarding God's ultimate goodness. Once we eliminate Satan as some type of quasi-deity who can be blamed for all of the evils that befall humanity, we are left asking if God has a dark side. What is more, if Satan is only carrying out God's divine will, then does this mean that God is the ultimate trickster? ✳

# Epilogue

*If Christ were here, there is one thing he would not be—a Christian.*
—Mark Twain

*Nothing is easier than to denounce the evildoer; nothing is more difficult than to understand him.*
—Fyodor Dostoevsky

The manuscript is ready to be sent to the publisher; nevertheless, we as authors are uneasy about some of the outcomes from our investigation into the life and times of Satan. We consider ourselves men of faith, specifically Christians, and yet our historical quest for Satan has led us to some disturbing revelations about our own beliefs, the nature of Christian leadership and authority, and what we consider to be true. As we survey all that has been done in the name of Christ by invoking the power of absolute Good over absolute Evil, we are unfortunately left wondering if it is the Christians who were the ones in league with the Devil. So much torture, killing, and conquering has been done by Christians that we must respectfully ask if there is something inherently evil within our faith tradition's way of treating other faith traditions, belief systems, religions, and cultures—none of which would have been condoned by Christ. Maybe that great modern-day theologian, Woody Allen, said it best: "If Jesus Christ came back today and saw what was being done in his name, he'd never stop throwing up."

How did our ancestors go from singing hymns of praise to the Prince of Peace to being the masters of the Inquisition? How did we descend from the lofty and liberating message of the gospel to the damning doctrines and exclusivity of so many writers and leaders among the Early Church Fathers? As authors and scholars with faith commitments to Christianity, we are deeply concerned that our quest for Satan's historical origins has led us to Christian priests, ministers, and bishops; to Christian politicians, rulers, and kings; and to persons who generally identified as Christians. Why? What does this mean?

Perhaps part of the answer already lies in the discursive patterns and the historical periods surveyed throughout the present work. Early Christianity personified absolute Evil as Satan, and for centuries transferred or projected this perceived "evil" onto those who stood in the way as Christians strove to accumulate power and privilege. Thus, we modern Christians, and those who came before us across all denominations, are partly responsible for all the while justifying our own fears and malice by defining ourselves as "good" and "godly" and then simultaneously labeling our various opposing Others (and internal dissenters, that is, heretics) as "evil" or "demonic." How true are the words of St. Paul, who warned: "You who teach others, why not teach yourselves. You teach against stealing, yet you steal. You prohibit adultery, yet you commit adultery. You detest idols, yet you rob their temples. You boast about the Law and then dishonor God by disobeying it. For it is written, it is your fault that the name of God is blasphemed among the nations" (Rom 2:21-24). If indeed a tree is known by its fruits, then history reveals for us a poisonous tree called Christendom, and those who have partaken of the serpent's temptation for godlike control over Others have tasted the demonic *will-to-power* and then wreaked havoc upon their local communities and the broader realm of humanity.

Readers will argue that our concern as authors about these disturbing characteristics and trajectories of the Christian ethos is nothing new and that many writers have pointed this out before us. It might even be objected that our closing reflections run the risk of rendering a relativistic diminishment of Christ's "Great Commission" to make disciples of all nations and spread the "Good News" of salvation and spiritual freedom contained in the Gospels (Matt 28:14-20). And we will reply: "Yes! Of course we knew that these violent tendencies and persecuting sentiments were present in the historical record of Christianity as well as in our own contemporary times." But academic and ethical integrity compel us to share with our readers that we were not fully prepared for the extensive degree to which the story of the life and times Satan, and of his legions of demons and malevolent spirits, was so persistently derived by Christians time and time again from the gods and goddesses, nature spirits and animistic practices, and philosophical and religious beliefs of Christianity's perceived religious or cultural rivals. The testimony of millions, slaughtered across the centuries and throughout the world by the Christian zeal to rid the earth of Satan's influence rise up and bear witness against those claiming to be faithful followers of Christ. *What does this mean?*

As discussed throughout the present work, firm belief in the worldly presence of elemental and ethereal spirits was a well-known conviction and profound fear among the ancient Mediterranean cultures that flourished during the life and times of Jesus of Nazareth. The tendency among the Church Fathers was to equate all of these spirits and lesser deities with the demonic realm, which over time increased the early Christian preoccupation and discourse about Satan. After all, even Jesus battled Satan during a forty-day period of intense prayer and reflection in the desert before resuming the high point of his public ministry in Galilee (Mark 1:12-13). As the early Christian movement spread from it nascent Jewish and Greek roots in Palestine to become a major force for social change and moral transformation throughout the Hellenistic-Roman Empire, it took on and struggled against many of the polytheistic beliefs, spiritual fears, and social concerns that weighed heavily in the hearts and minds of those who were touched by the gospel message and eventually converted to the new faith. In the Gospel of Mark (1:21-45), after Jesus preaches in the synagogue at Capernaum, we find an example of how persistent the fear of spiritual uncleanliness and demonic possession was among the people of those times. A man in the synagogue cried out: " 'What have you to do with us, Jesus of Nazareth? Have you come to destroy us? I know who you are, the Holy One of God.' But Jesus rebuked him, saying, 'Be silent, and come out of him!' " (1:23-26). As one reads or hears in these verses how the man began convulsing and crying out in a loud voice, we are left wondering if it was really the man speaking for himself, or if it was the voice of the demon speaking to Jesus while possessing this poor man's soul and mind.

It is also clear in these passages that Satan and his demons already know who Jesus is and are quite prepared to battle against him both on earth and in the interior regions of the human soul: "And he healed many who were sick with various diseases, and cast out many demons; and he would not permit the demons to speak, because they knew him" (1:34). The crowd was astonished and "they questioned among themselves, saying, 'What is this? A new teaching? With authority he commands even the unclean spirits, and they obey him.' And at once his fame spread everywhere throughout all the surrounding region of Galilee" (1:27-28). Such episodes and examples of demonic possession and Satan's presence in the human soul present a spiritual conundrum to contemporary men and women who live in the scientifically emancipated and technologically savvy times of the early twenty-first century. Just one hundred years ago, Freud and the psychoanalytic movement invited the Devil to lie down on the couch for a therapy session on the life and times of the Prince of Darkness and somehow helped convince most of modernity that demonic influences and religious superstitions would be healed or conquered by the year 2000.

How then can Christians be saved from Christendom? From the church? From those who call themselves "Christians" and crusade against modern-day demons? Over the past twenty centuries, did the demons of lust for power and control over others invade the soul of Christian leadership and authority time and time again so that, as in the Gospel of Mark, we now need Christ's gentle and humble power once again to rid us of these malevolent and unclean spirits? Where is the healing balm needed to change these poisons into medicine? Maybe our only hope and salvation is to stand in solidarity and compassion with the so-called heathens, pagans, and infidels against the holy persecutors misusing the name and message of Jesus Christ, who humbly ministered to the poor and the powerful around Galilee while loving God with all his heart and mind. If we truly believe that Jesus is found among "the least of these"—those who are hungry, thirsty, naked, alienated, incarcerated, and ill, those who are oppressed, dispossessed, and repressed—then Jesus was with the pagan philosopher stoned by a Christian mob, the witch burned by Christian officials, the indigenous tribe massacred by a conquering Christian army, as well as with the non-European men and women enslaved by Christian nations seeking a cheaper colonial labor force and with the innocent children and adults who died by the tens of thousands following the terrible January 12, 2010, earthquake in Haiti. Jesus, and many devout believers among the ranks of those who truly wish to follow his teachings, are forced to stand against Christians and their religious and secular institutions that are on a holy quest to rid the world of Satan and the demons.

We have ended our quest for the historical Satan by finding him in the mirror. We have seen Satan, and much too often over the past twenty centuries he has been us Christians. The real quest that now lies before us is finding a way to exorcise this Satan and the demonic legions lodged within the heart and mind of an exclusivist and persecuting tradition. Perhaps too many Christians have been overly preoccupied for far too long with the old biblical question about the source of malice and sin: *"From whence commeth evil?"* Perhaps Christians need to spend more time pondering the meaning of Jesus' cryptic question to Peter (Matt 16:13-16) about faith in his purpose and mission: *"Who do you say that I am?"* And perhaps herein lies the key to the quest for the historical Satan: Who or what do you say that Satan is?

*—De nobis fabula narratur—*

# NOTES

## Introduction: Desperately Seeking Satan

1. With a margin of error of ±4.

2. With a margin of error of ±3.

3. "The ACFA, that infamous association—one could say conspiracy—of professional, idealistic legal technicians, whitewashed, virtuous, and all-for-freedom on the exterior, but viciously liberal and anti-Christian in its motives and agenda" (1989, 71).

## Chapter 1 • Satan in the Modern World

1. For a complete exposé on the falsehood of Hollywood's version of *The Exorcist*, see the research and interviews conducted by Henry Angar Kelly (1974, 94–102).

2. As quoted and discussed in *The Omen: Two-Disc Collector's Edition* (1976); see Disc 1: *Omen 666 Revealed* (Twentieth Century Fox Film Corporation, June 2006).

3. For an authorized biography of Anton LaVey, see Barton 1992.

4. It is interesting to note that each of the seven deadly sins was paired with a particular demon. Bishop Peter Binsfeld, in 1589, made the following classifications: greed—Mammon; pride—Lucifer; envy—Leviathan; anger—Amon; gluttony—Beelzebub; lust—Asmodeus; and sloth—Belphegor.

5. See http://www.xeper.org/pub/gil/xp_FS_gil.htm. LaVey took responsibility for the split by instituting a reorganization that "phased out" those "disgruntled ex-members" who "were counterproductive," eliminating "much of the dross and administrivia that . . . obscuring the organization's true destiny" (Barton 1992, 119–21).

6. See http://www.xeper.org/pub/gil/xp_FS_gil.htm.

7. Although it is beyond the scope of this book to explore all of the criminal accusations made against the Satanists, author Gareth J. Medway in his book *Lure of the Sinister* (2001) attempts to do so.

8. See http://www.papalencyclicals.net/Paul06/p6devil.htm.

9. For the authors of the series, the symbol of Babylon is the Roman Catholic Church, a contaminated Christianity. Even though in the series the Pope is among those in rapture (some Catholics are portrayed as good Christians), it is the archbishop of Cincinnati, the fictional character Peter Matthews, who is made pope of a one-world religion.

10. There exists a third group known as amillennialists who believe that the thousand-year reign of God is neither a literal thousand-year term nor a physically established kingdom. This view, made popular after World War I, holds that Christ's thousand-year reign is a spiritual event.

11. As explained and quoted by Marie Louise von Franz on the 2004 DVD, *Matter of Heart: The Extraordinary Journey of C. G. Jung* (Kino International Corporation).

## Chapter 2 • The Birth of Satan: A Textual History

1. It is worth recalling that after Cain murdered Abel, Adam and Eve's younger third son, Seth, emerged as the virtuous and learned leader of their family line who was destined to be the father of the human race and of the Messiah. See Louis Ginzberg's classic multi-volume study, especially 1909–38, 120–24.

2. Psalm 109:6 is another possibility, but it remains ambiguous. The word "satan" in that verse could be read either as "Set a wicked person over him, and let an *accuser* stand at his right hand," or ". . . let *Satan* stand at his right hand." The same ambiguity can be found in the story of Balaam (Num 22:22-35), which has already been discussed.

3. The Greek translation of the Hebrew Bible is known as the Septuagint. Work on the Septuagint began in the third century BCE in Alexandria, Egypt.

4. *Dictionary of Deities and Demons in the Bible*, 2nd ed., s.v. "Azazel," by B. Janowski.

5. Scholars sometimes speak of "the intertestamental period," meaning the era between the composition of the writings of the Hebrew Bible and the New Testament, approximately from 350 BCE to 50 CE. Many pseudepigraphic Jewish writings were composed later than 50, however, so we prefer here to speak of "postbiblical" writings, that is, those written after the composition of the Hebrew Bible.

6. Apocalyptic literature is a genre that deals with the "end-times" and takes its name from the book of Revelation (*apokalypsis*). This genre can also be found in the Hebrew Bible in the form of the book of Daniel. Most apocalyptic literature was written in times of upheaval and distress within the community, i.e., the Jewish persecution of 168 BCE or the aftermath of the destruction of Jerusalem in 70 CE.

7. *Dictionary of Deities and Demons in the Bible*, 2nd ed., s.v. "Lilith," by M. Hutter.

8. "Pseudepigrapha" is the name given to some sixty-five books that are related to the Hebrew Bible, written by Jews and Christians during the three centuries before Jesus and the two centuries CE Some of these books are named after biblical figures who plainly did not write the texts but whom tradition has linked with

the works. Although not considered to have the same authority as scriptures, the pseudepigraphal works nevertheless have greatly influenced religious ideas, many of which found expression in the New Testament.

9. Regardless of the fact that the written account of Solomon's ring comes after the Matthew account, portions of the *Testament of Solomon* seem to reflect the first-century Jewish religious worldview.

10. The term "Apocrypha," from the Greek term "hidden," is used to refer to a collection of fifteen books, or portions of books, that do not form a part of the Hebrew Bible but are found in the early Christian versions of what was labeled the Old Testament. These books, for the most part, precede the fall of Jerusalem in 70 CE. Protestant practice has been to omit these books from the Scriptures.

11. *First Enoch* 20 lists six of the seven archangels. They are: Suru'el (Uriel), "of eternity and of trembling"; Raphael "of the spirits of man"; Raguel, who "take[s] vengeance for the world and for the luminaries"; Michael, who is "obedient in his benevolence over the people and the nations"; Saraqa'el, who is "set over the spirits [human]kind who sin in the spirit"; and Gabriel, who "oversees the garden of Eden, and the serpents, and the cherubim."

12. Cherubs appear eighty-eight times in the Hebrew Bible and once in the New Testament. They are responsible for three basic functions: (1) as guardians and bearers of God's throne (Ezek 10:8-22); (2) as guardians of the Garden of Eden (Gen 3:24); and (3) as guardians of the Temple's carved palm trees and rosettes (1 Kgs 6:23-35).

13. Seraphs are winged serpentine creatures that appear twice in the Hebrew Bible, both times in Isaiah 6. Their responsibilities are (1) to sing God's praises (vv. 2-3), and (2) to carry out acts of purification (v. 6). *First Enoch* 71:7 describes a third function of the seraphim. They, along with the cherubim and ophanim, are the "sleepless ones who guard the throne of [God's] glory."

14. Ophanim do not appear in the Hebrew Bible but are mentioned in the books of Enoch, especially in *3 Enoch*. As already mentioned, they are the "sleepless ones who guard the throne of [God's] glory" (*1 En.* 71:7). They also praise God. They are full of eyes with corresponding wings. Their garments contain 144 sapphires. From them, light like the morning star shines (*3 En.* 24:5-6).

15. Nations have their own guardian angels, protector figures who can act according to God's purposes or act against those chosen by God to help Israel (Dan 10:13).

16. Guardian angels are assigned to organize and write down the lives of people (*2 En.* 19:5).

17. Some texts place natural forces under the jurisdiction of angels, including the movement of sun, moon, and stars (*2 En.* 4:2), the seasons, rivers, oceans, and growth of living things (*2 En.* 19:4), or rain, wind, snow, thunder, and fire (*Jub.* 2:2)

18. In reality, angels can be grouped into more classes. *Second Enoch* 20 tells us there are ten classes of angels in the seventh heaven. Among those not mentioned in this Enoch verse, but appearing elsewhere, are: galgallim; creature (*hayyot*) (Ezek 1);

watchers ('*irin*) and holy ones (*qaddišin*) (Dan 4:14); '*elim*, '*er'ellim*, and *tapsarim* (*3 En.* 14:1); *hašmallim* and *šin'anim* (*3 En.* 7).

19. During the sixteenth and seventeenth centuries, grimoires became a "learned" magic where the practitioner (whom could also be professing Christians) was able to, like King Solomon and Jesus of old, control demons, treating them as slaves. See Medway 2001, 27–28.

20. As previously mentioned, Belial appears in the Hebrew Bible as the personification of wickedness. For example, Psalm 18:4 exclaims that "the torrents of Belial burst upon me," and Paul draws a distinction between the forces of Christ and those of Belial (2 Cor 6:15-16). Also, Belial is referred to as "the Worthless One," with most Bibles translating "sons of Belial" as "worthless men," i.e., 1 Sam 2:12.

21. Personified in the book of *Jubilees*, Mastema is the Hebrew word of "hostility," as used in Hos 9:7. Before becoming the Prince of demons, Mastema was the Angel of Yahweh responsible for executing punishments. After the Flood, Mastema received permission from God to allow a tenth of the demons to impose his will upon humanity.

22. Asmodeus's appearance in *Tobit* is probably a derivative of the Persian demon Aeshma; along with the generous almsgiving and the story of the dog in *Tobit,* this may indicate Zoroastrian influences.

23. Sammael, originally one of the chief archangels, is credited with tempting Eve in the Garden. He is referred to as Malkira, which in Hebrew means "king of evil."

24. Semyaz is the angel that led the other angels to have intercourse with human women.

25. Beelzebub, or Beelzeboul, is named the Prince of the Demons who once was the highest ranking angel in Heaven but now resides in the evening star.

26. The oldest accepted part of the Hebrew Bible was the Torah, the first five books of the Bible. These books, which become the central documents of the faith, reached their final form sometime between the mid-sixth and the fourth century BCE. An additional, less-authoritative set of writings, called "the Prophets," was accepted by most Jews in the first century CE. The Prophets included Joshua through 2 Kings (excluding Ruth), along with Isaiah, Jeremiah, Ezekiel, and the Twelve Minor Prophets. The third part of scripture, known as "the Writings," reached its final form during the latter part of the first century CE under the direction of the rabbinic courts at Jabneh. The Writings were the books from Esther through Song of Songs, plus Ruth.

27. Disagreement among scholars exists as to when the five books of Enoch were compiled. Dates range from 163 to 80 BCE. *Jubilees* is believed to have been written somewhere between 153 to 105 BCE. What is important for our purposes is that these texts were available to, and more than likely known by, the writers of the New Testament.

28. The Synoptic Gospels are Matthew, Mark, and Luke, so named because of the similarities in content and order, as opposed to what appears in John.

29. Paul is probably influenced by the Septuagint (Greek) translation of Deut 32:17, which uses the word "demon."

30. Much literature has sprung up in modern times about the Anti-Christ. Although the previous chapter explored this character, it is important to point out that there exist scant biblical passages upon which to develop the concept of Anti-Christ. Probably Henry Angar Kelly says it best: "So where did the infamous Anti-christ come from, the great enemy of Jesus in his Second Coming? Answer: he comes out of nowhere. He is an invention of creative readers of Prester John's Epistle and John the Divine's Book of Revelation, who fuse two different texts into one. An example of *creatio ex nihilio*" (Kelly 2006, 161).

31. Justin Martyr, *First Apology* 5.2; *Second Apology* 5.3; and *Dialogue with Trypho* 95.1.

32. Justin Martyr, *First Apology* 28; and *Dialogue with Trypho* 94.2.

33. Tertullian, *De Anima* 39.

34. Irenaeus, *Against Heresies* 3.18.7.

35. Origen, *Contra Celsus* 7.17.

36. Origen, *Commentary on Matthew* 13.9.

37. Origen, *Commentary on Matthew* 16.8 and 12.28; *Homily on Exodus* 6.9.

38. Origen, *Contra Celsus* 3.66.

39. Origen, *De Principis* 1.5.

40. Origen, *De Principis* 1.6.

41. The first Latin translation of the Bible.

42. Augustine, *De natura boni contra Manichaeos*.

43. For our purposes, we will concentrate on the Babylonian Talmud.

44. The Shema is the first Hebrew word of the Jewish declaration of faith found in Deut 6:4: "Hear O Israel, Yahweh our God is one Yahweh."

45. The Queen of Persia who lost her position to the biblical character Esther.

46. An animal's horn (that is, a ram's horn) that is formed into a musical instrument.

47. Also referred to as Gehinnom, the Pit, and Tophet (the Valley of Slaughter). It is interesting to note that the word "Hell," derived from Gehenna, only appears about five times throughout the Talmud.

48. That is, the first five books of the Hebrew Bible.

49. Although some of the Talmudic rabbis argue that the fire was created on the second day.

50. It is interesting to note that those who cause their community to sin will not be provided with an opportunity to repent.

51. Also spelled Koran in English, the Qur'an is Islam's holy book, which was revealed by Allah to the Prophet Mohammed starting in about the year 610 CE.

52. For a concise discussion of the Islamic development and conception of Iblīs as the personification of evil, see Waardenberg 2002, 35–40.

## Chapter 3 • Satan through the Ages

1. A quote from website of Dove World Outreach Center (August 22, 2010): www.doveworld.org/the-sign.

2. A quote from a t-shirt offered for sale on the website of Dove World Outreach Center (August 22, 2010): www.doveworld.org/the-sign.

3. Origen, *Contra Celsum* 1.1, 31.

4. Irenaeus, *Against Heresies* 1.6.3; 1.27.4.

5. Tertullian, *Prescription Against Heretics* 40.

6. Hubaux and Carcopino conducted their studies in the mid-1940s. Their work is discussed and cited in Eliade 1974, 133–37.

7. From Augustine's *Enarratio I in Ps. 34, 7*, as quoted in Brown 1996, 9 n.15, 80.

8. Augustine, *De natura boni contra Manichaeos*.

## Chapter 4 • Satan Comes of Age

1. Eusebius, *Vita Constantini* 1.27-32.

2. Lactantius, *De mortibus persecutorum* 44.5.

3. Epiphanius of Salamis, *Panarion* 26.3.3–5.7.

4. Tertullian, *Apologeticus* 43.

5. Justin Martyr, *Dialogue with Trypho* 45.4.

6. Justin Martyr, *First Apology* 5.

7. Justin Martyr, *Dialogue with Trypho* 79.

8. Justin Martyr, *Dialogue with Trypho* 105.

9. Homer, *Odyssey* X.240.

10. *Theodosian Code* IX.16.3, 7.

11. Pope Innocent VIII, *Summis Desiderantes* 1484.

12. The misogamy that undergirds the *Malleus Maleficarum*, especially Part 1 Question 6 (Kramer 1486, 41–54), helps explain the sadistic persecution of women that took place during the late medieval witch hunts. One is also struck with how many pages are dedicated to issues dealing with sexuality.

13. Tertullian, *The Apparel of Women* I.1.2.

14. Accused witches were usually stripped naked before their male judges, who were looking for the Devil's concealed mark made upon her body to signify their pact. The mark was usually on her left side and at times consisted of a claw mark.

15. Thomas Aquinas, *Summa Theologica* I.51.3, 6.

16. Thomas Aquinas, *De Trinitate* III.

17. John Calvin, *Institutes* I.XIV.18.

18. John Calvin, *Institutes* I.XIV.18.

19. Martin Luther, *Weimar Edition*, WA XVI.551.

20. John Calvin, *Institutes* I.XIV.17.

21. John Calvin, *Institutes* I.XIV.18.

22. For a more complete analysis of how Girard's concept of "scapegoat" applies the marginalized communities, see De La Torre 2007, 69–72.

23. The English later gave her the nickname "Isabella," meaning "little Elizabeth," which was an insult aimed at diminishing her status when compared with England's own very powerful ruler, Queen Elizabeth I.

24. Jonathan Edwards, *Sermon on Matthew 7:13-14*, January 1751.

25. Jonathan Edwards, *Sermon on Luke 19:10*, June 1751.

26. Jonathan Edwards, *Sermon on Revelation 3:15*, Spring 1729.

## Chapter 5 • The Devil Made Me Do It

1. Another event influencing Voltaire's novel was the Seven Years' War (probably the first global conflict ever fought), which occurred from 1756 to 1763. Triggered by Frederick the Great of Prussia's invasion of Saxony, it involved all of Europe's major powers and was fought on several continents, including North America, where it was better known as the French and Indian War.

2. For a more detailed account on the life of Padre Pio, see Chiffolo Pio 2000 and Preziuso 2000.

3. It would be helpful to have a working definition of power. To that end we reference Michel Foucault: "It seems to me that power must be understood in the first instance as the multiplicity of force relations immanent in the sphere in which they operate and which constitute their own organization; as the process which, through ceaseless struggles and confrontations, transform, strengthens, or reverses them; as the support which these force relations find in one another, thus forming a chain or a system, or on the contrary, the disjunction and contradictions which isolate them from one another; and lastly, as the strategies in which they take effect, whose general design or institutional crystallization is embodied in the state apparatus, in the formation of the law, in the various social hegemonies. . . . [Thus,] power is everywhere; not because it embraces everything, but because it comes from everywhere" (Foucault 1990, 92–93).

4. In 1964, Justice Potter Stewart, in *Jacobellis vs. Ohio*, attempted to define what constituted as hard-core pornography by stating, "I know it when I see it."

5. Trickster figures are usually portrayed as male figures.

6. The Greek word *exaiteomai* is a *hapax legomenon*, meaning that the word appears only once in the New Testament. Most translations render *exaiteomai* as "asked," "desired," or "demanded." However, *exaiteomai* is a verb (aorist middle indicative, third person singular) that is best translated as "has obtained permission for demands to trial or test."

# Bibliography

Acosta, José de. 1985 [1590]. *Historia natural y moral de las Indias*. Mexico, D.F.: Fondo de Cultura Económica. Translated by Edward Grimston as *The Natural and Moral History of the Indies*. New York: Franklin, 1970 [1604].

Adorno, Theodor W. 1973. *Negative Dialectics*. Translated by E. B. Ashton. New York: Seabury.

———. 1983. *Prisms*. Translated by Shierry Weber, Samuel Weber, and Shierry Weber Nicholsen. Cambridge: MIT Press.

Allason-Jones, Lindsay. 1996. "Coventina's Well." In *The Concept of the Goddess*. Edited by Sandra Billington and Miranda Green, 107–19. London: Routledge.

Arendt, Hannah. 1977 [1963]. *Eichmann in Jerusalem: A Report on the Banality of Evil*. New York: Penguin.

Aslan, Adnan. 2001. "The Fall and the Overcoming of Evil and Suffering in Islam." In *The Origin and the Overcoming of Evil and Suffering in the World Religions*. Edited by Peter Koslowski, 24-47. Dordrecht: Kluwer.

Auffarth, Christoph, and Loren T. Stuckenbruck, eds. 2004. *The Fall of the Angels*. Leiden: Brill.

Augustine, Saint. 1958. *On Christian Doctrine*. Translated by D. W. Robertson. Upper Saddle River: Prentice Hall.

———. 1991 [398]. *Confessions*. Translated by Henry Chadwick. Oxford: Oxford University Press.

Bailey, Michael D. 2003. *Battling Demons: Witchcraft, Heresy, and Reform in the Late Middle Ages*. University Park: Pennsylvania University Press.

Barnett, Paul. 2005. *The Birth of Christianity: The First Twenty Years*. Grand Rapids: Eerdmans.

Baroja, Julio Caro. 1965 [1961]. *The World of the Witches*. Translated by O. N. V. Glendinning. Chicago: University of Chicago Press.

Barton, Blanche. 1992 [1990]. *The Secret Life of a Satanist: The Authorized Biography of Anton LaVey*. London: Mondo.

Baudelaire, Charles. 1975. "The Generous Gambler." In *Baudelaire, Rimbaud, Verlaine: Selected Verse and Prose Poems*. Edited by Joseph M. Bernstein, 133–35. New York: Citadel.

Billington, Sandra, and Miranda Green, eds. 1996. *The Concept of the Goddess*. London: Routledge.

Bocaccio, Giovanni. 1930 [1353]. *Tales from the Decameron of Giovanni Bocaccio*. Translated by Richard Aldington. Chicago: Puritan.

Boureau, Alain. 2006. *Satan the Heretic: The Birth of Demonology in the Medieval West*. Translated by Teresa Lavender Fagan. Chicago: University of Chicago Press.

Bradley, Marion Zimmer. 1984. *The Mists of Avalon*. New York: Del Rey.

Brown, Peter. 1981. *The Cult of the Saints: Its Rise and Function in Latin Christianity*. Chicago: University of Chicago Press.

———. 1996. *Authority and the Sacred: Aspects of the Christianisation of the Roman World*. New York: Cambridge University Press.

Burr, David. 2001. *The Spiritual Franciscans: From Protest to Persecution in the Century after Saint Francis*. University Park: Pennsylvania State University Press.

Campenhausen, Hans von. 1997. *Ecclesiastical Authority and Spiritual Power in the Church of the First Three Centuries*. Peabody: Hendrickson.

Cantor, Norman F. 2002. *In the Wake of the Plague: The Black Death and the World It Made*. New York: Harper Perennial.

Carter, George William. 1970. *Zoroastrianism and Judaism*. New York: AMS.

*Catechism of the Catholic Church*. 2000. 2nd ed. Revised in Accordance with the Official Latin Text Promulgated by Pope John Paul II. Imprimi Potest by Cardinal Joseph Ratzinger. Vatican: Libreria Editrice Vaticana.

Cieza de León, Pedro de. 1553. *La crónica del Perú*. Colección Austral 507. Madrid: Espasa Calpe. Translated by Luis N. Rivera in *A Violent Evangelism: The Political and Religious Conquest of the Americas*. Louisville: John Knox, 1992.

Cigman, Gloria. 2002. *Exploring Evil Through the Landscape of Literature*. London and Bern: Lang.

Cohn, Norman. 1970. *The Pursuit of the Millennium: Revolutionary Millenarians and Mystical Anarchists of the Middle Ages.* Rev. and Exp. ed. New York: Oxford University Press.

Collins, John J. 1977. *The Apocalyptic Vision of the Book of Daniel.* Harvard Semitic Monographs 16. Missoula: Scholars.

Cook, J. M. 1983. *The Persian Empire.* New York: Barnes & Noble.

Copenhaver, Brian P. 1992. *Hermetica: The Greek Corpus Hermeticum and the Latin Asclepius in a New English Translation, with Notes and Introduction.* Cambridge: Cambridge University Press.

Cuevas, Mariano. 1975 [1914]. *Historia de la inéditos del siglo XVI oara la historia de México.* Mexico, D.F.: Porrúa.

Cunliffe, Barry. 1979. *The Celtic World.* New York: McGraw-Hill.

Dante. 2010. *The Divine Comedy.*Translated by Burton Raffel. Evanston: Northwestern University Press.

———. 1982. *The Inferno: Dante's Immortal Drama of a Journey through Hell.* Translated by John Ciardi. New York: Penguin/Mentor.

De La Torre, Miguel A. 2007. *Liberating Jonah: Forming an Ethics of Reconciliation.* Maryknoll, N.Y.: Orbis.

———. 2010. *Latina/o Social Ethics: Moving Beyond Eurocentric Moral Teaching.* Waco, Tex.: Baylor University Press.

De Lubac, Henri. 1993. *At the Service of the Church.* San Francisco: Ignatius.

D'Encausee, Helene C. 1979. *Decline of an Empire: The Soviet Socialist Republics in Revolt.* New York: Newsweek.

Dendle, Peter. 2001. *Satan Unbound: The Devil in Old English Narrative Literature.* Toronto: University of Toronto Press.

Desilet, Gregory. 2006. *Our Faith in Evil: Melodrama and the Effects of Entertainment Violence.* Jefferson: McFarland.

Donn, Linda. 1988. *Freud and Jung: Years of Friendship, Years of Loss.* New York: Collier/Macmillan.

Doorn-Harder, Nelly van, and Lourens Minnema, eds. 2008. *Coping with Evil in Religion and Culture: Case Studies.* Amsterdam: Rodopi.

Douie, Decima L. 1932. *The Nature and the Effect of the Heresy of the Fraticelli.* Manchester: Manchester University Press.

Edwards, Emily D. 2005. *Metaphysical Media: The Occult Experience in Popular Culture.* Carbondale: Southern Illinois University Press.

Edwards, Jonathan. 1851. *The Works of President Edwards, in Four Volumes*, Vol. 1. New York: Leavitt & Co.

———. 1989. *The Works of Jonathan Edwards*. Vol. 9, *History of the Work of Redemption*. Edited by John F. Wilson. New Haven, Conn.: Yale University Press.

Eliade, Mircea. 1974. *The Myth of the Eternal Return, or Cosmos and History*. Translated by William R. Trask. Bollingen Series XLVI. Princeton, N.J.: Princeton University Press.

Ellingsen, Mark. 1999. *Reclaiming Our Roots: An Inclusive Introduction to Church History*, Vol. 1. Harrisburg, Pa.: Trinity.

Faivre, Antoine. 1995. *The Eternal Hermes: From Greek God to Alchemical Magus*. Translated by Joscelyn Godwin. Grand Rapids: Phanes.

Flesher, LeAnn Snow. 2006. *Left Behind? The Facts Behind the Fiction*. Valley Forge, Pa.: Judson.

Foucault, Michel. 1990 [1976]. *The History of Sexuality*. Vol. 1, *An Introduction*. Translated by Robert Hurley. New York: Vintage.

———. 1995 [1975]. *Discipline and Punish: The Birth of the Prison*. 2nd ed. Translated by Alan Sheridan. New York: Vintage.

Frankfurter, David. 2006. *Evil Incarnate: Rumors of Demonic Conspiracy and Ritual Abuse in History*. Princeton, N.J.: Princeton University Press.

Freeman, Charles. 2009. *A.D. 381: Heretics, Pagans, and the Dawn of the Monotheistic State*. New York: Overlook.

Friedman, Lester D. 2004. "Darkness Visible: Images of Nazis in American Film." In *Bad: Infamy, Darkness, Evil, and Slime on Screen*. Edited by Murray Pomerance, 255–72. Albany: State University of New York Press.

Freud, Sigmund. 1961 [1927]. *The Future of an Illusion*. Edited by James Strachey. New York: Norton.

———. 1961 [1930]. *Civilization and its Discontents*. Edited by James Strachey. New York: Norton.

Garcia, Ismael. 2009. "Ethics." In *Hispanic American Religious Cultures*, Vol. 2. Edited by Miguel A. De La Torre, 627–35. Santa Barbara: ABC-CLIO.

Geary, Patrick J. 2003. *The Myth of Nations: The Medieval Origins of Europe*. Princeton, N.J.: Princeton University Press.

Gillis, Stacy, and Philippa Gates, eds. 2002. *The Devil Himself: Villainy in Detective Fiction and Film*. London: Greenwood.

Ginés de Sepúlveda, Juan. 1951. *Demócrates segundo o de las Justas causas de la Guerra contra los indios.* Edited and translated by Angel Losada. Madrid: Consejo Superior de Investigaciones Científicas.

Ginzberg, Louis. 1909. *The Legends of the Jews: From the Creation to Jacob,* Vol. 1. Philadelphia: Jewish Publication Society.

Girard, René. 1986. *The Scapegoat.* Translated by Yvonne Freccero. Baltimore: Johns Hopkins University Press.

———. 1987. *Things Hidden Since the Foundation of the World.* Translated by Stephen Bann and Michael Metteer. London: Athlone.

Goodrick-Clarke, Nicholas. 1992. *The Occult Roots of Nazism: Secret Aryan Cults and Their Influence on Nazi Ideology.* New York: New York University Press.

Gort, Jerald D., Henry Jansen, and Hendrik M. Vroom, eds. 2007. *Probing the Depths of Evil and Good: Multi-Religious Views and Case Studies.* Amsterdam: Rodopi.

Graf, Fritz. 1997. *Magic in the Ancient World.* Translated by Franklin Philip. Cambridge: Harvard University Press.

Green, Miranda, ed. 1996. *Celtic Goddesses: Warriors, Virgins, and Mothers.* New York: Braziller.

Gunning, Tom. 2004. "Flickers: On Cinema's Power for Evil." In *Bad: Infamy, Darkness, Evil, and Slime on Screen.* Edited by Murray Pomerance, 21–37. Albany: State University of New York Press.

Hafez, Mohammed M. 2006. *Manufacturing Human Bombs: The Making of Palestinian Suicide Bombers.* Washington, D.C.: U.S. Institute of Peace.

Hume, David. 1948. *Dialogues Concerning Natural Religion.* New York: Social Science Publishers.

Iannucci, Amilcare A., ed. 2004. *Dante, Cinema, and Television.* Toronto: University of Toronto Press.

Janowitz, Naomi. 2001. *Magic in the Roman World: Pagans, Jews, and Christians.* New York: Routledge.

Jones, Terry D. 2010. *Islam Is of the Devil.* Lake Mary, Fla.: Creation.

Jung, Carl G. 1978. *Aion: Researches into the Phenomenology of the Self.* 2nd ed. Translated by R. F. C. Hull. The Collected Works of C. G. Jung, Vol. 9, Part II. Princeton, N.J.: Princeton University Press.

———. 1989. *Memories, Dreams, Reflections.* Edited by Aniella Jaffe. Translated by Richard and Clara Winston. New York: Vintage.

Justin Martyr. 1997. *St. Justin Martyr: The First and Second Apologies*. Translated by L. W. Barnard. Mahwah, N.J.: Paulist.

Kant, Immanuel. 1960 [1793]. *Religion within the Limits of Reason Alone*. Translated by Theodore M. Greene and Hoyt H. Hudson. New York: Harper & Brothers.

Kelly, Henry Ansgar. 1974. *The Devil, Demonology, and Witchcraft: The Development of Christian Beliefs in Evil Spirits*. Eugene, Ore.: Wipf & Stock.

———. 2006. *Satan: A Biography*. Cambridge: Cambridge University Press.

Kidwell, Clara Sue, Homer Noley, and George E. "Tink" Tinker. 2001. *A Native American Theology*. Maryknoll, N.Y.: Orbis.

Kieckhefer, Richard. 1989. *Magic in the Middle Ages*. Cambridge Medieval Textbooks. New York: Cambridge University Press.

Klauck, Hans-Josef. 2003. *Magic and Paganism in Early Christianity: The World of the Acts of the Apostles*. Translated by Brian McNeil. Minneapolis: Fortress Press.

Koester, Helmut. 1987. *History, Culture, and Religion of the Hellenistic Age: Introduction to the New Testament*, Vol. 1. New York and Berlin: de Gruyter.

Koslowski, Peter, ed. 2001. *The Origin and the Overcoming of Evil and Suffering in the World Religions*. Dordrecht, The Netherlands: Kluwer.

Kramer, Heinrich, and Jakob Sprenger. 1971 [1486?]. *Malleus Maleficarum*. Edited and translated by Montague Summers. New York: Dover.

Kriwaczek, Paul. 2003. *In Search of Zarathustra: The First Prophet and the Ideas That Changed the World*. New York: Knopf.

LaHaye, Tim, Jerry B. Jenkins, and Sandi L. Swanson. 2005. *The Authorized Left Behind Handbook*. Wheaton, Ill.: Tyndale.

Lane, Tony. 2006. *A Concise History of Christian Thought*. Revised ed. Grand Rapids: Baker Academic.

Las Casas, Batolomé de 1967. *Apologética historia sumaria*. 2 vols. Edited by Edmundo O'Gorman. Mexico, D.F.: Universidad Nacional Autónoma. Translated by Luis N. Rivera in *A Violent Evangelism: The Political and Religious Conquest of the Americas*. Louisville: John Knox, 1992.

LaVey, Anton. 1969. *The Satanic Bible*. New York: Avon.

———. 1992. *The Devil's Notebook*. Los Angeles: Feral House.

Levack, Brian P. 1987. *The Witch-Hunt in Early Modern Europe*. London: Longman Group.

Lindsey, Hal. 1970. *The Late Great Planet Earth*. Grand Rapids: Zondervan.

———. 1972. *Satan Is Alive and Well on Planet Earth*. Grand Rapids: Zondervan.

———. 1980. *The 1980s: Countdown to Armageddon*. New York: Bantam.

López de Gómez, Francisco. 1946. *Historia General de las Indias (1552)*. Vol. 22, *Biblioteca de Autores Españoles*. Edited by Enrique de Vedía. Madrid: Ediciones Atlas.

Loomis, Roger Sherman. 1963. *The Grail: From Celtic Myth to Christian Symbol*. New York: Columbia University Press.

Luke, Helen M. 1989. *Dark Wood to White Rose: Journey and Transformation in Dante's "Divine Comedy."* New York: Parabola.

Lurker, Manfred. 1980. *The Gods and Symbols of Ancient Egypt: An Illustrated Dictionary*. London: Thames & Hudson.

———. 1987. *Dictionary of Gods and Goddesses, Devils and Demons*. Translated by G. L. Campbell. London: Routledge & Kegan Paul.

Luther, Martin. 1807 [1531]. *A Commentary of St. Paul's Epistle to the Galatians*. Edited by Edwinus London. Translated by George Roerer. London: Matthews & Leigh.

Malory, Sir Thomas. 1970. *Le Morte d'Arthur*, Vol. 1. Edited by Janet Cowen. New York: Penguin Classics.

———. 1962. *Malory's Le Morte d'Arthur*. Translated by Keith Baines. New York: Bramhall.

Marsden, George M. 1980. *Fundamentalism and American Culture: The Shaping of Twentieth-Century Evangelism 1870–1925*. New York: Oxford University Press.

Mason, Peter. 1990. *Deconstructing America: Representations of the Others*. New York: Routledge.

McDermott, Gerald R. 2000. *Jonathan Edwards Confronts the Gods: Christian Theology, Enlightenment Religion, and Non-Christian Faiths*. New York: Oxford University Press.

Medway, Gareth J. 2001. *Lure of the Sinister: The Unnatural History of Satanism*. New York: New York University Press.

Mehr, Farhang. 2003. *The Zoroastrian Tradition: An Introduction to the Ancient Wisdom of Zarathustra*. Costa Mesa, Calif.: Mazda.

Mendieta, Gerónimo de. 1980 [1596]. *Historia eclesiástica Indiana.* 3rd facsimile ed. Mexico, D.F.: Editorial Porrúa. Translated by Luis N. Rivera. In *A Violent Evangelism: The Political and Religious Conquest of the Americas.* Louisville: John Knox, 1992.

Meyer, Marvin W., ed. 1999. *The Ancient Mysteries: A Sourcebook of Sacred Texts.* Philadelphia: University of Pennsylvania Press.

Moore, Robert I. 1991. *The Formation of a Persecuting Society: Power and Deviance in Western Europe, 950–1250.* Oxford: Blackwell.

Moulton, James Hope. 1913. *Early Zoroastrianism.* London: Williams & Norgate.

Muchembled, Robert. 2003. *A History of the Devil: From the Middle Ages to the Present.* Translated by Jean Birrell. Cambridge: Polity.

Neusner, Jacob. 1993. *Judaism and Zoroastrianism at the Dusk of Antiquity: How Two Ancient Faiths Wrote Down Their Great Traditions.* Atlanta: Scholars.

Nirenberg, David. 1996. *Communities of Violence: Persecution of Minorities in the Middle Ages.* Princeton, N.J.: Princeton University Press.

Pagden, Anthony. 1982. *The Fall of Natural Man: The American Indian and the Origins of Comparative Ethnology.* Cambridge: Cambridge University Press.

Pagels, Elaine. 1996. *The Origin of Satan.* New York: Vintage.

Paolucci, Anne. 2008. *Dante Revisited.* Middle Village, N.Y.: Griffon.

Pearce, Roy Harvey. 1953. *Savagism and Civilization.* Baltimore: Johns Hopkins University Press.

Peretti, Frank E. 1986. *This Present Darkness.* Westchester, Ill.: Crossway.

———. 1989. *Piercing the Darkness.* Westchester, Ill.: Crossway.

Peters, Edward M. 1989. *Inquisition.* Berkeley: University of California Press.

Pfister, Oskar. 1928. "Die Illusion einer Zukunft." *Imago* 14: 149-84.

Polycarp. 1977. Polycarp to the Philippians. In *The Apostolic Fathers,* 293–346. Vol. 1. Translated by Kirsopp Lake. Cambridge: Harvard University Press.

Pomerance, Murray. 2004. "Introduction: From Bad to Worse." In *Bad: Infamy, Darkness, Evil, and Slime on Screen.* Edited by Murray Pomerance, 1–20. Albany: State University of New York Press.

Rahn, Otto. 1933. *Crusade against the Grail.* Fribourg: Urban.

Rauschning, Hermann. 1939. *Hitler Speaks.* London: Chapel River.

Rivera, Luis N. 1992. *A Violent Evangelism: The Political and Religious Conquest of the Americas*. Louisville: John Knox.

Robisheaux, Thomas. 2009. *The Last Witch of Langenburg: Murder in a German Village*. New York: Norton.

Rorty, Amélie Oksenberg, ed. 2001. *The Many Faces of Evil: Historical Perspectives*. New York: Routledge.

Rosenberg, Donna. 1987. *World Mythology: An Anthology of the Great Myths and Epics*. Lincolnwood: National Textbook.

Rosenfeld, Nancy. 2008. *The Human Satan in Seventeenth-Century English Literature: From Milton to Rochester*. Burlington, Vt.: Ashgate.

Scott, James C. 1990. *Domination and the Arts of Resistance*. New Haven, Conn.: Yale University Press.

Stausberg, Michael. 2008. *Zarathustra and Zoroastrianism: A Short Introduction*. London: Equinox.

Takaki, Ronald. 1993. *A Different Mirror: A History of Multicultural America*. Boston: Back Bay.

Thompson, Bard. 1996. *Humanists and Reformers: A History of the Renaissance and Reformation*. Grand Rapids: Eerdmans.

Tilley, Terrence. 1991. *The Evils of Theodicy*. Washington, D.C.: Georgetown University Press.

Twain, Mark. 1979. *A Connecticut Yankee in King Arthur's Court*. Berkeley: University of California Press.

Ulansey, David. 1988. *The Origins of the Mithraic Mysteries: Cosmology and Salvation in the Ancient World*. New York: Oxford University Press.

Underhill, (Captain) John. 1638. *Newes From America or, A New And Experimentall Discoverie of New England* London: J.D. for Peter Cole.

Voltaire. 1991 [1759]. *Candide*. New York: Courier Dover.

———. 2001 [1756]. Poem on the Lisbon Disaster, or an Examination of the Axiom, "All is Well." In *The Enlightenment: A Sourcebook and Reader*. Edited by Paul Hyland, Olga Gomez, and Francesca Greensides, 75–82. New York: Routledge.

Waardenberg, Jacques. 2002. *Islam: Historical, Social, and Political Perspectives*. Berlin: de Gruyter.

Wallis Budge, E. A. 1969. *The Gods of the Egyptians: Studies in Egyptian Mythology*. 2 vols. New York: Dover.

Warnke, Mike. 1972. *The Satan-Seller*. Plainfield, N.J.: Logos International.

————. 2002. *Friendly Fire: A Recovery Guide for Believers Battered by Religion.* Shippensburg, Pa.: Destiny.

Wilken, Robert L. 1984. *The Christians as the Romans Saw Them.* New Haven: Yale University Press.

Williams, Robert A., Jr. 1990. *The American Indian in Western Legal Thought: The Discourses of Conquest.* New York: Oxford University Press.

Yenne, Bill. 2010. *Hitler's Master of the Dark Arts: Himmler's Black Knights and the Occult Origins of the S.S.* Minneapolis: Zenith.

# INDEX

divine feminine, 52, 54, 79, 99–102, 104–5, 111–14, 122, 128, 131, 137–38, 140–42, 144–47, 149, 159, 201–2, 219

Girard, René, 167–68, 229n22
Gnosticism, 83–85, 111, 125, 128
goddess cults. *See* Divine Feminine
grace of God, 9, 20, 33, 35, 39, 83, 94,
121–23, 125, 128–30, 135, 182,
186, 190, 198, 206, 210, 212
Graham, Franklin, 7
Gregory the Great, 29, 116

Haitian earthquake, 49–50, 93, 184,
220
Harry Potter book series, 122
Heaven, 3, 32–33, 38, 60, 65–68, 70,
72–74, 79–83, 85, 90, 93, 101, 108–
9, 111–12, 114–15, 118, 122–23,
130, 137, 154, 158, 180, 193, 197,
207, 225n18, 226n25
Hell, 3, 8, 18, 22–23, 33–34, 37, 43,
55, 62–65, 67–69, 73–75, 82, 91,
98, 116–17, 150, 154–58, 162, 168,
176, 180, 190, 197, 227n47
as place of eternal fire, 68, 73–75,
80, 88–89, 91, 109, 173, 197. *See
also* Gehenna
Hellboy, 22–23, 32
Hellenism, 52, 66–67, 79, 83, 99–105,
107–15, 117–21, 123–24, 126, 131,
136–38, 142, 157, 201–3, 219
heresy, 79, 81, 84–85, 95, 124–25, 127,
131–32, 136, 141, 157, 161, 164,
169, 218
Hermes (Greek god), 108–9, 118–22,
201–2
Himmler, Heinrich, 23, 26, 45–47
Hitler, Adolph, 5, 23–27, 44, 187
Hollywood, 16–27, 32, 76, 223n1
Holocaust, x, 4, 5, 24–25, 42, 44, 47,
179, 182, 187, 192, 198
Holy Spirit, 66, 98, 102, 105, 114–16,
121, 128, 131, 152–53, 162, 170, 203

homosexuality, 34, 36, 171. *See also*
sexuality
Horus (Egyptian god), 54–56
humanism
Christian, 42; secular, 36, 39

Iblīs. *See* Satan
Illuminati, 30
*imago Dei*, 33, 81, 122–23, 158, 162
incarnation, 34, 81, 106, 108, 110–11,
114–16, 118, 122–23, 131, 135, 203
Inglis, Florida, 1–2, 4, 7, 9
Inquisition, 5, 43, 47, 169, 179, 213,
217
Irenaeus of Lyons, 81, 116, 125
Islam, 6–8, 27, 37, 50–51, 66–68,
89–91, 94, 97–99, 136, 149, 151,
169
radical, 6–7, 15, 177–78
Israel. *See* Judaism

Jenkins, Jerry, 36–39
Jerusalem, 56, 63, 75, 85, 100, 105,
114, 156, 175, 180, 210, 224n6,
225n10
Temple of, 37, 63–65, 69, 72, 85, 87,
121, 225n12
Jesus, xi, 1–2, 4, 9, 11, 14, 20, 27, 34,
40, 42, 55, 60, 65, 68–69, 75–78,
80–82, 85, 90, 93, 98, 101–3, 105–
6, 108–12, 114–25, 127, 129, 134,
138, 140, 144, 149, 152, 156, 160,
161, 165, 169–73, 175, 179–81, 183,
188, 190, 206–7, 209–14, 217–21
death of, 35, 39, 77, 81, 99, 109, 111,
116–17, 128, 137, 162, 169, 173,
191, 198, 202; as King of Kings,
105, 148, 152; as Lucifer, 82;
name of, 1–2, 4, 9, 34, 77–78,
114–16, 125; as Prince of Peace,

oppression (*continued*)
    social structures, xii, 39, 47,
    50, 111, 115, 124, 153, 171,
    184, 193, 196, 199, 201, 205–6,
    214–15
Origen, 16, 81–82, 99, 116
Osiris, 53–56
"Other," the, 5, 8, 37, 98–99, 125, 131,
    134–35, 162–63, 169–78, 193–94,
    218

paganisms, 13, 36, 100, 102, 105,
    107–8, 110–19, 121–22, 124–25,
    128, 130–31, 135–38, 140–42,
    144–45, 147–48, 155, 163, 173, 197,
    201–3, 220
Pagels, Elaine, 98–99, 165, 173
Pan (Greek god), 13, 138
papacy, xi, 35, 142–44, 152–54, 157,
    164, 168
paradise, 67–68, 72, 88, 155
*Passion of the Christ*, 117
Paul, apostle, 9, 59–60, 76–77, 79, 85,
    107, 118, 213–14, 218, 226n20,
    227n29
Peretti, Frank E., 3–4, 7, 196–97
Peter, apostle, 75–76, 82, 153, 207,
    210–12, 214, 221
Pio (Padre), 191–92
Platonism, 107–10, 129–30, 155
Polycarp, 124–25
pop culture, 24, 35
Pseudepigrapha, 68, 70, 72–74, 87,
    208, 224n8

Qumran, 60, 72–73
Qur'an, 89–91, 97, 227n51
    burning of, 97–98

race, 14, 24, 26, 45, 59, 71, 117, 131,
    154, 172–77, 214
Rand, Ayn, 28
rapture, 36–37, 224n9. *See also* Left
    Behind
Reagan, Ronald, 7, 177
Reformation, Protestant, 14–15, 95,
    132, 164–65, 188
Renaissance, 27, 119, 121, 188
resurrection
    of Christ, 75, 77, 81, 101, 109–10,
    114–15, 118, 124, 129, 130, 183;
    of the dead, 36, 38, 73, 88; of
    Satan, 187, 191–95
Risher, Mayor Carolyn, 1–4, 7, 9
Robertson, Pat, 49–50, 184
Rome. *See also* empire
Roman emperors, 105, 117, 133–34
    Caesars, 74, 106–7, 109, 124;
    Constantine, 130, 133–37, 143;
    Diocletian, 99, 133; Hadrian,
    108, 146; Julius, 52, 105–6,
    157; Licinius, 133–34; Marcus
    Aurelius, 110, 113; Maxentius,
    133; Maximinus Daia, 133–34;
    Octavius, 105; Theodosius, 106,
    127, 136, 140; Valens, 138; Val-
    entinian, 138; worship of, 74,
    105–6, 124–25

saints, xi, 102–3, 119, 140, 146, 172,
    182, 191
Salem Witch Trials. *See* witchcraft
salvation, 6, 33, 34, 36, 41, 51, 58–59,
    67–69, 73, 80–81, 83–85, 91, 100,
    112–17, 124, 128, 162, 173, 177,
    180, 190, 194, 196, 201, 206, 213,
    215, 218–20
    history, 110, 123–24

Santería, x, xi, 203
Satan
    as accuser, 28, 57, 61–63, 79,
        87; as archenemy of God, 63,
        71, 73–74, 92, 94, 115, 131,
        151, 190, 193, 197, 206, 215;
        as Beelzebub, 68–69, 72, 78,
        223n4, 226n25; church of, 13,
        28–31, 78, 169, 223n7; death
        of, 179–87, 191–92; as deceiver,
        14, 27, 32, 74–75, 79–81, 83,
        110–11, 124–125, 153, 159, 172,
        212; depictions of, 14, 17, 79; as
        the Devil, xi, 2–3, 11, 22, 25, 31,
        34–36, 44, 47, 49–50, 55, 60,
        68, 73–74, 76–78, 81–82, 84,
        89–90, 97–98, 116, 125, 137–38,
        149, 153, 157–65, 167–68,
        173–77, 179–82, 188–89, 196,
        209, 217, 220, 228n14; as Edenic
        serpent, 60, 74–75, 80–81, 116,
        123; enslavement to, 33–35, 60,
        76, 116, 173, 198; as fallen angel,
        27, 32, 73, 80–83, 91, 128,
        130, 158, 163; as Iblīs, 89–91,
        227n52; image of, 3, 55, 87, 131,
        154, 175, 196; as instrument of
        God, 62–63, 80, 83, 130, 201,
        206, 211; as Lucifer, 17–18, 27,
        30, 32–33, 80, 82, 137, 140,
        190, 223n4; pact with, 13, 18,
        49–50, 157–58, 160, 163, 168,
        171, 188–90, 201; personification
        of, 69, 85, 135; as prince of dark-
        ness, 17–18, 20–21, 27, 30, 41,
        51, 73, 79, 94, 114, 131, 135, 152,
        157, 180, 188, 191–92, 220; as
        prince of this world, 75, 79–82,
        116, 165; resurrection of, 187,

        191–95; as the satan, 57, 61–62,
        87; as tempter, 15, 17, 33, 35, 43,
        48, 60–63, 71–72, 79, 82, 87,
        90, 99, 102, 115–16, 123–24,
        138, 140, 152, 159, 162, 187,
        207, 209–10, 218; as trickster, 27,
        47–48, 62, 95, 100, 123, 130–31,
        190, 198–99, 205–15; as voodoo
        spirit, 50; worship of, 13, 28–31,
        136, 143, 161, 174–77. *See also*
        demonic forces
Satanism, 13, 28–31
Saul (king), 58, 61, 63, 94, 137, 215
secularism, 4, 16, 35–36, 39, 192, 220
Seth (Egyptian god), 51–57, 72, 105,
        224n1
sexuality, 14, 19, 30, 34, 36, 40–41, 59,
        70–71, 80, 88–89, 108, 127, 129,
        134–35, 147–48, 160–62, 164, 171,
        202, 214, 228n12
Sheol, 73
sin, 17–18, 27, 29, 33–34, 72–73, 77,
        79, 85, 88, 91, 94, 101–2, 112, 116–
        17, 123, 126, 129–30, 140, 144–45,
        155–57, 162–63, 166–68, 172, 184,
        187, 194–95, 197–98, 213–15, 221,
        223n4, 225n11, 227n50
    original, 9, 33–35, 80–81, 90–91,
        116, 186
slavery
    to the demonic, 33–35, 60, 76, 84,
        116, 118–19, 166, 173, 198; to
        the political, 38, 166–67, 172,
        177, 203, 220, 226n19
Socrates, 109, 113
Solomon, King, 57, 68–69, 72, 87,
        225n9, 226n19
sorcery. *See* magic
Soviet Union, ix, 7, 20, 177